ANTHROPOLOGICAL PAPERS OF
THE UNIVERSITY OF ARIZONA
NUMBER 35

BASKETMAKER CAVES IN THE PRAYER ROCK DISTRICT, NORTHEASTERN ARIZONA

ELIZABETH ANN MORRIS

THE UNIVERSITY OF ARIZONA PRESS
TUCSON, ARIZONA
1980

About the Author . . .

ELIZABETH ANN MORRIS became familiar with the Prayer Rock collections spread out on her father's laboratory tables at an early age, never dreaming that she would eventually be responsible for recording their meaning. Earl H. Morris of the Carnegie Institution of Washington excavated the Prayer Rock caves in northeastern Arizona in 1931. After his death in 1956, the final analysis and description of the materials, as well as their comparison to other Basketmaker remains, constituted Elizabeth Morris's Ph.D. dissertation at the University of Arizona in 1959. Dr. Morris revisited the Prayer Rock caves in 1957, 1958, and 1959 clarifying details about locations and descriptions of specific sites, recording the rock art, and cataloguing the numerous large stone tools that had been left in the field by the original expedition. Dr. Morris has excavated with the Oriental Institute in Iran and with Harvard University in France. She has worked at the Laboratory of Tree-Ring Research in Tucson, at Temple University in Philadelphia, and became Chair of the Department of Anthropology at Colorado State University in Fort Collins in 1977 where the major focus of her research was establishing a regional chronology and defining settlement patterns in northeastern Colorado.

THE UNIVERSITY OF ARIZONA PRESS

Copyright © 1980
The Arizona Board of Regents
All Rights Reserved
Manufactured in the U.S.A.

Library of Congress Cataloging in Publication Data

Morris, Elizabeth Ann, 1932–
      Basketmaker caves in the Prayer Rock district,
northeastern Arizona.
      (Anthropological papers of the University of
Arizona; no. 35)
      Shortened and rev. version of the author's
thesis, University of Arizona, 1959.
      Bibliography: p.
      1. Basket-Maker Indians. 2. Prayer Rock
region, Ariz. — Antiquities. 3. Caves — Arizona —
Prayer Rock region. 4. Arizona — Antiquities.
I. Title. II. Series: Arizona. University.
Anthropological papers; no. 35.
E99.B37M67   1979   979.1'37   79-20149

ISBN 0-8165-0499-7

Dedicated to the memory of
A. V. Kidder

EPIGRAPH

Some spell it in two separate words; . . . some hyphenate it; a few telescope the two into one. I prefer this form, Basketmaker, as the simplest version of an awkward and essentially meaningless term, for most of the world's people are makers of baskets.

Charles Avery Amsden
*Prehistoric Southwesterners from
Basketmaker to Pueblo*

CONTENTS

FIGURES

TABLES

PREFACE

The archaeological remains discussed in this volume were excavated by Earl H. Morris of the Carnegie Institution of Washington. In 1928 Morris noted the presence of cave sites in the Prayer Rock area at the north end of the Lukachukai Mountains in the extreme northeastern corner of Arizona. In 1930 he spent several weeks excavating in these caves as a member of the Bernheimer Expedition of the American Museum of Natural History. The specimens recovered during that period are in the American Museum in New York City. In 1931, for 10 weeks, Morris directed a Carnegie Institution of Washington expedition in the Prayer Rock country. He undertook intensive examinations of Broken Flute Cave, Obelisk Cave, Pocket Cave, Cave 1, Cave 2, and Cave 8, and he tested a number of other sites in the immediate vicinity. Some of the remains recovered in the 1931 season have been described (see beginning of Chapter 1).

Precise information is lacking on the composition of the field crew and the conditions of excavation. The group, under the direction of Earl Morris, was in the field from the middle of July to the first of October, 1931. Ann Axtell Morris, Ole Owen, Omer Tatman, Oscar Tatman, and Roger Thomas (Thomas Roger ?) can be identified from the available photographs. Eugene Tapahonso and Slim Saltwater were among the Navajo workmen. Maps used in the field were drawn by Ezekial Johnson. Willard Fraser, Laura Gilpin, A. V. Kidder, Dwight Morrow, Jr., Deric Nusbaum, Gustav Stromsvik, and Mrs. Walter Trumbull were in camp for part of the season.

Several employees of the Carnegie Institution analyzed some of the artifactual remains under Morris's direction. The published portions of that work are summarized in this volume for the sake of completeness, and the unpublished portions have been reorganized for presentation here. The analysis and initial illustrations of the dog hair sashes were done by Verna Cinema, then a student at the University of Colorado. Analysis of the multiwarp tapestry-weave sandals is taken from work done by Kisa Noguchi and Jean Zeigler. Robert F. Burgh drew the original illustrations of the tump bands (Fig. 60), the tapestry-weave aprons (Fig. 65), and the cradle board (Fig. 89). The plans and sections of caves and houses are adapted from field maps prepared by E.

Johnson. David A. Breternitz and Robert C. Euler supplied information on unpublished sites in the Museum of Northern Arizona survey files. Harry L. Shapiro, Chairman of the Department of Anthropology, American Museum of Natural History, graciously gave permission to include descriptions of a cradle board, a feather box, and three nets.

A number of individuals were called upon to assist in the analysis of the remainder of the materials. Thomas W. Whitaker of the Crops Research Division, U.S. Department of Agriculture, La Jolla, California, analyzed the squash and gourd remains. Paul C. Mangelsdorf of the Botanical Museum, Harvard University, examined the corn specimens. The beans were identified by Lawrence Kaplan of Roosevelt University, Chicago. C. W. Ferguson of the Laboratory of Tree-Ring Research, Tucson, Arizona, and the Forest Products Laboratory of the U.S. Department of Agriculture, Madison, Wisconsin, identified a selected sample of floral material. The Smith, Kline, and French Pharmaceutical Laboratory in Philadelphia made chemical analyses of the alkaloid content of the yucca-fiber quids, which was later identified as tobacco (Raffauf and Morris 1960). Volney H. Jones of the Ethnobotanical Laboratory, University of Michigan, Ann Arbor, examined other plant foods, a sample of the cordage remains, and the feces specimen. He was also responsible for recognizing the tobacco remains that were stored in a jar and those that were wrapped inside of the yucca fiber quids. The Research and Development Department of Philip Morris, Inc., Richmond, Virginia, obtained positive indications of nicotine and nicotinic acid in "cake" and "dottle" material from Prayer Rock pipes by microscopic examination and chromatographic analyses (Johnson, Gager, and Holmes 1959; Jones and Morris 1960; Gell and Jones 1962).

Lowell Swenson of the University of Colorado Museum, Boulder, identified some of the animal remains. J. T. Marshall of the Department of Zoology, University of Arizona, Tucson; Lyndon L. Hargrave of the Southwest Research Center, National Park Service, Globe; Herbert Friedmann of the U.S. National Museum, Washington; and Kenneth E. Stager of the Los Angeles County Museum provided identifications of the bird remains.

Robert W. Wilson of the Museum of Natural History, University of Kansas, examined some of the antelope remains. Robert J. Drake, then of the Department of Zoology, University of Arizona, identified the shells used in the jewelry and those used as accidental temper in some of the pottery. David E. Johnson of the Division of Mammals, Smithsonian Institution, identified the dog hair used in the sashes.

At the time of Morris's death in 1956, the Carnegie Institution authorized the distribution of the specimens in his laboratory to museums that could preserve the materials and arrange for them to be studied. The Basketmaker collection and the field notes from the Prayer Rock district excavations were placed in the Arizona State Museum in Tucson. The other specimens (including remains from Canyon del Muerto, Kawaika-a, Solomonsville, the Mimbres valley, the Gobernador area, the upper Rio Grande valley, western New Mexico in general, and the Durango area in Colorado), were sent with the associated field notes to the University of Colorado Museum in Boulder. Before this time, a large number of pottery vessels had been given to the Museum of the University of New Mexico, and some of these pieces have been illustrated (E. H. Morris 1939).

This study is a report on the Prayer Rock Basketmaker remains that are in the Arizona State Museum collections. It is a shortened and revised version of my doctoral dissertation completed in 1959 at the University of Arizona with the addition of more recent references.

I am indebted to Emil W. Haury, my dissertation chairman, for his suggestions concerning the content and organization of the textual material. I am also grateful to Raymond H. Thompson for his assistance with the arrangement and presentation of the subject matter. Frederick S. Hulse and Richard B. Woodbury read the manuscript and made helpful suggestions. Nathalie F. S. Woodbury made useful comments on the concluding chapters. Sincere appreciation is expressed to Gail Hershberger for her careful editorial assistance and her special abilities in clarifying tables. Carol Gifford and Gail Hershberger prepared the manuscript for the Press, thus concluding an endeavor involving numerous people and extending over many years. During the 30 years of excavation and description of the Prayer Rock materials there were no doubt others, unknown to me, who made contributions, and to them I would like to express my thanks.

Finally, I am grateful to the staff of the Arizona State Museum for permitting me to analyze this collection and thus bring to completion an interesting piece of work initiated by my father. It is unfortunate that Earl Morris could not have finished describing the materials that he found, since inevitably some details of occurrence and meaning are only in the mind of the excavator. It is my sincere hope that he would have been gratified to see the results of his work as they appear in this volume.

ELIZABETH ANN MORRIS

BASKETMAKER CAVES
IN THE
PRAYER ROCK DISTRICT,
NORTHEASTERN ARIZONA

1. INTRODUCTION

The prehistoric manifestation that is labeled "Basket-maker" has long been of interest to Southwestern archaeologists. Early workers recognized that some of the materials they were finding were different from the artifacts associated with the great cliff dwellings that initially attracted their attention. They decided that this different material must be older on the basis of its crudity and sometimes its location beneath other remains. A large number of investigations steadily increased the range of available knowledge of Basketmaker material culture, and taxonomic systems that related the Basketmaker complex to the rest of Southwestern prehistory were defined and redefined. Today the Basketmaker period is considered to have been of fundamental importance in Anasazi development.

The cave sites in the Prayer Rock district of northeastern Arizona produced a large well-preserved assemblage of Basketmaker materials. Here, for the first time, quantities of architecture, ceramics, and perishable remains were found in association and were carefully excavated. Only a portion of the objects have been reported. Morris wrote an article to accompany the tree-ring dates that were published by A. E. Douglass (Douglass 1936; E. H. Morris 1936), and an article on the human figurines (E. H. Morris 1951). The basketry was the basis for a large analytical monograph by E. H. Morris and Robert F. Burgh (1941). Several articles by various collaborators and me have appeared concerning an early projectile point type found in the area (E. A. Morris 1958), flutes (Bakkegard and Morris 1961, E. A. Morris 1959a), textiles (E. A. Morris 1975), and a complex series of remains related to the use of tobacco at this early time (Gell and Jones 1962; Johnson, Gager, and Holmes 1959; Jones and Morris 1960; and Raffauf and Morris 1960). Abel (1955) examined the Obelisk Gray vessels in defining that ceramic type.

The present study is an attempt to provide an analysis of the entire collection of Basketmaker remains excavated by Earl Morris and now housed at the Arizona State Museum. It is hoped that the integration of the Prayer Rock material into Southwestern prehistory will offer a new perspective on the significance of the Basketmaker III period in Anasazi development.

DEVELOPMENT OF THE BASKETMAKER CONCEPT

Early in the development of Southwestern archaeology came the realization that differences existed among assemblages of prehistoric materials. Some of these could be ascribed to the normal variation between any two groups of people; others, occurring within a localized area and sometimes within a given site, needed further explanation. Notable among the hypotheses advanced were several concerning seriation and stratigraphic methodology. It was discovered that ceramic remains obtained from several places could be ordered to reveal temporal variation. Kidder on the Pajarito Plateau (1915), Nelson in the Galisteo Basin (1916), and Kroeber (1916) and Spier (1917), both working in Zuni country, laid the foundations for the more detailed ceramic sequence that is recognized today.

As early as 1893, Richard Wetherill was impressed with the diversity of the remains he was finding in Butler Wash in southern Utah (E. H. Morris 1939: 11). Some were like the Cliff Dweller remains he had found in the Mesa Verde. Others, sometimes occurring beneath Cliff Dweller remains, appeared to be different, and these he labeled "Basket Maker." Nordenskiöld (1893: 169) noted poorly fired, clumsily shaped vessels from Step House in the Mesa Verde and correctly postulated that they might be ancestral to the later remains. According to Brew (1946: 20), the first published notice of this early work was a statement in *The Archaeologist* ("H" 1894: 154). In 1897 Richard Wetherill and T. Mitchell Prudden each published an account using the term "Basket Maker," and it became firmly implanted in the literature.

In 1902, George H. Pepper of the American Museum of Natural History formalized the "Basket Maker" concept, listing physical and cultural traits as they were understood at that time (Pepper 1902). The work of A. V. Kidder and S. J. Guernsey in the Kayenta country produced the first well-documented accounts of excavations of Basketmaker sites (Kidder and Guernsey 1919; Guernsey and Kidder 1921; Guernsey 1931). Specimens recovered on their expeditions of 1914–17 and 1920–23 constitute the original core of Basketmaker perishable remains. The excavation of DuPont Cave in Kane

County, Utah, augmented the knowledge of prepottery material culture (Nusbaum, Kidder, and Guernsey 1922).

Thus the major constellation of traits was established by the early 1920s. Work done since then has increased the depth and complexity of our knowledge without altering the basic structure. It has been accompanied by theoretical and classificatory treatises of an increasingly perceptive nature.

The earliest detailed definition of the sequence of cultures in the Basketmaker area was published by Kidder and Guernsey (1919: 204–6). They listed three successive cultural periods: "Basket Maker," "Slabhouse," and "Cliff-house." For the "Basket Maker" culture they specified the following traits:

1. Undeformed dolichocephalic skulls
2. No domesticated turkeys
3. Flint corn only (?)
4. Apparently no beans
5. Fine-cord square-toed sandals with bottom reinforcement covering the whole sole
6. Guitar-shaped cradles; grass-edge and cedar-bark cradles abundant
7. Coiled basketry, somewhat coarser than Pueblo
8. Hair string, twined bags, and fur cloth common
9. Cotton cloth, loom cloth, and turkey feather cloth absent
10. Atlatl
11. Short, squat pipes
12. Pottery rare, perhaps even absent

An early theoretical construct placing the Basketmaker complex in a developmental scheme was made by Morris (1921). The earliest period, which he also labeled "Basket Maker," was characterized by:

Pronounced dolichocephalic crania, without artificial occipital flattening; apparent total absence of permanent habitations; absence of bow and arrow; use of the atlatl; high development of textile manufacture, with specialized types of sandals and burial baskets; absence of pottery and the cultivation of one very primitive type of corn.

This was followed by the "Pre-Pueblo" period, for which E. H. Morris noted dolichocephalic and a few brachycephalic crania with artificial flattening. Flimsy one-storied structures were built near circular subterranean chambers. The pottery was crude; less than 30 percent was plain, and some corrugated may have been present.

In 1924, Kidder described the prepottery "Basket Maker" period in more detail (Kidder 1924), following the criteria suggested by Morris and adding the information obtained by Guernsey (Guernsey and Kidder 1921). He distinguished between a "Post-Basket Maker" and a "Pre-Pueblo" complex largely on the basis of the degree of proficiency in ceramic technology. The "Post-Basket Maker" people were responsible for the acquisi-

tion and development of pottery making and for the earliest attempts at decoration. Their skulls were undeformed and they exhibited a number of traits previously considered to be Basketmaker. The associated architectural complex was of slab and mud construction, which had been attributed by Morris to the "Pre-Pueblo" people.

Here, then, was a transitional complex between the Basketmaker and Pre-Pueblo periods. Kidder described the Pre-Pueblo people as making neck-banded but not corrugated pottery and a little black-on-red ware. Their houses were semisubterranean, with walls of upright slabs and mud, of wattle and daub, or of mud "turtle backs." In at least some cases the roofs were pitched. The houses were round or rectangular in shape, placed in unconnected aggregations of a few to many. Occasionally there were deep subterranean rooms associated with the surface structures. The Pre-Pueblo skulls exhibited marked occipital flattening.

In 1927, A. V. Kidder called the First Southwestern Archaeological Conference at his camp at Pecos, New Mexico. Kidder states (1927: 489–91):

The purposes of the meeting were: to bring about contacts between workers in the Southwestern field; to discuss fundamental problems of Southwestern history, and to formulate plans for a coordinated attack upon them; to pool knowledge for facts and techniques, and to lay foundations for a unified system of nomenclature.

The development of prehistoric peoples in the Southwest was considered in detail, the described periods were refined, and a revised terminology was suggested. A postulated preagricultural level was called "Basket Maker I"; "Basket Maker," the agricultural, prepottery stage, became "Basket Maker II"; and "Post-Basket Maker," the slab-house period in which pottery first appeared, was supplanted by "Basket Maker III." "Pre-Pueblo" became "Pueblo I," the first period when cranial deformation was consistently practiced; neck-banded pottery and contiguous-walled living rooms built of true masonry are the major diagnostics of this period. The above terms are still adequate for the purpose of developmental classification or temporal ordering. The most serious criticism of them is that they lack the regional distinctions that have become apparent as a result of continued excavation.

After the establishment of the Pecos system of classification, major contributions to the problem of culture sequence were made by Frank H. H. Roberts. His report on Shabik'eschee Village (1929), a Basketmaker III site in Chaco Canyon, lists traits of the Basketmaker periods. Squash and fiber-tempered mud trays are added to the Basketmaker II complex. Formalized pit house architecture, several kinds of corn and beans, and the bow and arrow are added to the Basketmaker III assemblage. Certain traits thought previously to be Pueblo are now placed at the end of the Basketmaker III complex; notable among these are the bow and arrow and beans. The listing indicates a greater cultural difference between Basketmaker II and Basketmaker III than between Basketmaker III and Pueblo I — in contrast to the division established by the initial Pecos conference, which emphasized the differences between the Basketmaker sequence and the Pueblo sequence.

Roberts continued to produce a major contribution to Southwestern archaeology almost every year until 1940. Some of these concerned the Basketmaker concept (Roberts 1930; 1931), and some dealt with later developments. Two major, culminating theoretical works (Roberts 1935; 1937) were intended to present the Pecos classification in flexible enough terms so that it could include the diverse kinds of remains that deserved a place in the Anasazi continuum. Roberts sought to clarify the relationships between the Anasazi cultural complex and the Hohokam and Mogollon developments, which were becoming more than "outlying peripheral areas where the system did not seem to work." He suggested that the name Basketmaker II be altered to "Basket Maker" and that Basketmaker III be renamed "Modified Basket Maker." These changes were designed to charactertize the periods more clearly and to eliminate the implication that all areas passed through all of the sequentially numbered periods of the Pecos classification.

In 1939, E. H. Morris published a summary of his excavations in the La Plata district. He applied the Pecos system to remains in the San Juan drainage, utilizing the more fluid period boundaries proposed by Roberts. This considerably augmented the detail known for each taxonomic unit and clarified the period diagnostics.

One of the most acute evaluations of the utility of the Pecos classification was advanced by Clyde Kluckhohn (Kluckhohn and Reiter 1939). Like Roberts, he noted that the period sequence does not apply to all sites in the Anasazi area, and he discussed some of the potentials and limitations of taxonomic systems. Kluckhohn states (Kluckhohn and Reiter 1939: 162):

> Human activity notably fails to exhibit exceptionless uniformities.... All classifications can but, at best, express modal tendencies and must be used purely heuristically with constant awareness that they are at most crude categorizations of the human acts we are trying to reconstruct.

Rather than utilize the modified Pecos classification suggested by Roberts, Kluckhohn leaned toward new systems, such as those being formulated by H. S. Gladwin and H. S. Colton at that time.

Succeeding excavations undertaken in the Anasazi area have been reported in terms of the Pecos system, with the modifications of details and period boundaries contributed by Roberts and Morris, and in some areas

with the application of the branch and phase system devised at Gila Pueblo by Harold S. Gladwin and his staff. The establishment of branches as geographical units and phases as temporal subdivisions of branches serves to segment the Anasazi area into similar but distinguishable localities. These units catalog temporal and geographical differences between traits in a more concise and complete fashion. The Chaco Branch (Gladwin 1945) and the Mesa Verde Branch (O'Bryan 1950), with which this report is concerned, have been established within this system. The account of the Mesa Verde Branch includes references to the Prayer Rock Basketmaker material and serves as the most adequate existing frame of reference with which to integrate these remains — although, as will be noted below, it is not perfect. Because the phase concept has not been applied to the Anasazi area as a whole, the period designations established at the first Pecos conference will be used for comparative purposes, with reference to the other systems in use when necessary.

H. S. Colton (1939) applied the Museum of Northern Arizona adaptation of the Gladwin system to the archaeology of the Kayenta country. The foci he defines differ only slightly from the periods of the Pecos classification. This system will be referred to in the discussion of the Kayenta materials.

THE PRAYER ROCK STUDY

When archaeologists present their material, they have several related obligations. One of these is the integration of the data into a spatial and temporal framework that is consistent both with the evidence at hand and with the evidence of other prehistoric remains recovered in the past. Another obligation is the interpretation of the material and its technological aspects so as to reconstruct the life of the people in as complete a form as possible. With the consideration of theoretical schemes of development that involve the whole North American continent, the Basketmaker complex gains new significance as a relatively well-preserved assemblage that developed out of a Desert culture base as defined by Jennings (Jennings and Norbeck 1955; Jennings 1957). With the addition of traits derived from the high culture centers of Mesoamerica, it serves as the foundation for the Pueblo III efflorescence.

In the cave sites of the Prayer Rock district a large number of well-preserved architectural, ceramic, and perishable remains of the Basketmaker III level of development were found in association. It was thought that an analysis of these materials would shed new light on the importance of the Basketmaker III period as a level of prehistoric achievement, and to this end several approaches to the problem of ordering archaeological materials were used in my original presentation (E. A. Morris 1959b).

In that report an evaluation was made of features that distinguish Basketmaker remains from earlier manifestations in western North America. The Anasazi region is culturally subdivided on the basis of the ceramic and architectural attributes common to restricted localities, and the Prayer Rock Basketmaker assemblage was compared to other Basketmaker remains in the Anasazi area in an effort to establish the nature of its prehistoric affiliations. In some places this attempt was limited by the lack of excavated sites representing this time horizon; in others the record is particularly detailed and informative. The origin of traits and trait complexes was also the subject of considerable attention. The cultural remains were presented in functional groups in the original analysis. The functions of some artifact classes were inferred from such qualities as material, morphology, indications of use, context, and ethnographic analysis. Some of the functional units considered were houses, subsistence, containers, weapons, and clothing. In a number of cases, these categories cross-cut two or more kinds of material. A group such as "containers" included specimens of pottery, mud, wood, juniper bark, yucca fiber, and gourd. This functional grouping was an attempt to portray the articles as seen by their manufacturers and users. This discussion has not been included in this publication, but can be found in my dissertation (E. A. Morris 1959b), on file in the Arizona State Museum Library, Tucson.

In the interests of compiling a useful catalogue of the remains recovered during the excavations in the Prayer Rock district, the material culture is described primarily on the basis of material composition. Secondary groups and subgroups are established within the material classes on the basis of morphology and manufacturing techniques. Thus, several kinds of foreshafts and mainshafts are described under "Arrows," which are listed under "Wood." It is believed that this basic categorization by physical and chemical properties of the specimens minimizes the possibility of variation in interpretation by different individuals.

In an attempt to reconstruct the cultural inventory of the residential unit, the artifacts were examined by material and functional groupings for each house and cist. It was thought that the cultural materials inside such structures would reflect an actual domestic situation, and that conclusions could be drawn concerning the place of certain artifacts in daily life.

This method of analysis assumes that houses occupied by people of equivalent social status in the same culture at the same time will have similar cultural contents. More precisely, they will range about a norm — some houses having more and some less than the average number of particular cultural items, of associated complexes, and of total artifacts. Departure from this normative range theoretically suggests differences in social status, lack of contemporaneity, location of specialized activities within the structure, or other such anomalies.

The consideration of remains by residential units proved to be less revealing than was expected since the variables involved in the occurrence of artifacts obscured some of the ideally predictable conclusions. The variable of deposition involves the material culture present in the house at the time of abandonment. Ideally, all of the belongings that were normally kept in the house would be there when the last person left for the last time. In actuality, the structure may have been more or less cleaned out. The variable of preservation involves the human and environmental agents that might remove, alter, or destroy all or part of the contents between the time of abandonment and the time of discovery by the archaeologist. The variable of discovery involves the position of the site, the techniques of excavation, and the interpretation of the findings.

It is obvious that these complicating variables preclude the derivation of precise information that would enable the archaeologist to predict the range of material culture items that will be present in a given site. In fact, the occurrence of regular distributions or informative associations could almost be termed valuable accidents. Yet the examination of archaeological data for patterned distribution of remains is a rewarding study. This has been demonstrated in numerous site descriptions and has been treated theoretically in some detail (Steward and Setzler 1938; Taylor 1948).

The pit houses in the caves of the Prayer Rock district provided an opportunity to establish the material culture components of a typical residential unit with some degree of accuracy. Some houses in particular appeared to have been abandoned with a large number of items inside. These remains do not precisely follow patterns, because of the factors mentioned above, but some trends were noted. Fire had burned most of the houses, charring some of the contents and destroying other material within the structures and in neighboring areas of trash. The remains of human occupation in post-Basketmaker times might have introduced error into the interpretation; however, most of the activity of these later people was apparently concentrated on some of the cists. The Basketmaker pit houses were protected by their own collapsed superstructures and by deposits of trash. The caves were excavated and the artifacts catalogued by sector or by the architectural unit in which they were found. Most of the sectors have been dropped from the artifactual presentation as they proved to reflect nothing of distributional significance but were considered in this evaluation. More precise locations even than these were provided for many specimens in the field notes.

Specimens listed in the field notes are here designated by descriptive category where possible; this could not be determined in all cases because some specimens were too poorly preserved to bring in from the field and because it has not been possible to account for every artifact. Many heavy stone artifacts were not catalogued; most of those that were field catalogued by the present author in 1958 could not be assigned to house units. These various difficulties notwithstanding, the artifactual assemblage for each house is presented in as complete a form as possible. About half of the pit houses were well enough preserved to permit a tabulation of their contents.

Although no precise patterning was observed, some concentrations of artifact types were noted for some rooms. The remains give some indication of what constituted the typical material culture assemblage for a household unit. Some houses seemed to have concentrations of specialized cultural remains reflecting their place of manufacture and use; although in some cases this is probably the product of the combined variables of deposition and discovery, in many instances it is believed to indicate the prehistoric distribution.

Most of the houses were equipped with a shallow trough metate, one to several manos, and several rubbing stones. Many houses had a boulder mortar and a stone pestle. It is believed that a thin stone cooking slab was present in most houses, although the lack of identification during excavation led to their description under a variety of terms. A number were noted on the surface of Broken Flute Cave in 1958. Flattish, round or oval, river-worn cobblestones of many sizes were found in almost every house.

Most houses had more than one each of plain gray pots, unfired mud trays, and baskets. There were many gray vessels of diverse shapes, a few decorated vessels, and occasionally a polished red jar. From one to five unfired basket-impressed trays were present, often stacked with the pottery.

The majority of houses contained from one to many worn sandals, often in piles on the floors or benches. Footprints on the floor of one house indicate that people went barefoot at least some of the time. The piles of characteristically unpaired sandals may be interpreted as common stores from which a person would take two to wear outside. From one to many bone awls were found in most houses, and usually there were one or two digging sticks on the floor.

Aside from these essential components, the houses contained a tremendous miscellany of random artifacts, consisting of occasional occurrences of practically every specimen type noted in the descriptive section. A pair(?) of human hair leggings or anklets was found in Pit House 9 in Broken Flute Cave. A pair of flutes was cached beneath the floor of Pit House 4 in the same cave. Fragments of two other flutes were in the trash fill of a burial in a cist; perhaps they had belonged to the individual interred. The stone bowl with a handle was on the bench in Pit House 6 in Broken Flute Cave, and the flat-bottomed stone bowl was near a wall on the floor of Pit House 4 in Pocket Cave. This latter room was apparently the workshop of an arrow maker, as evidenced by the minute flakes of chalcedony which littered the floor. To what extent this kind of occurrence is more than accidental is a matter of question.

A number of rooms had caches of valuables beneath the floors or at the backs of benches. These ranged from jewelry to rodent-skin sacks full of possibly sacred items to a cache of six perfect ears of corn, intended possibly for seed corn or ceremonial usage.

Besides these specific artifacts there were many generalized items found in quantity in most houses. Among these were worked sticks, bundles, twists and aprons of fiber, hundreds of pieces of cordage, and scraps of material. The identity of some of these would be apparent only to the maker, and some must have sifted into the houses during the time of their ruin, but all had some place in the lives of the people.

The contents of the excavated cists consisted of wind-blown sand, fallen wall and roof material, and in some cases a certain amount of culture-bearing trash. The few artifacts found in the trash appeared to be completely random. Apparently the effects of accidents of deposition, preservation and discovery were such that there was no associational information to be derived from the contents of cists. It is believed that if any cists were left intact by the Basketmaker inhabitants, they were disturbed by later people prior to excavation.

Most of the surface areas of the caves had a layer of trash superimposed on the sterile materials of the natural formation of the caves, and in some cases on previously abandoned pit houses. This was examined in detail for a patterned distribution of artifacts by material or function. The only seemingly significant trend was that most of the wood and clay human figurines came from Pit House 9, or the trash overlying it, in Broken Flute Cave. Other than this it can only be said that some caves and some areas within caves were richer in total number of artifacts than others.

It was possible to derive some information on what would compose a normative household, but some of the most suggestive specimens were so scarce that only their presence in the total assemblage could be noted. This suggests that recording the range of occurrence of specimens may be more productive than a house-by-house listing. A useful approach is that by Amsden (1949), portrayed especially for the Basketmaker. The range of items is presented with the range of probable uses and activities with which they were associated. Within this is a consideration of the associations which occur with varying frequencies, ethnographic examples, and a certain amount of intuitive interpretation. The large amount of information to be obtained from the number, variety, and distribution of artifacts in Pit House 6 in Broken

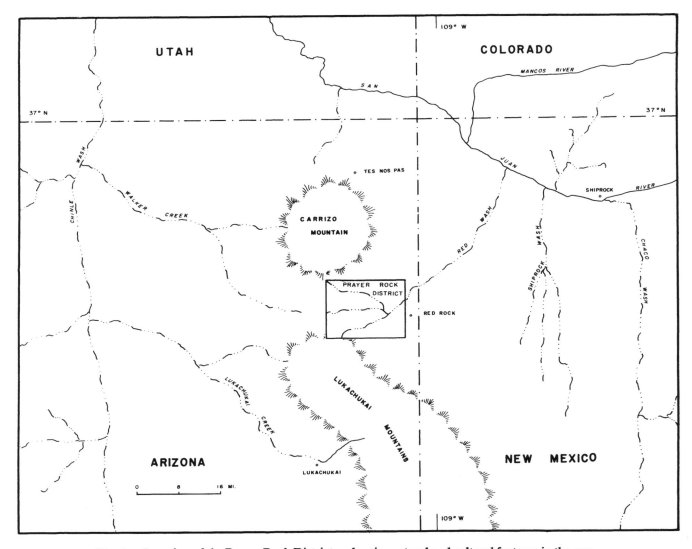

Fig. 1.   Location of the Prayer Rock District and major natural and cultural features in the area.

Flute Cave, for instance, or the pit houses in Cave 8, provides more information pertinent to the reconstruction of Basketmaker life than carefully charted qualitative and quantitative distribution studies. The results of these latter efforts are more useful in the establishment of the degree of likeness between sites with possible areal and temporal differences.

THE PRAYER ROCK DISTRICT

The Prayer Rock district lies in the extreme northeast corner of Arizona, within the Navajo Indian Reservation, 30 miles south of the Arizona-Utah border and 45 miles southwest of the town of Shiprock, New Mexico. The area considered here is on the east side of a forested ridge that connects the Lukachukai and Carrizo mountain masses. These mountains are composed of metamorphosed sandstones with some admixture of

igneous rocks. They rise 2,500 feet above the valley floor to altitudes of more than 9,000 feet. The Prayer Rock valley is composed of several box canyons drained by the western tributaries of Red Wash, which flows north to the San Juan river (see map, Fig. 1).

East of the cave area is Red Rock trading post, located on Red Wash; nearby are a school, some mission buildings, and a cluster of Navajo hogans. About ten miles to the west of the trading post, south of the caves described in this report, is Cove, a uranium mining settlement. There are Navajo hogans scattered over most of the area, with rough tracks leading between them.

Toward its head Black Horse Creek valley narrows between walls of rock with a few southern ramifications and many pockets and canyons extending toward the north. About three miles west of the mouth of the canyon the main watercourse becomes narrow and a wider branch comes in from the northwest. The Navajo wagon

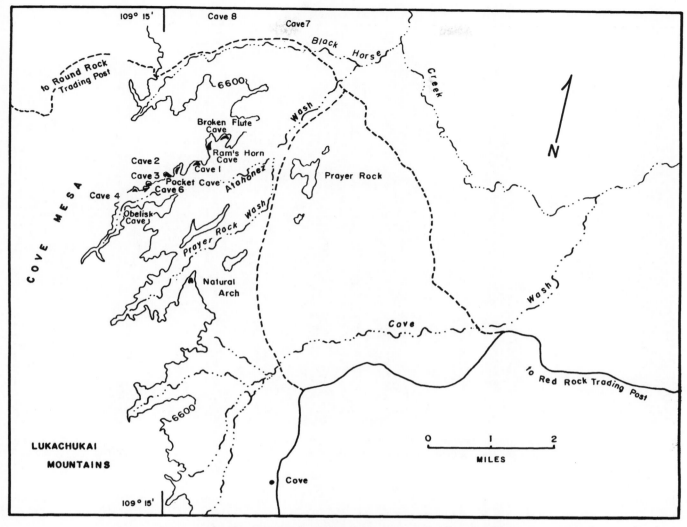

Fig. 2.   Map of Atahonez Wash showing the caves in which excavations were conducted,
and prominent cultural and physiographic features in the area.

track that crosses the divide to the Chinle valley winds
up between the two tributaries. The eastern side of Red
Wash opens out onto a flat plain, which rises to an
imperceptible divide separating this valley from that of
the Chaco Wash. The Prayer Rock itself is a prominent
sandstone monolith that stands directly east of the mouth
of Atahonez canyon (see map, Fig. 2). The U.S. Geological Survey quadrangle for Redrock Valley may be
consulted for topographic details.

The Prayer Rock canyons have flat floors deeply
incised by modern arroyos. The perpendicular sandstone
cliffs on the north sides of the tributaries are dotted with
rock shelters (Fig. 3).

The southernmost canyon is called Atahonez (Navajo
for "long trap-like box canyon"). On its north side lie
Broken Flute Cave, Ram's Horn Cave, Pocket Cave,
and Caves 1, 2, 3, 4, and 6 (see Fig. 2). Obelisk Cave
lies in the south-facing wall of the open-mouthed canyon

adjacent to the south, and Caves 7 and 8 lie side by side
on the east wall of the northern tributary of Black Horse
Creek, about two miles to the north. Cave 9 is described
as being in the next canyon north of the tributary of
Black Horse Creek in which Caves 7 and 8 are located.

Caves 5, 10, 11, and 12 are not specifically located
or described in the field notes, but there is every reason
to believe that they are in the described canyons or the
immediate vicinity, and that the archaeological remains
are consistent with the main body of Prayer Rock
Basketmaker materials.

Geology

The basal strata of the Lukachukai Mountains are
composed of massive red sandstone, and most of the
range is capped with a basalt formation. The lower
portion of the dissected sandstone is a member of the
Triassic Wingate formation and it forms the canyons

Fig. 3.   View of Atahonez Canyon, looking west. Note the caves in the north wall, the arroyo in the center of the valley floor, and the distribution of vegetation over the physiographic features.

in which the Prayer Rock caves are located. The formation exhibits crossbedding, which weathers into sheer cliffs (Harshbarger and others 1957: 10).

Heads of the canyon ramifications consist of overhanging cliffs; these are designated caves in the Southwest, although in reality they are rock shelters. Typically they occur above the valley floor at the junction of two distinct strata in the red sandstone. Water seepage occurs along the contact between the strata, and the moisture has worn away the base of the upper stratum more rapidly than its upper levels, producing the recesses that were used as shelters by ancient peoples.

At the present time, small pools of water can be observed standing below some of the caves where the floors of the tributary canyons abut the sides of the main canyon. This water may derive from rainfall runoff or from ground water seepage or both. In any case, the pools probably constituted a major source of water for the inhabitants of the caves.

The fact that the occupied caves are consistently on the north sides of the canyons might be attributed to two possible factors: first, the erosion of the south slopes usually did not produce caves with floors that were large enough to be used by the prehistoric peoples; second,

the southern exposure to the sun may have been considered an important requirement in choosing a habitation (as in the case of the Pueblo sites).

The valley floors are cut by arroyos and lined with minor escarpments of sandstone. Here and there, fantastically eroded remnants tower above the sage, and occasionally black volcanic necks project through the red sandstone formations.

Climate

The U.S. Weather Bureau station closest to the Prayer Rock district is 45 miles away at Shiprock, New Mexico (elevation about 4,900 feet). The Shiprock records were compared with those from Tohatchi, New Mexico, about 70 miles distant, because its elevation, 6,800 feet, is closer to that of the Prayer Rock valley and both locations are at the eastern edge of the mountains (see Table 1). There was variation between the two stations from one year to the next, but annual precipitation curves plotted for the last 30 years were roughly parallel. Elevation above sea level appears to determine the relative amounts of moisture at these two stations. The entire area receives most of its moisture from summer storms in July, August, and sometimes September. The winter

TABLE 1
Climatic Data from Shiprock and Tohatchi, New Mexico, 1931–1961

	Shiprock	Tohatchi
Average annual precipitation	7 inches	9 inches
Range in annual precipitation	2.1–15.9 inches	4.4–15.7 inches
Average annual mean temperature	53.5 degrees	52.4 degrees
Average annual frost-free days *	159 days	176 days
Range in annual frost-free days *	131–178 days	142–193 days

* Indicates data taken from 1953–1961.
Source: United States Weather Bureau Records.

months of December, January, and February are some-what damper than spring and fall because of snowfall. Although the higher station at Tohatchi records a greater rainfall and a slightly colder annual mean temperature than the Shiprock station, it also has more frost-free days. The shorter growing season at Shiprock is presumably a phenomenon related to cold air drainage in the immediate vicinity of the San Juan River valley.

Flora

The high mesas, talus slopes, and rocky ridges throughout the Prayer Rock district are overgrown with piñon pine and juniper trees (see Fig. 3). Along the ledges on the south slopes of the canyons are occasional Douglas fir trees, supported by shade, seepage, and the presence of waterfalls during storms. The level spaces of the valley floor support only a growth of sage. The adjacent mountains are covered with a heavy stand of ponderosa pine and Douglas fir trees. On the mountain-tops and on north slopes the forest is spotted with clumps of quaking aspen. Several kinds of oaks grow in more exposed places. Numerous types of brush and bushes line the watercourses today and presumably did so in the past.

The following kinds of wood were noted among the archaeological remains. The list is not exhaustive but represents a sample of the vegetative materials used by the Basketmaker people. The range of genera present would seem to parallel those available in modern times.

Arizona Cypress (?), *Cupressus arizonica*
Barberry, *Berberis* sp.
Boxelder, *Acer negundo*
Carrizo cane, *Phragmites communis*
Douglas fir, *Pseudotsuga taxifolia*
Gambel's oak, *Quercus Gambelli*
Hop sage, *Grayia* sp.
Juniper, *Juniperus* sp.
Mountain mahogany, *Cercocarpus* sp.
Piñon pine, *Pinus edulis*
Ponderosa pine, *Pinus ponderosa*
Sage, *Salvia* sp.
Silk tassel, *Garrya* sp.
Shrub live oak, *Quercus turbinella*
Willow, *Salix* sp.

Fauna

The area is largely devoid of game today as a result of the activities of the Navajo Indians, but archaeological remains indicate considerable diversity in the range of species once available. Again, the listing below is not complete but gives an indication of the species utilized by the prehistoric inhabitants.

Birds

Eagle (?), *Aquila* sp.
Hawk, *Buteo* sp.
Oriole, *Icterus* sp.
Piñon Jay, *Cyanocephalus cyanocephalus*
Red-naped sapsucker, *Sphyrapicus varius nuchalis*
Red-shafted flicker, *Colaptes cafer*
Roadrunner, *Geococcyx californicus*
Steller's jay, *Cyanocitta stelleri*
Trumpeter swan, *Olor cf. buccinator*
Turkey, *Melagris gallopavo*

Mammals

Antelope, *Antilopcapra americana*
Badger, *Taxidea taxis*
Bear, *Ursus americanus*
Deer, *Odocoileus* sp.
Dog, *Canis familiaris*
Lion, *Felis concolor*
Mountain sheep, *Ovis canadensis*
Rat, *Crisetinae*, gen. et sp. indet.
Rodents, *Rodentia*, gen. et sp. indet.

Prehistoric Occupation

At present the valley floors of the Prayer Rock district are incised by straight-walled washes that have cut deeply into the light red sandy soil. As a consequence, although the rainfall is adequate and spring water is available, only occasional spots are suitable for cultivation. This condition, however, is distinctly recent. Navajo Indians living nearby in 1931 recalled a time when the valleys were not cut by arroyos and the rainwater that came down from the rocks flooded the canyon floor.

Under aboriginal conditions the Prayer Rock valley would have been an excellent place for habitation. Shelter was available in the large numerous caves in the canyon walls. Moisture derived from snow and rainfall was supplemented by springs at the edges of the canyons, and the relatively flat valley floors provided space for cultivation. A large number of animal and plant species were available in the different ecological zones in the immediate vicinity. However, there is not a single large Pueblo ruin to be found in the entire area. Small sites of all ages are numerous, but they appear to have been only temporary settlements.

Morris's survey of the district indicates that the heaviest population was present during the Basketmaker III period. Characteristic Basketmaker sherds are to be observed at open sites out in the valley and are plentiful on the narrow ridges that run down from the mesa edges.

But the caves seem to have been the preferred locations of these Basketmaker people. Every overhang with a sunward exposure and with a remaining floor shows traces of their presence. In a few overhangs where the floor is weathered away, pictographs along the wall suggest that they, too, were once inhabited.

Superimposed on the Basketmaker refuse in some of the caves is a thin discontinuous layer of Pueblo remains. In large part, these consist of crude masonry storage cists and bins, built against the back wall. The small size of the rooms and the lack of Pueblo pottery indicate the nonresidential nature of this late occupation. Sherd areas exhibiting wares associated with the Chaco, Mesa Verde, and Kayenta areas in Pueblo III times were noted throughout the valley. These were uniformly small and no masonry was visible.

The Prayer Rock area was neglected archaeologically during the early exploration of prehistoric remains in the Southwest, and many sites remain to be dug. Morris made the only organized excavations after the preliminary work of the 1930 Bernheimer Expedition. He offers the following explanation in his field notes:

It lay well off the beaten track, and there was nothing to suggest to those who passed by across the Reservation to the eastward that the valley might contain early remains of conspicuous interest and importance. In the summer of 1928, chance took me to the topmost peak of the Carrizos. From that vantage point the valley lay in panorama beneath me, and I could see in the canyon walls at its western side the black shadows that filled the mouths of scores of caves. In 1930 I joined the Bernheimer Expedition of the American Museum of Natural History, which spent three weeks in reconnaissance of the district lying between the Red Rock Store and the Chinle Valley. As a result of what I saw on the reconnaissance trip, the summer of 1931 was spent in exploring these caves.

2. THE SITES

Fig. 4.   View of Broken Flute Cave, looking north.

Examination of the sites described in the following pages was performed by Morris in 1931. Broken Flute Cave, Obelisk Cave, Pocket Cave, Cave 1, Cave 2, and Cave 8 were excavated or intensively examined and the remainder were tested. Although much of the material in the site descriptions has been taken directly from his field notes, the verb tenses have been regulated somewhat for consistency and readability.

BROKEN FLUTE CAVE

Broken Flute Cave faces south from the head of the easternmost cove on the north side of Atahonez. It is about 50 m below the brink of the cliff and some 80 m above the valley floor (Fig. 4).

The floor of the cave is roughly horseshoe-shaped, 120 m in length and varying from 3 to 25 m in width (Fig. 5). As indicated by the absence of the forward edges of several pit houses, the cave floor was broader at the time of occupation than it is at present. The entire floor of the cave is covered by an overhanging cliff that extends beyond the existing edge of the talus slope. Bedrock slopes abruptly downward, falling at about the same angle as the rise of the roof.

The floor of Broken Flute Cave is almost completely covered by remains of human occupation, which in some areas is overlain by an intermittent layer of occupation debris and sterile sandstone detritus fallen from the roof. Sixteen pit houses, 65 cists, several walking surfaces, and a probable great kiva were built on trash, sterile earth, and bedrock. Nowhere in this cave is seen the waterlaid clay deposit or "hardpan" that occurs in a number of the caves in northeastern Arizona.

Occasional large blocks of sandstone were not built over but had served as tool-shaping areas or as space for petroglyphs. Traces of pictographs (Fig. 6a) and petroglyphs (Fig. 6b) may be seen on the back wall of the cave but many have been destroyed by the scaling of the rock. Doubtless some of the art work and some portions of the ceramics and architecture can be attributed to people who came to the cave after the Basketmakers had left.

The eastern portion of the cave has an extremely irregular surface with huge sandstone blocks protruding from beneath it. Numerous cists and at least two pit houses had been built in the available space, but these were so crushed by a subsequent rockfall that their number and character could not be determined with certainty. Some deposits of trash and many rat nests were noted in this area.

In the broadest part of the cave, west of the debris in the east end, is a large circle of sandstone slabs, interpreted by the excavator as a Great Kiva. The floor level of this structure appears to be that of the ground level

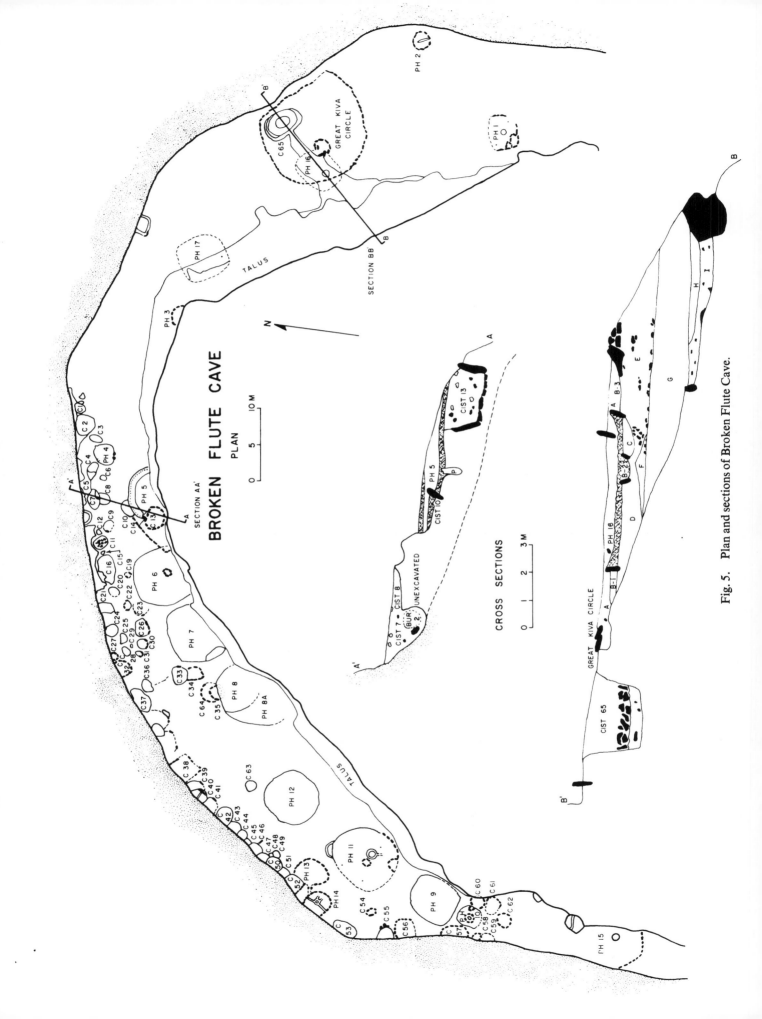

BROKEN FLUTE CAVE

PLAN

SECTION AA'

0   5   10 M

N

TALUS

PH 3

PH 17

TALUS

SECTION BB

GREAT KIVA CIRCLE

PH 2

PH I

C 65

PH 16

C I

C 2

C 3

C 4

(PH 4)

C 5

C 6

C 7

C 8

C 9

PH 5

C IO

C I4

C I3

C II

C I2

C I5

C I6

C 20

C I9

C 21

C 22

C 23

C 24

C 25

C 29

C 26

C 27

C 28

C 30

C 31

C 32

C 36

C 33

C 34

C 64

C 35

C 37

PH 6

PH 7

PH 8

PH 8A

C 38

C 39

C 40

C 41

C 63

PH 12

C 42

C 43

C 44

C 45

C 46

C 47

C 48

C 49

C 50

C 51

C 52

PH 13

PH II

PH I4

C 53

C 54

C 55

PH 9

C 56

C 57

C 58

C 59

C 60

C 6I

C 62

PH 15

CROSS SECTIONS

0   1   2   3 M

A'

CIST 7

CIST 8

(BUR. 2)

UNEXCAVATED

CIST IO

PH 5

CIST 13

A

GREAT KIVA CIRCLE

A

B-1

PH 16

A

B-2

B-3

C

D

E

F

G

H

I

B

CIST 65

B'

Fig. 5.   Plan and sections of Broken Flute Cave.

at the time of the Basketmaker occupation, and the ring of slabs is considered to be the edge or the facing of a bench.

In the central part of the cave is a nearly continuous row of cists built against the back wall, which in many cases serves as a portion of the cist walls and floors. A row of closely spaced pit houses is built at the edge of the talus slope. Erosion of the edge of the slope has removed portions of four of these structures.

The rows of cists and pit houses meet at the narrowest portion of the cave floor, near the west end. The areas between Cists 57, 58, and Pit House 10 and south of Cist 59 show remnants of mud surfacing. Whether these pertained to cists or to part of a level yard could not be determined.

The space from Pit House 10 to the end of the cave was probably filled with cists and rooms that have completely weathered away. Rain coming down the cliff has moistened the entire area and wind has removed a great deal of material. The stain of ashes and decayed refuse was seen in several test pits, but Pit House 15 was the only structure found.

Great Kiva Circle

A section was made through the Great Kiva Circle in Broken Flute Cave (B-B′ in Fig. 5). Because of the lack of cross referencing, most of the description below is taken verbatim from the field notes. There is an intriguing possibility of one or more earlier occupation levels, and thus it is desirable to preserve precisely the impressions of the excavator.

Layer A. At the surface was a deposit laid down during the Basketmaker III occupation of the cave. It was composed of sand, small rocks, and a considerable amount of trash.

Layer B. Pit House 16, which was burned, was under the fill of Layer A. Its age is uncertain. The lack of fired pottery suggests a Basketmaker II age, but some Basketmaker III pit houses in the cave lacked pottery. Since the rest of the houses and most of the artifacts in the cave are assigned to the Basketmaker III period, it would seem likely that this structure was also built in that period.

B-1. Between the real wall of Pit House 16 and the natural material of the rising cave floor, there was a layer of clean sand, with a streak of ash and vegetation at the top of it.

B-2. The pit house itself was not excavated extensively enough to recover many constructional details.

B-3. The Basketmaker III living surface, hard-tramped and black from use, sloped down from the surface of the rockfall at the front of the cave to the wall of Pit House 16; the living surface and the pit house wall were contemporaneous.

Layer C. This dug hole had been filled with cave sand containing some of the juniper bark and other vegetative material originally deposited above the rockfall in the top of Layer E and in front of Pit House 16. Its age cannot be stated positively; possibly it dates from the Basketmaker II period.

Layer D. This layer consisted of wind-blown sand and fine scale from the roof. In it were darker laminations containing small amounts of organic material. Very fine charcoal was present in both the sand and the laminations. Although hairlike rootlets were present at least throughout the upper two-thirds of this layer, indicating some degree of moisture at one time, the decay of other organic materials was not complete; bits of acorn shells and fragments of leaves were observable. The strata sloped upward toward the front of the cave.

Layer E. This deposit was like that in Layer D except that the strata were horizontal. At the brink of the cave floor Layer E was overlain with a rockfall, which had come down upon clean material with no trace of a definite habitation level.

Layer F. This layer consisted of a ridge of clean sand containing a series of dark laminations. Charcoal was observed throughout the deposit. It is difficult to explain the origin of this ridge, and appearances where the section was taken may not have revealed an original condition. Forward of the ridge there was a quantity of sandstone fallen from the roof. Into the upper part of this a hole (*Layer C,* described above) had been dug by the occupants of the cave, so that the depth and mass of the fall could not be determined. It seems possible that the impact of a heavy block of stone coming down from a height of at least 15 m onto a soft damp surface would have compressed the material underneath, interrupting continuous strata and creating the impression of a ridge behind the point of break as indicated in the cross section. Surface ridges of similar shape have been noted near the back walls of several caves by the author.

Layer G. This layer was a stratified deposit of sand and organic material. The strata were generally horizontal but were somewhat wavy in form. The most conspicuous bands were dark in color and relatively hard, varying in thickness from 1 to 5 mm. In some places single bands were separated by several centimeters of softer material, while in others the bands were grouped close together, forming compact masses as much as 6 cm in thickness. The dark color of these laminations is due to the large proportion of charcoal, ash, and organic material. The softer material between them was of relatively clean sand. Occasional chunks of charcoal up to 3 mm in diameter were observed. Half way down in the deposit there was a portion of a charred gourd or squash seed. Fragments of at least two species of snail shells and some small white spherical objects of calcareous

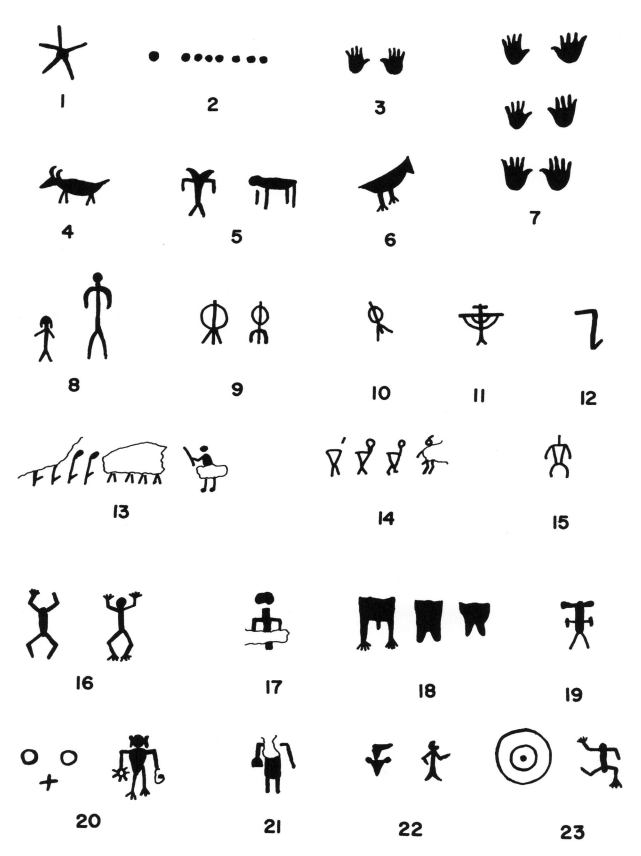

Fig. 6a. Pictographs on rear wall of Broken Flute Cave in 1958, 1–23 (red, 1, 7, 12, 15; white, 2, 4–6, 8–11, 16, 18–20, 22, 23; green, 3; black, 13, 14; yellow, 17; white with black object in hand, 21).

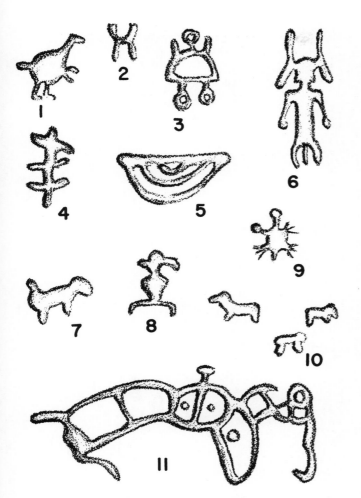

Fig. 6b. Petroglyphs on rear wall of Broken Flute Cave in 1958, 1–11. (Not to scale.)

composition were observed. The forward edge of the layer was laid down against a large block lying at the front of the cave. This deposit may be interpreted as a mass laid down by the alternating action of wind and water, with the clean sand strata blown in during relatively dry intervals. The thin bands, containing the larger proportions of charcoal and other organic material, represent the residue left by rain water that ran into the cave and filtered into the surface. The fact that the deposit was repeatedly wet would account for the absence of the leaves and twigs that inevitably would have found their way into such an accumulation. On top of Layer G was a layer up to 6 cm thick of sandstone scaled off of the roof.

Layer H. This basin-shaped deposit of stratified material consisted of coarse sand, fine sandstone particles, and pebbles with rounded edges. The surface of this deposit bore a clearly defined stratum, very fine-grained and dark gray in color, presumably because of the presence of a considerable quantity of ash. In this stratum chunks of charcoal were discernible, and at the lower

edge of it there were three pieces of charcoal slightly larger than cherry stones. As can be seen in the cross section, Layer H is apparently the initial element of a deposit laid down in a pre-existing cavity. The lines of the strata and the presence of the weathered gravel suggest water deposition.

Layer I. The natural cave floor consists of large blocks of stone and of finer stone debris. There is no indication of vegetable or other foreign matter.

Comment. It would appear that at the time much of the material in this cross section was being deposited, a barrier existed across the front of the cave. The basinlike shape of Layer H and the great block at and partly beneath its forward edge show plainly enough that there was higher ground farther forward. The great block is an indication that the barrier may have been composed of stones fallen from the cliff above. The presence of so much charcoal and decayed organic material from the lower limit of Layer H to the top of Layer E should have left no question as to the human origin of this deposition, but positive proof of inhabitation of the cave, in the form of artifacts and definite living surfaces, was not recovered until Level C, the dug hole beneath the forward edge of Pit House 16, was excavated. The charcoal in the strata laid by wind and water beneath and forward from this point resulted from manmade fires, and the length of time since the lowest portions of it were laid down must have been great.

RAM'S HORN CAVE

Ram's Horn Cave is in the west wall about one-half mile southwest of Broken Flute Cave, and is the only other habitable shelter in this cove of Atahonez Canyon (see Fig. 2). The cave has a small circular opening protected from the prevailing wind. Rainwater cascades over the natural flying buttress at its eastern end and falls as a fine spray from the other extremity. This in part accounts for the heavy growth of pine, oak, and underbrush on the ledge beneath the talus slope. The floor of the cave is crescent-shaped, 44 m long across the talus slope and 2.25 m at its greatest width. The overall depth of the cave, from the front ends of the floor to the back of the crescent, is about 8 m. At least one-third of the floor space was unavailable for occupation because of rain drip, despite the overhang of the roof, which is nearly double the width of the cave floor.

On the back wall were pictographs and petroglyphs characteristic of Basketmaker III and modern Navajo Indians. At the north end, faint cist marks and pecked sockets for the butts of timbers were traceable. The poorly preserved remains of two pit houses and three cists were uncovered. A test trench through the center of the floor encountered dampness at a depth of 30 cm, probably seepage through the back wall. A few Basketmaker III artifacts were recovered.

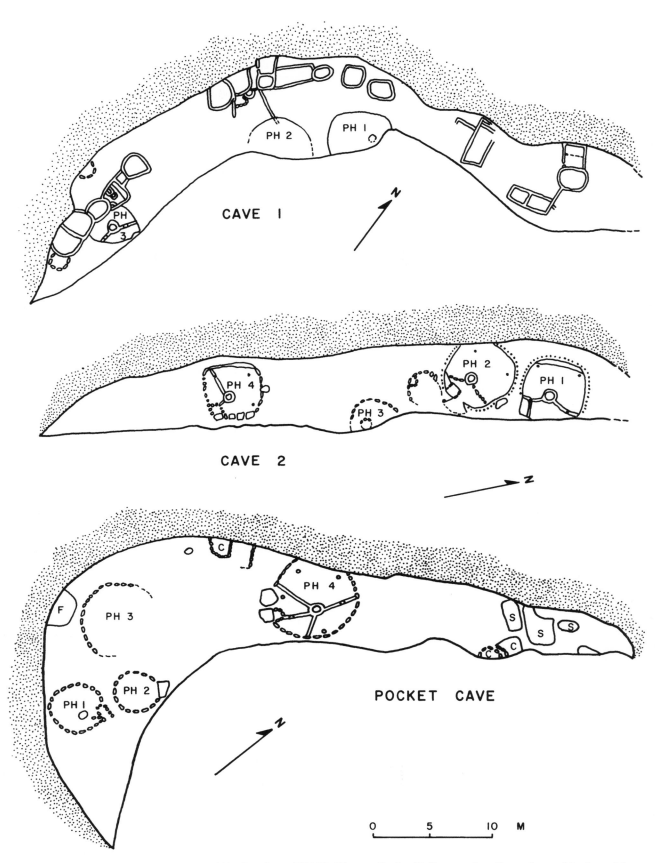

Fig. 7. Plans of Cave 1, Cave 2, and Pocket Cave. PH, Pit House; C, cist; F, floor pocket; S, sandstone block or slab.

Fig. 8.   Pueblo storage rooms built over Basketmaker III remains at the back of Cave 1.

CAVE 1

Cave 1 is situated at the back of the next tributary canyon west of the cove containing Broken Flute and Ram's Horn caves (see Fig. 2). It faces southeast and overlooks the Atahonez valley. The cave is about 50 m long and 8 m wide (see plan, Fig. 7). Most of the floor was covered with a hard crust of sheep manure, indicating use of the cave as a corral by the Navajo Indians.

A row of masonry rooms was located along the back wall (Fig. 8). With the exception of the highest structures, the rooms were piled full of wall debris covered with sheep droppings. In front of these rooms was a relatively smooth floor dipping slightly toward the mouth. Immediately under the layer of manure were neckbanded and decorated Pueblo I potsherds and fragments of coarse plaited sandals presumably dating from the same period. Any pit houses in the central part of the cave had been trampled into oblivion. Two large Basketmaker III pit houses were found in the central part of the cave and one similar structure was found in the southwest end. These chambers had burned and were in a poor state of preservation. Where the pit houses came closest to the back wall of the cave, the cave fill debris was moist, and there were indications that at one time the cave floor had been much wetter than at present. This caused the decay of any perishable substances that had not been charred, and for this reason the remainder of the cave was not cleared.

Cave 1 was first occupied during the Basketmaker III period, of which Pit Houses 1, 2, and 3 and possibly some of the slab elements of the small enclosures are representative. Subsequently, the floor of the cave was completely occupied by Pueblo people who erected the small rectangular and oval surface chambers with masonry walls in which mud was a major component. It is notable that these people had practically ceased to use vegetal reinforcement in their masonry.

CAVE 2

Cave 2 is 100 m upcanyon from Cave 1, west of the first shoulder of cliff (see Fig. 2). It is a relatively deep cave, commanding a magnificent view of the valley and of the north end of the Lukachukai Mountains, which are visible through a gap in the south side of Atahonez Canyon.

The drip line of the cave roof is about 25 m forward of the rear wall at the deepest point of the crescent. The occupied floor area is about 50 m long and 5 to 8 m wide (see plan, Fig. 7); at one time the floor was much larger, but erosion has removed large areas of fill and exposed the bare bedrock at both ends. Two or three vestiges of cists were discovered against the back wall in areas where the floor was missing.

Under a layer of modern sheep dung were found remains of four Basketmaker III pit houses and at least three cists. The flat area west of Pit House 3 probably contained architectural remains at one time, but all traces have weathered away.

CAVE 3

Cave 3 is situated high in the west wall of the next tributary canyon west of that containing Cave 2. The existing floor level is about 175 m long. The roof has a considerable overhang, but the debris forming the floor of the cave has weathered away so that only a narrow space suitable for habitation is left against the back wall. The floor area has an uneven surface with masses of rockfall projecting at intervals. Most of the hummocks and depressions were at one time covered with prehistoric construction.

The remains of at least six Basketmaker pit houses were found. Between them were vestiges of storage rooms and of large slab and masonry cists, some of them with slabs standing shoulder-high. Little of the cave was considered worth excavating. One structure had burned after removal of its contents, and the timber had been taken out of the other pit houses for use elsewhere. There was little fill in any of the cists or storage rooms. The cave was apparently abandoned while others in the neighborhood continued to be occupied.

POCKET CAVE

Pocket Cave is upcanyon from Cave 3, in the next overhang of the north wall in which any floor remains (see Fig. 2). It faces southeast, commanding a magnificent view of Prayer Rock and the line of three pinnacles of which Shiprock is the most distant member.

The cave is pouch-shaped, about 60 m long, and 12 m at its greatest width (see plan, Fig. 7). The floor has weathered back for some distance beyond the drip line of the overhanging cliff and is very irregular. All of the strata found in superposition in the cave were exposed in some part of the uneven surface.

Overlying the bedrock at the bottom of the cave fill was a sterile deposit of sandstone detritus. The upper portion of this sterile layer consisted of a layer of "hard-pan," a clay deposit presumably laid by water. Two amorphous depressions had been sunk to a maximum depth of 1.8 m in the hardpan layer; these were filled with trash composed largely of ashes with a light admixture of juniper bark and chips. Two chipped stone blades and a few plain Basketmaker III sherds were the only artifacts found, and there was not a single potsherd in the lowest 1.5 m of deposit. Several burials had been dug into the uppermost portion of the hardpan.

The trash layer above the hardpan was lying exposed at the south end of the cave, thickened toward the center, and as the cave floor rose, thinned out to a thickness of less than 1 meter at the edge of Pit House 4. Overlying and partially sunken into this trash deposit were the remains of four Basketmaker III pit houses and a large number of cists. The similarity of the contents of the deposit in and around these features, as well as the presence of Basketmaker III sherds in the immediately underlying trash, indicates that there was no significant temporal difference between the structures and the trash on which they were built.

The pit houses were built in the southern and western portions of the cave where the floor was broadest. In size and construction they were consistent with others in the Prayer Rock pit house complex. The excavated portions of the rest of the cave contained the remains of a number of badly ruined cists, and an area east of Pit House 3 had been used as a turkey pen. A compact mass of turkey droppings, juniper bark, and shredded corn leaves and tassels was 20 cm deep at the brink of the talus, thickening to a depth of 95 cm at a point 5 m in from the slope, and then thinning out toward the cliff wall. A stone pendant and two or three strings were the only artifacts found; not a single potsherd was seen. In the overlying trash was a wide-mouthed gray jar containing a clay stopper. It had been cached lying on its side and held the stripped-back husks of two ears of corn.

Many of the cists were located along the back of the cave floor. A few artifacts were found in these features, but in most cases only incomplete floors and badly crushed slab or mud walls could be seen. The trash surrounding and filling these ruined structures contained burned stones, chunks of vegetal-reinforced mud, some Basketmaker III sherds, and a few artifacts. This mass of material varied in depth from 0 to 1.73 m. In the east end of the deposit near the back of the cave were the jaw and other bones of an adult.

Overlying the Basketmaker debris in the end of the cave east of Pit House 4 was a large rockfall. This area was not excavated. A second area of rockfall, as much as 60 cm thick, was found on top of the deposit of turkey droppings east of Pit House 3. Between the blocks, rats had built nests incorporating Basketmaker remains. On a large block at the inner edge of this fall were a row of "axe-grinding" slots, four of which had pecked depressions above and below the troughs, and several petroglyphs. This block was on top of Basketmaker III trash and therefore is later than at least some of the Basketmaker III occupation. Some indications of additional rockfall were seen in the north end of the cave, where large chunks of sandstone were mixed in with the trash and ruined cists.

CAVE 4

There is a heavy overhang that appears to be the head of Atahonez as one looks westward up the canyon. Cave 4 is in the west side of the first northern cove downstream from this overhang (see Fig. 2). The shelter is some 40 m long by 8 m wide at its deepest point, and the floor is approximately level, sloping slightly downward toward the front.

Against the back wall there were the stubs of two slab and mud cists. Toward the southern end were the badly ruined remains of a few other cists that had been excavated in the cave floor and lined with slabs. It would seem that this cave was never a place of habitation and was used only minimally for storage.

The cave had been extensively used as a burial place, and the burials had been robbed in prehistoric times. As a result, human skeletal material and artifactual remains were scattered over the surface in great disarray. Basket fragments, parts of arrow shafts, an occasional sandal, and a few other objects were found in the trash. Only one gray sherd was found in the cave.

CAVE 6

Cave 6 lies to the west of a thin rock partition that comes down from the cliff a short distance upstream from Pocket Cave (see Fig. 2). The entire floor had weathered away since the time of prehistoric occupation, and only the vestiges of three pit houses and two or three cists remained.

The length of the area once covered with buildings was probably about 300 m. The black refuse stretching down the talus beneath the west end of the cave showed that at one time it was a veritable hive of people.

The three pit houses had burned. From the few centimeters of charred material on their floors, several construction timbers and a representative sample of fired and unfired pottery were collected; these included five plain gray and two fiber-tempered vessels. At the extreme south end, a neck-banded Pueblo I jar was cached at the back of one of the Basketmaker houses. Scattered over the surface in the same area were fragments of Pueblo III corrugated vessels.

CAVE 7

The cliffs bordering the north branch of Black Horse Creek, some two miles north of Atahonez, end in a sharp point above broken timbered ridges about one-half mile north of the stream bed. Just west of this point is a cove containing Cave 7.

The shelter is about 100 m long and 7 m wide. A burned Basketmaker III pit house was found in the west end at the edge of the talus. The forward edge of the structure had been eroded away and the back had been destroyed by Pueblo construction. Among the charred contents were undecorated sherds, unfired mud bowls, and half of a clay figurine.

Scattered along the remaining floor area were Pueblo structures built of crude masonry, and Pueblo III sherds exhibiting Mesa Verde influence were noted on the surface. A corrugated pot was found near the center of the cave about 1 m from the back wall.

CAVE 8

Cave 8 lies immediately north of the sharp tongue of cliff that forms the western end of Cave 7. The floor curves deeply, opening toward the southwest, and is more than 175 m long. Except at the southern end, the level space is quite narrow, and the seepage of water from the cliff makes the natural floor unsuitable for habitation. However, at the price of considerable labor, this sloping surface was made suitable for house construction.

A retaining wall consisting of logs and roughly piled stones was built along the front of the cave to an average height of 4 m. The space behind the wall was filled with large stones, and occasional timbers were laid horizontally at right angles to the wall. Three Basketmaker III pit houses were built above the level of the cribbing, partially resting on the constructed mass and partially excavated 0.75 m to 1.25 m into the natural cave floor. The outer edges of the northern two structures were at the surface of the constructed floor mass. A third of the floor of the southern pit house had weathered away by the time of excavation. In the southern end of the cave, a fourth pit house of the same type was built in an open spot between large sandstone blocks. All four pit houses had burned, and a large number of typical Prayer Rock Basketmaker III artifacts were recovered.

Among the sandstone blocks at the south end of the cave, along the back wall behind the pit houses, and along the back wall to the north were numerous cists, but these had been almost entirely destroyed by sheep that had been penned in the cave in recent years.

CAVES 5, 9, 10, 11, AND 12

No field notes or maps have been located for Caves 5, 10, 11, or 12; Cave 9 is described as being in the next canyon north from Caves 7 and 8 in Black Horse canyon. Specimens from these sites are listed in the field catalog and have been included in the artifact description. These

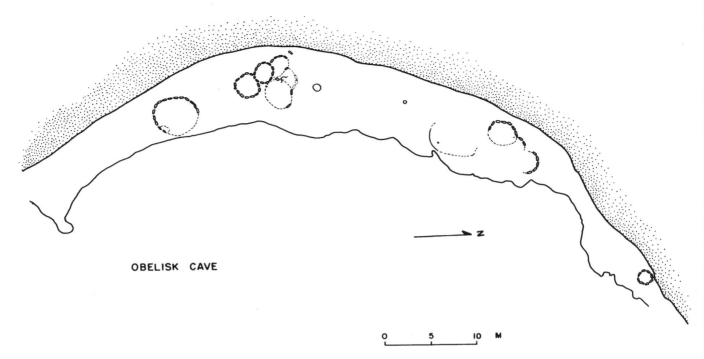

OBELISK CAVE

Fig. 9.   Plan of Obelisk Cave.

items fit satisfactorily into the Basketmaker artifact classes derived for specimens from the described caves. From this fact and from the small quantity of remains involved, it is assumed that the caves were similar in architectural details and were relatively insignificant (Morris 1936). A specimen is listed from Cave 5, Pit House 3, which indicates that this cave had at least three pit houses.

OBELISK CAVE

The cave is located south of Atahonez in the parallel adjacent valley, and it faces south (Figs. 2, 9). This site is an exception to the relative insignificance of the other undescribed caves. The Bernheimer Expedition recovered a number of fine artifacts there, and the Carnegie Institution Expedition found some exceptionally inform-

ative remains. No field notes on Obelisk Cave have been found to date. A summary description included in Morris (1936: 35) indicates a prehistoric occupation that fits into the Prayer Rock complex in detail.

A problem arises concerning the tree-ring dates that range from A.D. 470 to 489. If these are cutting dates and if the year designations can be applied to the houses and the plain gray pottery that was recovered, then this is the earliest Basketmaker III site that has been dug and dated. However, if the dates do not relate to the houses — or if they do and the timbers were salvaged from some earlier structure(s) — then we are not justified in dating the Obelisk Cave remains so early. The evidence at hand does not clarify the situation. It is hoped that further work in the cave or the recovery of the field notes may shed some light on the problem.

3. ARCHITECTURE

The architectural remains were similar in all of the caves excavated and are briefly described. There are occasional discrepencies between the excavator's field notes and the plans of the pit houses — for instance, the notation of a feature in the original plan but not in the field notes, or vice versa. An effort has been made to coordinate the text with the plans, but where discrepencies occur it has been deemed best to include all of the information given both in the descriptions and in the plans.

The pit houses and some of the cists are attributed to the Basketmaker occupation. The remainder of the cists and the masonry rooms belong to the later Pueblo inhabitants. The pit houses were places of residence, as is evidenced by the domestic features and the contents. For the most part the cists were storage chambers, although a few had indications of human habitation. The masonry rooms are small and lack level floors and floor features; this is interpreted to mean that they were constructed primarily for storage, although like the cists they may occasionally have served as shelter for human beings. The consistency of the architectural patterns corresponds with the uniformity of the other material remains and indicates the close relationship between the occupants of the different caves.

SUMMARY DESCRIPTION OF ARCHITECTURAL FEATURES

Pit Houses

The Basketmaker pit houses in the Prayer Rock caves have a distinct and fairly complex type of architecture. There is a certain amount of minor variation from house to house, but the component parts of the complex are almost invariably present. A few houses differ markedly from this pattern in that they lack most of the features discussed below.

Location. The pit houses are scattered along the floors of the caves, occupying no set relationship with respect to one another. The narrow width of most of the caves served to limit their position to a single alignment of structures. Typically, the outward edges of the houses were built on material that has subsequently eroded away. Insofar as can be determined, the houses were oriented toward the talus slope — that is, the hearths are off center in that direction, the radial timbers and wingwalls set off a portion of the floor on that side, and the wall openings interpreted as entryways face in that direction. The number of houses occupying a given cave seems to have been limited by the amount of floor space available. While there were several cases of pit houses superimposed over cists and vice versa, in only one instance were two pit houses overlapping (Pit Houses 8 and 8A in Broken Flute Cave).

Form. Pit house shapes varied from rectangular with rounded corners to round. The wall and floor positions were frequently determined by the position of the bedrock or of roof spalls. The pit houses ranged between 2.25 and 8.5 m in diameter or in greatest dimension, most of them being between 5.0 and 8.0 m. Typically the depth increased from only a few centimeters at the outward edge to as much as 1.5 m on the side nearest the back of the cave.

Benches. Most pit houses had an irregular sand bench, poorly preserved, along the portions of the wall that remained. These benches were constructed over finished floors and varied considerably in height and width within a single room. Heights varied from 10 to 60 cm, with most of them between 20 and 35 cm; widths varied between 25 cm and 30 cm. In a few cases the benches were faced with sandstone slabs, neatly plastered in place. More often a thin mud mortar was used for surfacing. Some benches had a plastered rim along the outside edge; on others the slabs protruded, forming a small rim. In many instances a variety of small artifacts were tucked in next to the wall timbers at the back of the bench. On the tops of two benches, two small sticks were set 45 and 55 cm apart, midway from the wall to the face of the bench. Their use was not apparent.

Walls. Most pit houses had a row of wall timbers set into the ground at the edge of the floor. These varied from 8 to 17 cm in diameter and were 13 to 25 cm apart. In some houses, where the fill beneath the floor was thin, sockets were dug into bedrock. The posts sloped inward, presumably to rest on a log rectangle that served as a frame for the roof (see below). A layer of horizontal reeds or juniper bark was laid on the outside of the wall logs. In some houses a second covering of vertical reeds was laid over the first layer. Slender withes were placed perpendicularly over the outside layer of reeds and were fastened to the wall poles by strips of bark tied through the reeds and around the wall posts. Then the whole was plastered over with mud. At the base of the wall timbers, where the house was built into trash and sand, layers of juniper bark or of sandstone slabs were laid to keep the sand from sifting into the house. An interesting indication of the time of year some of the houses were built is seen in the appearance of the reeds. Carrizo cane is still immature and green in color at the first of August, and sometime during the early winter the large mature green canes turn yellow. Some houses were built with green canes and some with yellow, indicating cutting and probably building in the fall and during the winter.

Roofs. Most houses had four primary roof support posts set away from the walls in an irregular rectangle. In one house a fifth upright was placed for additional support. In two houses the two remaining supporting timbers were set at the base of the wall. Posts varied from 13 to 27 cm in diameter and were made from juniper, fir, or pine. They supported a rectangular frame of logs that held up the flat central part of the roof. On the frame were laid parallel timbers, up to 15 cm in diameter, placed 5 to 8 cm apart, then coated with as much as 13 cm of mud. On one house the timbers were first covered with juniper bark, but in the others the mud was placed directly on the logs. In some houses board shelves had been suspended from the roof. In the construction of such chambers the roof supports and the horizontal rectangle resting upon them were the first elements to be put in place. Then the peripheral timbers were stood up, their ends resting against the sides of the rectangle. The space around the butts was filled with clay, which was wiped up to form a collar about each timber.

Floors. Floors were composed of a thin layer of mud laid over trash, natural earth, bedrock, or some combination of these substances. One house had a floor covering of clean unaltered sand. In some cases, bedrock or fallen roof spalls that had projected through the floor were broken or battered off to produce a level surface. Typically the floors were somewhat irregular and sloped downward toward the center. In one house the thickness and appearance of the floor indicated a number of replasterings. In many houses the floor curved up slightly at the edge, making a rounded angle with the base of the wall. In one house (Pit House 12, Broken Flute Cave) the floor was 7 to 15 cm higher in the area toward the edge than in the main part of the house.

Hearths. Most pit houses had a clearly defined fire hearth. It was a round, or occasionally D-shaped, slab-walled basin located somewhat toward the talus slope from the center of the house. The cracks between the slabs and often the rounded rims of hearths were plastered with mud. The hearths ranged from 10 to 50 cm in total depth, with half or more of that distance below

floor level. They varied from 0.50 to 1.20 m in maximum diameter, with the walls sloping inward toward the bottom. In some instances subfloor blocks of stone necessitated the manufacture of fire basins of irregular size and shape. The lack of a hearth in a pit house is attributed to the erosion of the forward edge of the floor or to poor conditions of preservation.

Ashpit. One house (Pit House 14, Broken Flute Cave) had an ashpit located adjacent to the south side of the fire hearth. It was slab lined, and the cracks and edges were plastered with mud to the same height as the fire hearth. The ashpit was square, about 37 by 37 cm.

Deflector. One house (Pit House 3, Broken Flute Cave) had the base of a wooden deflector, approximately 90 cm long, placed 70 cm from the hearth toward the edge of the slope. It was fashioned from slabs split from a tree at least 50 cm in diameter. The tops of the slabs were burned off just above the ground. Its presence indicates that there was an opening in the house wall, but erosion had removed the wall at the appropriate point. A trough metate was set on edge where the opening should have been, and it may have served as a cover for the aperture.

Radials and wing walls. In many pit houses one to four low mud partitions extended from the hearth to the walls or to cists adjacent to the walls, in the half of the house nearest the front of the cave. Typically these mud ridges had a log for a core, base, or cap. The logs were sometimes raised on a mud and stone base 5 to 15 cm high. In some instances, the use of sandstone slabs set on end increased the height of the wing wall to as much as 40 cm. In some houses one or two of the roof supports were included in the partition wall. The mud bases of the radial partitions ranged up to 27 cm in total width. In one house (Pit House 12, Broken Flute Cave) the portion of the floor near the front of the cave was 7 to 15 cm higher than the portion on the back side of the wing wall.

Storage bins and floor-level cists. Most pit houses had at least one storage bin built inside the house at floor level; some had as many as five. These bins were usually adjacent to a roof support, a radial timber, or the house wall. Most often they were placed at the junction of the radial with the wall. Sometimes they were independent of other floor features. If more than one bin was present in a house, the bins were usually adjacent. Size and shape were irregular; the greatest dimension ranged from 0.35 m to 1.35 m and depth ranged up to 0.75 m. The forms were unstandardized, sometimes determined by the position of the pre-existing features that were to be incorporated into the bin walls. The walls of the bins were constructed of sandstone slabs, sometimes plastered with mud; vertical poles set at intervals and completely plastered over; wooden slabs; or pure mud. One bin was roofed over with small timbers and mud. Another had a stone mortar plastered into it, with mud packed around the top of the mortar to fill the space between it and the wall slabs.

Subfloor cists. Subfloor cavities were found in about half of the houses. They were of two general types — deep irregularly shaped holes and shallow mud-lined basins. The deep holes were less than a meter in diameter and depth, and seem to have been placed anywhere on the house floor. Frequently they were covered with mud flooring material. Some of these may have been abandoned postholes; others may have antedated the house construction. One contained an assemblage, perhaps a cache, consisting of pumpkin seeds, grass stems, and the cordage of a feather fan; another contained six perfect ears of corn. The shallow mud-lined cists were usually located near the fire hearth. Their diameter was less than a meter and the depth less than the diameter. They did not exhibit baking due to heating. It has been suggested that they served as built-in pot rests. One of these basins had a mud partition dividing it into two parts.

Entries. At least three houses had central roof openings and probably others did as well. In one house the indication was a ladder pole with one end in a socket next to the hearth. In two others, fallen smoke holes were found, 40 and 56 cm in diameter. Estimated heights of the roofs, based on the angle of convergence between the roof support and the wall timbers, ranged from 1.59 to 2.30 m. Six houses had indications of openings through the walls. Three of these were tentatively interpreted as entries, but the evidence is not conclusive. One was a tunnel 1.0 m wide and at least 1.8 m long, separated from the room by a masonry sill 0.45 m in height. The second was a passage 50 cm wide and 95 cm long, with walls of plastered poles and boards; it was 50 cm higher than the floor of the house. The third was a long rectangular chamber leading from a depression in the pit house wall, 0.50 m above the floor; the chamber had a closed end, and if it was an entry, access must have been through its roof. Three other wall openings were less clearly identifiable as entries. One was a round aperture 0.35 m in diameter, 1.2 m above the floor. Another was suggested by the presence of a metate lying on its side in a line with the deflector and hearth; it may have covered an opening. The third was an inclined passage connecting two houses, descending 0.65 m in 1.65 m; it was about 0.35 m in diameter.

Cists

Most of the cists found in the Prayer Rock caves were built during the Basketmaker occupation. This was indicated by the extensive mixture of the clay with vegetal material, consisting of juniper bark, corn husks, bean pods, oak leaves, and carrizo canes. Some cists were made of unreinforced mud and some utilized a poor coarse masonry; these are attributed to sporadic Pueblo occupation in post-Basketmaker times. In some instances, the Pueblo people had used or remodeled a Basketmaker cist. More recently, Navajo Indians had used some of the old cists and may also have made some of their own.

All of the cists were characterized by lack of formal structure. Often one or more walls consisted of the sloping bedrock at the back of the cave and of walls of adjacent cists. The cists varied from round to rectangular to irregular in vertical section. The shape was largely controlled by the space available at the spot chosen for building the cist.

Many cists were dug into natural earth, the walls showing the scars of digging sticks. Others were composed of sandstone slabs joined with mud, and the floors were plastered with the same substance. Variations included the use of angular rock spalls, wooden logs or slabs, and occasionally pure mud. Indications of the nature of the roof structure consisted largely of impressions of ends of logs in the mud at the rim of the cist. Rows of parallel logs and cribbed roofs were the two types noted.

Most cists were empty or were filled with trash or wind-blown sand. Whether they had been left empty by the Basketmakers or cleaned out by later people is impossible to determine.

Masonry Rooms

The post-Basketmaker structures built in some of the Prayer Rock caves (see Fig. 8) can be attributed to later Pueblo occupation. Generally speaking, the rooms were small and poorly constructed. Their size and lack of interior features, particularly hearths, seem to indicate their use as storage chambers. Most of these structures were built next to the back wall of the cliff, and the sloping bedrock was often utilized as a floor and possibly as a portion of the back wall. Some were two stories high, and in some cases a double row of rooms was built, with doors occurring in any of the three walls away from the cliff.

The masonry was crude, with quantities of mortar used between the irregularly shaped stones. The exterior surfaces were heavily plastered and often retained deep finger impressions from the plastering process. Corners were generally square and the doorways constructed with some care. Some openings were flanged — presumably to support a door slab — and some were blocked with masonry.

A few rooms had openings in the walls, so small that they could only have served as peep holes or as openings for ventilation. Rows of wooden pegs were found on two walls of one room.

These rooms may be attributed to temporary habitation by people who used the caves and valleys to some extent, but who were not present long enough or in great enough numbers to leave extensive remains in the form of architecture and trash.

BROKEN FLUTE CAVE

Pit House 1

Form. Pit House 1 was situated at the extreme edge of the rockfall at the east end of the cave. Its dimensions could not be determined because the northwest portion of the floor had weathered out at the surface. The boundaries of the chamber conformed to the irregular space available between the blocks of stone.

Floor. The floor was a thin uneven film of mud spread over natural earth.

Hearth. Slightly southwest of center there was a nearly circular fireplace 70 cm in diameter. It was walled with rough stones slanting slightly inward and protruding about 12 cm above the floor line to form a raised rim. It varied in depth from 20 to 25 cm.

Cists. Fallen slabs at the back of the southwest roof support indicated the presence of a bin about 90 cm square and 40 cm high. In line between the eastern pair of posts, beginning 20 cm from the northern one, there was an excavation 40 cm in width and depth and 60 cm in length.

Roof supports. The four juniper roof supports were 13 to 15 cm in diameter.

Fill. On the southeast side of the house the fill was about 30 cm deep. The lower half of it was composed of burned roof material and large stones that had evidently been stood up behind the wall. The upper half consisted of fine sandstone detritus. All inflammable materials in the roof had burned, and ashes and chunks of charcoal formed a continuous layer over the remains of the floor. A metate, several pecking stones, a bone awl, a bone paddle, some cordage, a sandal fragment, and a portion of a burned basket containing small seeds had survived the fire.

Pit House 2

Form. Pit House 2 had a diameter of 2.25 m at the base of the walls and was dug into the sandy cave floor to a depth of 0.70 m on the west side and 1.35 m on the east side. The walls sloped backward as they rose, giving the chamber a diameter of 3.0 m at a height of 1.50 m above the floor of the house. The natural earth of the sides had been plastered over with clay reinforced with shredded corn husks and yucca fiber waste. The original height of the room could not be satisfactorily estimated. The walls appeared to have continued for some distance above the cave floor, since in the fill there were many blocks of sandstone embedded in a matrix of clay reinforced with vegetation. Opposite the entry at a height of 1.1 m above the floor was an irregular recess 20 cm deep.

Floor. Scattered across the sandy floor were ashes and charcoal. Lying from north to south across the center was a piñon pole 30 cm in diameter at the butt. It was smoked black, suggesting use as a roof timber.

Hearth. In spots the base of the wall was smoked black, further indicating that fire had been maintained within the room.

Entry. On the south side there was evidence of a possible entry passage 35 cm in height and width. Its sill was 1.2 m above the floor.

Fill. The fill consisted of sandy earth containing many large blocks of stone and a few artifacts.

Pit House 3

Form. Nearly all of Pit House 3 had weathered out at the front of the cave. There remained a semicircle 2.0 m deep and 4.75 m across. The wall consisted of a row of slabs leaning slightly backward, rising 30 cm above the floor.

Bench. Extending outward from the tops of the slabs at the base of the wall was a bench 45 cm in width. The slab work of the bench face was good, the stones placed at a uniform height and the cracks between them smoothed with mud. The tops of the slabs extended 5 to 10 cm above the bench level, forming a rim at the front.

Roof supports. At the center of the floor was the butt of a post 20 cm in diameter.

Wall posts. Behind the bench were the butts of the wall timbers. Judging from their fallen position, the tips had rested against a rectangular frame supported by roof posts, but the existence of this frame was not indicated by the single post. The peripheral timbers were about 15 cm apart and measured from 10 to 14 cm in diameter. Covering them on the outside was a thick layer of juniper bark. It was not evident how this had been held in place against the timbers. It is possible that this pit house had a conical roof and a single post, like Pit House 1 at Site 145 in the Mesa Verde (O'Bryan 1950: 55).

Fill. The chamber was destroyed by fire and there were no artifacts remaining. Refuse from the slopes above had buried the inner side of the room to a depth of 1.0 m.

Pit House 4

Form. Pit House 4 was a basin-shaped chamber excavated 90 cm into the cave floor. The lack of the usual architectural features may indicate that the structure was a roofed cist. The walls consisted of natural earth and of flat stones set on edge and sealed together with mud containing shredded vegetation.

Walls. The walls sloped slightly inward toward the bottom and curved to join the floor. The original height of the room could not be estimated. About 15 cm eastward of the eastern post and 10 cm above the floor was a circular wall niche some 18 cm in diameter. At a depth of 10 cm the walls of the niche flared outward to join the boundaries of a cavity cut into the soft sandstone, 40 cm across, 30 cm deep, and 30 cm high.

Floor. The thin mud floor curved up at the base of the wall.

Hearth. Absent. The wall plaster was blackened, but this probably happened when the roof burned.

Roof supports. Against the cliff, 1.69 m apart, the stubs of two vertical posts 8 cm in diameter were found embedded in the floor. The butts were wedged in place by upright stones.

Fill. About 25 cm west of the east roof support lay a horizontal timber evidently fallen from above. Quantities of charcoal lay directly upon the floor. The fill was 1.20 m deep and consisted of large stones and clods from dismantled cists and trash. At the west end of the south wall of the pit house, a slot had been gouged in the floor, its western end extending under a natural stone at the base of the room wall. In this cavity, not more than 5 cm below the floor, were hidden two wooden flutes tied together with strips of yucca. One of them was stopped at each end with wads of yucca fiber; the other was plugged at one end with a corn cob. There was a wad of yucca fiber placed to protect the feather ornamentation bound at one end of each flute.

Additional artifacts from the fill included two snare sticks, two flutes, a fire hearth, a digging stick, and five miscellaneous artifacts of wood; four sandals, an apron, and some yucca fiber cordage; a yucca root, a corn cob with a stick placed in one end, a turkey feather, a squash shell fragment, a paint-smeared stone chip, and a bundle of roots; a La Plata Black-on-white bowl and a few unfired clay sherds.

Pit House 5

Form. The forward half of Pit House 5 had eroded off the edge of the cliff. The remaining portion of it was 5 m wide and 1.50 m deep.

Bench. A low bench varying from 0.55 to 0.75 m in width encircled the chamber. It rose from the floor to a height of 0.25 m at a gradual slant, receding about 20 cm; then it sloped to the wall of the room with a rise of about 10 cm more. Set into the bench 18 cm from the back were the stubs of two upright sticks 2.5 cm in diameter and 42 cm apart. The western one was directly north of the west roof support. There was nothing to indicate the purpose of these sticks.

Roof. A continuation of the angle formed by the stubs of the wall posts in position, extended to the line between the roof supports, indicated that the ceiling height had been 2.95 m.

Floor. The level floor consisted of a layer of mud spread over the irregular surface of the original excavation. At the east side the tip of a sandstone block about 75 cm across had been battered down to bring it to the desired floor level.

Hearth. The place where the hearth should have been had eroded away.

Roof supports. The butts of two pine posts, 20 cm in diameter, were adjacent to the bench, 3.10 m apart.

They were the northern pair of the four uprights that had supported the central portion of the roof.

Wall posts. Set into the back of the bench was a row of timbers inclining slightly toward the center of the room and set an average of 25 cm apart. The timbers had been covered with a layer of horizontally placed reeds, 5 to 7 cm thick. These reeds were mature, and bright green in color, indicating a cutting date early in the fall. At intervals of about 50 cm, upright withes had been bound against the outer side of the reeds to hold them in place. Behind the reeds, where the wall extended below the level of the adjoining cists or rock masses, a considerable thickness of juniper bark kept the loose cave dirt from trickling into the house. Above the level of the bark the reeds were coated with a layer of mud containing shredded juniper bark. This made the outer shell of the chamber extremely tough and resilient.

Fill. The chamber was destroyed by fire after abandonment, as indicated by an accumulation of 3 to 5 cm of clean sand between the floor and the burned roof material. Toward the west side were several burned two-rod-and-bundle baskets. Beneath one of them, three round-toed sandals lay in a pile. Over the charred remains a layer of trash had accumulated before the floor of Cist 10 was put down. (Cist 13 had been built and filled before the floor of Pit House 5 was laid.)

Pit House 6

Form. Pit House 6 (Figs. 10, 11) was less affected by weathering than the previously described chambers. The room was oval, with its longer dimension parallel to the cliff. Its length was 7.42 m and the remaining width was 5.56 m.

Bench. The bench was noncontinuous and irregularly shaped, as indicated in Figure 10. It varied from 12 to 35 cm in height. Back of the northeast roof support, a pocket had been dug into the bench. The sides were badly crumbled and the dimensions of this cavity could not be determined; it had been at least 40 cm square and more than 25 cm deep, with its floor parallel to the floor of the pit house. Where the bench was not present, the floor level continued unbroken to the wall timbers. Slightly west of the center of the north side of the bench, two upright sticks were set 18 cm from the forward edge. These were about 4 cm in diameter and 55 cm apart. The miserable condition of the benches in both Pit Houses 5 and 6 seems inconsistent with the otherwise careful construction. In both cases the floor levels of the rooms continued beneath the benches to the butts of the wall posts. The material composing the benches was soft cave sand plastered with a layer of mud. Because of the softness of the sand fill, it was difficult to excavate the benches without destroying them. At the southwest end of the bench on the north side was a pocket at floor level in which lay six perfect ears of corn. At several places

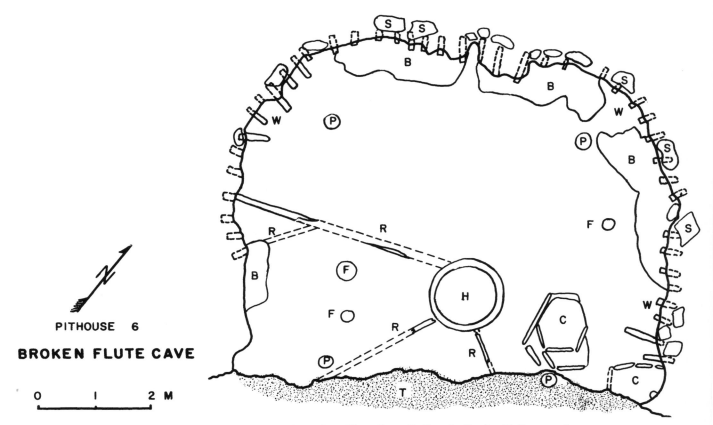

Fig. 10.   Plan of Pit House 6, Broken Flute Cave. B, Bench; C, cist; F, floor pocket;
H, hearth; P, posthole; R, radial; S, sandstone block or slab; T, trash; W, wall.

holes had been dug at the back of the bench next to the wall posts. In these were a bone awl, a small knife blade, corn grains, pumpkin seeds, a few piñon nuts, a few strands of red and yellow cordage, what appeared to be a chunk of charred flesh, and two ears of corn. At the northeast edge was a hole about 35 cm square extending through the bench and slightly into the floor below. This cavity had been open at the time of the fire; in it were the tips of two digging sticks, a burned sandal, and some cordage.

Roof. The angle between the northeast roof support and the line of the unmoved wall timbers nearest to it indicated a ceiling height of at least 2.30 m. The flat central rectangle of the roof had consisted of straight timbers up to 15 cm in diameter, spaced from 5 to 8 cm apart, and oriented northwest to southeast. There had been no reed covering on the roof, since the mud fallen from it showed parallel casts of the supporting timbers. Inflammable reeds near the smoke hole might have heightened the probability of fire. There was nothing to indicate the exact position or size of the roof vent.

Floor. The smooth floor of the house had been broken by the settling of the cave floor and the collapse of the roof. Along the rear half, the mud was spread over

original cave floor deposits, consisting mostly of small sandstone blocks, while the forward edge lay above trash.

Cists. There were five small floor pockets. In the one nearest the wall was a wad of animal hair. Midway between the fireplace and the east wall, the slab top of an earlier cist came flush with the floor.

Hearth. The fireplace was situated south of the center of the room. At floor level it measured 1.16 m by 0.97 m. The sides sloped abruptly inward so that it measured 67 cm by 45 cm at the bottom, and it was 50 cm deep. The walls were of rough stones sealed together with mud and continued above floor level to form a rim some 6 cm high and 12 cm wide.

Radials. A slot left by a burned-out radial timber 9 to 10 cm in diameter extended from the fireplace to the west wall. A smaller timber had branched south from this timber at a distance of 1.10 m from the wall, running to the southwest wall of the chamber. Upward curls in the floor plaster suggested that there had been two more of these radial timbers extending southeast and southwest from the south side of the fireplace.

Roof supports. The four deeply embedded pine or fir posts were from 21 to 27 cm in diameter. The two front posts stood at the very edge of the talus slope.

Fig. 11.   View of Pit House 6, Broken Flute Cave, looking east across remaining floor.

Wall posts. The slanting side timbers varied from 9 to 15 cm in diameter. A layer of horizontal reeds 4 to 5 cm thick covered the entire sloping framework. In some places there was a second layer of the same material placed upright on the outside of the horizontal layer. These reeds were bright yellow in color, indicating that they had been cut in the winter months. At every fourth or fifth wall timber, withes were laid against the reeds and tied to the timber to hold the reeds in place. Where the bottom of the rear wall was built against trash, brush and juniper bark were piled against it. Large rough blocks of sandstone formed a ring against the base of the wall.

Fill. This room was destroyed by fire during occupancy. At least six plain gray pottery jars (including one Lino Gray and one Obelisk Gray), four La Plata Black-on-white bowls, a polished red bowl, and six unfired fiber-tempered pieces stood on the floor. Several pots must have rested on the roof, for fragments of them were found high in the burned roof material instead of beneath it. The unfired mud vessels, the plain pots, and the few red and decorated pieces constitute a classic Basketmaker III assemblage. At least a score of shouldered bone awls were scattered about, some of them with cord-wrapped butts, and there were a few unshouldered specimens. Of more than 20 sandals, all except one had scalloped toes. A sandstone bowl with a thick stubby handle rested on the bench at the center of the north side. This and the other stone tools were shattered by the heat, but they were all restorable. A wooden ladle lay against the foot of the bench at the east side. About 1 m north of the fireplace was an artifact made from a massive antler. It contained a number of transverse perforations and may have been a wrench. Some chalcedony chips, charred cordage, and human hair (both in hanks and made into string) were noted. Midway between the fireplace and the northwest ceiling support there was a large, deep stone mortar.

Additional artifacts found in the fill included an arrow foreshaft bunt, a bone end scraper, some corn kernels and squash seeds, fragments of several sandals, 5 cores of petrified wood and chalcedony, 2 trough metates, 1

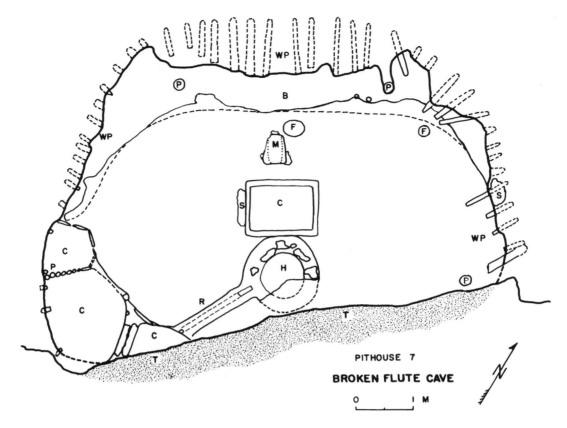

Fig. 12.   Plan of Pit House 7, Broken Flute Cave. B, Bench; C, cist;
F, floor pocket; H, hearth; M, metate; P, posthole; R, radial; S, sandstone slab; T, Trash; WP, wall posts.

rectangular mano, 2 one-hand manos, and 14 smooth cobblestones, three of which were very large and flat.

Beneath floor. On the east side of the pit house was a stone-lined subfloor basin that had been remodeled several times. Originally it had been 1.22 m long, with the sides sloping inward toward the bottom. The first remodeling consisted of placing a slab and mud wall across the southwest corner. Later another slab was placed in a comparable position at the west side, and a third slab was placed between the other two, making the recess rather coffin shaped, with a depth of 32 cm. The recess had been filled with clean earth and the floor of the room plastered across it. Under the floor of Pit House 6 were a number of caches, found in pockets gouged into the floor and filled in to hide the contents. In one of these, two braided bands of white dog wool were tied as if they were to be used as garters. Slightly north of the fireplace was a bag made from the skin of an animal resembling a young mink or weasel. At the north side there was a strip of tanned hide wrapped around a chalcedony flake. North of the hearth were some sections of charred timbers beneath the floor level, perhaps the remains of a previous chamber that had occupied a portion of the same area.

Pit House 7

Form. The forward edge of Pit House 7 (Figs. 12–14) had disappeared over the edge of the talus. The remaining floor was 8.50 m long and 5.25 m wide.

Bench. Along most of the remaining wall was a continuous bench composed of soft cave sand, which had been piled and tamped on the smooth floor. Irregular in shape, the bench sloped upward and backward from the floor to a maximum height and breadth of 45 cm at the northwest corner. Along the northwest side, its width was 1.30 m, enough to include the two rear roof supports. The bench was constructed after these timbers had been put in place.

Roof. The central section of the roof consisted of a thick layer of mud plastered over closely spaced timbers that ran from northwest to southeast.

Floor. The floor of the pit house was a fairly smooth surface of hard clay.

Hearth. The fireplace was circular, 90 cm in interior diameter, and 30 cm in depth. It was lined with thick stones that sloped rapidly toward the bottom and were coated with mud. Stones and mud together formed a raised rim 20 cm wide that reached from 10 to 15 cm above the floor.

Fig. 13.   View of Pit House 7, Broken Flute Cave, looking west across excavated floor.
Pit House 7 is at *lower left*, Cist 33 is at *right center*.

Radials. Extending from the edge of the southeastern-most bin to the raised rim of the hearth was a ridge of mud 27 cm wide and 5 cm high. In the crest of this ridge was a trough left by a burned-out radial timber 5 to 7 cm in diameter.

Cists. At the southwestern edge of the room, the bench ended against the north side of a slab bin, the floor level of which was 15 cm above that of the pit house. The cist was floored with slabs plastered with mud, which was smoothed upward to join the walls. One side consisted of mud plastered between the inclined side timbers of the room. The curved side facing the chamber was of thin slabs set upright; the tallest one remaining was 75 cm in height. The partition between the bin and the one east of it was composed of clay completely enclosing several wooden uprights, which were up to 7 cm thick and made from a large pine or fir. The floor of this second bin was of hard smooth clay, and it was 20 cm higher than the floor of the room. It is probable that a third bin had existed immediately eastward of the one

just described. A stone slab broken off at floor level indicated its inside boundary, 70 cm in length.

Roof supports. The roof supports, of pine or fir, were about 20 cm in diameter.

Wall posts. The inclined wall timbers varied from 6 to 14 cm in diameter and were spaced at intervals of 18 to 30 cm. Outside, in some places, there was a single layer of reeds laid horizontally against the supports. Along the entire north side a second layer had been placed vertically outside of the first layer. There were the usual upright withes tied against every third or fourth post to hold the reeds in place. Along the cliffward side, the level prepared for the floor was dug about 70 cm below the adjacent blocks of stone. Between the rocks and the base of the wall a great amount of brush had been piled. Some of this was sage twisted off or pulled up by the roots, and some of it was a small green bush that resembles the rubber weed growing in the vicinity today. It would appear that this room, like Pit House 6, had been built in the late fall or winter, since the reed

Fig. 14.   View of Pit House 7, Broken Flute Cave, looking east across
excavated floor. Metate is in place on a mud and sandstone base.

stems were yellow, but Pit House 5 must have been built considerably earlier in the season since the reed stems, though mature, were bright green in color. (As noted earlier in the summary description, the stems of carrizo cane are still small and immature at the beginning of August, which would place the collection of materials for constructing Pit House 5 between this time and whenever they turn yellow.)

Fill. On the floor at the time this room was destroyed by fire were a number of pottery vessels, including a deep bowl and a seed jar of La Plata Black-on-white, a plain gray bowl partitioned into two parts, at least one plain gray seed jar, and an unfired fiber-tempered bowl. A few sandals, some fragments of yucca fiber textiles, a good deal of yucca fiber cordage, and hanks of prepared yucca fiber were scattered about. A small twined bag containing a chunk of red paint was found tucked beneath the butts of two inclined timbers slightly north of the northernmost bin. There was a metate in place facing toward the fireplace. The miller had knelt between the

metate and the bench, which were separated by a distance of 60 cm. The mill was raised from the floor, 14 cm at the forward end and 20 cm at the rear, by three rough stones. Between the fireplace and the northeast wall were sections of a pine slab that had been at least 25 cm wide and about 7 cm thick; it might have been suspended from the roof to serve as a shelf. Above the layer of charred material the trash was 75 cm deep in some places. Above the trash there was fine sandstone detritus and wind-blown sand that brought the deposit to a depth of 1.5 m above the floor of the structure.

Additional artifacts found in the fill included a wooden wrench, a feathered prayer stick, four bone awls, a cooking slab, and miscellaneous scraps of yucca leaves, minerals, fur, and hide — including a mass of long, slender, furry strips coiled as though taken from a fur blanket.

Beneath floor. Extending slightly beneath the back rim of the hearth was a rectangular basin 1.38 m long and 1.06 m wide at the top, and 0.23 m deep; at the bottom it was 1.16 m long and 0.77 m wide. The sides were of clay plastered onto the banks of the excavation or onto thin inclined slabs. The recess was filled and the floor built over it. The fill was of mixed earth and occupational debris, including a few fired sherds, a section of a mud bowl, and several burned sticks. Beneath the floor of the pit house the earth had been disturbed to a depth of several centimeters; across the east end it consisted mostly of stone chips with enough vegetal rubbish to show that it had been turned. Conspicuous in the rubbish were bean pods and red beans, and near the north ceiling support there was a round-toed sandal and a bunch of feathers wrapped in prepared fiber. Beneath the forward edge of the bench there was an old pothole some 80 cm in depth and 50 cm in diameter; at the bottom there was a stratum of vegetal rubbish that yielded three ears of corn, two sandals, and a few other specimens. In the red sand behind the western ceiling support was a child's sandal.

Pit House 8

Form. The forward third of Pit House 8 (Figs. 15, 16) had weathered away, and the remaining portion of the chamber was 5.50 m square.

Walls. This chamber differed from those previously described in having a row of sandstone slabs that originally stood inside the wall timbers. Some of the slabs were thin and broad, while others were thick long blocks. They were set with the longer dimension upright and were about 65 cm in height.

Bench. The tops of the slabs constituted the margins of a bench that reached back to the sloping wall timbers. Where measurable it was 35 cm wide. The tops of the slabs were smoothed over with mud to make a rim.

Floor. The floor of the room was surfaced with mud as much as 3 cm thick in places. Originally it had been well smoothed, and it sloped upward to a height of 25 cm at the base of the sandstone slabs.

Hearth. A fireplace was situated somewhat south of the center of the pit house. It was D-shaped, 69 cm wide, 65 cm long, and 32 cm deep. Flat stones on edge formed the walls. The top was finished with a raised rim of mud about 8 cm in height and varying greatly in thickness. Embedded in this mud rim was a flat stone with a ladder pole socket 8 cm in diameter and 3 cm in depth pecked into the top. Lying flat upon this stone and pointing west from the socket was the butt of one pole of a runged ladder; it was of neatly trimmed pine and 7 cm in diameter. Portions of the uprights and rungs were observed among the charred material south of the fireplace; all were of hard wood polished by use. The socket for the other upright could not be found.

Radials. From the fireplace a ridge of mud 22 cm wide and 10 cm high extended to the inner side of a bin wall in the southern corner of the room.

Cists. Of the cist at the forward edge of the house, only a portion of the walls and floor remained. Its floor

was 20 cm higher than that of the room. The free boundaries of the structure were composed of round timbers and thin slabs split from a log; these were set upright and completely covered with mud. Presumably the bin had been rectangular, the northeast boundary continuing to the wall of the room. The south roof support stood adjacent to the northwest corner of this bin. In the angle between the bin and the southwestern wall was a second enclosure, triangular in shape, its floor at a level with that of the room. Its outer side was afforded by the slab ring that encircled the floor, and its boundary on the room side consisted of thin slabs set on end. Mud had been added to the tops of these slabs and neatly rounded off at the height of the bench, that is, 65 cm. In the angle between the wall and the bin just mentioned was a tiny triangular enclosure, 35 cm in greatest dimension; its inner boundary was of slabs set on edge. A fourth bin was built against the bench at the northeast side of the room. It was no more than a pocket sloping abruptly inward and downward; the bottom was a continuation of the sloping edge of the floor where it rose to the encircling ring of slabs. At a height of 40 cm slender poles had been laid across the top of the cist, parallel to the wall of the room, and had been plastered over with mud; probably at some point in this cover there had been a handhold to give access to the small enclosure. Southeast of the fireplace was an excavation in the floor, at least 25 cm deep, and filled about two-thirds full; in it lay a smooth cobblestone, its upper surface slightly below that of the floor. In the rear half of the room were five floor pockets lined with mud up to 3 cm thick; these were irregularly bowl-shaped, with the exception of one that had a partition through the center of it. Between the west ceiling support and the wall of the room, clean sand had been piled against the wall to form a slope behind the post. In the sloping sand was a pothole 17 cm in diameter, and a seed jar was found at the bottom.

Roof supports. Three of the roof supports were of juniper and the fourth was of pine or fir. Almost midway between the north and east posts and nearly aligned with them was the butt of a fifth vertical timber, intended perhaps to strengthen a weak log in the roof.

Wall posts. The side timbers were of juniper, varying from 9 to 15 cm in diameter and spaced from 14 to 25 cm apart. Outside them was a layer of horizontal reeds bound in position with upright withes. The reeds were mature but still light green in color, indicating that the pit house had been constructed early in the fall. Brush, juniper bark, and corn husks had been piled along the base of the wall at the uphill side.

Fill. Across the northwest side, the row of slabs and the stubs of the wall timbers had been knocked forward on the floor, presumably by the impact of a great mass of cliff roof that fell after the room had been occupied (the block was raised for excavation). Apparently there was

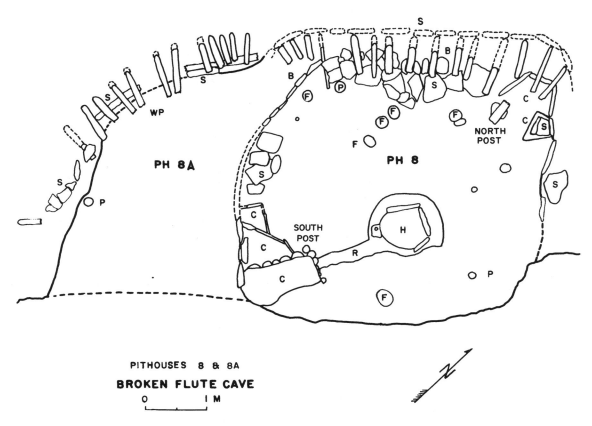

PITHOUSES 8 & 8A
BROKEN FLUTE CAVE
0   I M

Fig. 15. Plan of Pit Houses 8 and 8A, Broken Flute Cave. B, Bench; C, cist; F, Floor pocket; H, hearth; P, posthole; S, sandstone slab; WP, wall post.

a cavity beneath that permitted the collapse of the walls when the great weight came down upon them. The room had burned while it still contained many objects. Relatively undamaged were three seed jars (one Lino Gray, one Chapin Gray, and one plain gray with mixed temper), two plain gray wide-mouthed jars, and a mud bowl partitioned into two halves; a wooden awl, 19 shouldered bone awls, 2 tapered bone awls; at least 1 metate, a circular sandstone pot lid, many smooth cobblestones, a stone effigy, and a stone pendant. Fragments of carbonized textiles, two aprons, two tapestry-weave sandals, a net, bundles of yucca fiber and human hair cordage, and two baskets (one with a single rod foundation and cordage weft) were observed. Additional artifacts included a short blade-tipped digging stick, a fire hearth, a grooved stick, a tobacco quid, a shell disk, and a mountain-sheep horn. Trash was deposited above the burned layer to an average depth of about 30 cm. Directly over this lay the sandstone block fallen from the roof, and all but the thicker portions of this slab were buried in trash.

Beneath floor. About 1 m beneath the floor at the

southwest edge of Pit House 8, John Wetherill of the Bernheimer Expedition found a large decorated basket; it was at the bottom of an irregular pit presumably dug to hold it. The basket was two-thirds full of turkey feathers and covered with several bundles of basket splints. Above the basket splints were two large stone slabs and a fill of earth only slightly stained with refuse.

Pit House 8A

Form. Pit House 8 cut across the area of a more ancient chamber, Pit House 8A, whose floor was 40 cm deeper. Evidence for the more recent date of Pit House 8 was the fact that unburned refuse had trickled down over the bank of its pit to fill a cavity behind the line of wall slabs. The excavation for Pit House 8A was dug 1 m into the cave floor, which slopes up westward, toward Pit House 12. Pit Houses 8 and 8A were similar in construction. The undestroyed portion of Pit House 8A was faced with large flat stones standing to a height of 0.50 m. Behind them was a line of horizontal poles, and the butts of the wall timbers were behind the poles. It is interesting to note that the placement of horizontal

Fig. 16.   View of Pit Houses 8 and 8A, Broken Flute Cave, looking east across floors. The floor pockets (one covered with a cobblestone), mud-covered radials, fallen charred roof beam, and sandstone slabs can be seen.

poles at the base of the wall is a characteristic of the Basketmaker II houses at Talus Village (Morris and Burgh 1954).

Roof supports. One ceiling support was present at the west side, situated 30 cm from the slab boundary.

Wall posts. The wall timbers were of juniper and ranged from 9 to 16 cm in diameter. They were set as closely together as their tips would permit and were covered with juniper bark.

Fill. Outside the west wall, the excavation for the room had cut 55 cm into a deposit of irregularly stratified material, which lay above sandstone detritus from the roof. The stratified earth had been laid down by the alternating action of wind and rain; some layers were light in color and relatively clean, while others were dark, stained gray by ashes and containing a good deal of charcoal. Some of the charcoal was in granules as large as the end of a thumb. On top of the stratified level

was 20 cm of sterile sandstone detritus, and then a tangle of brush and rushes 1 m thick and weighted down with sandstone slabs. This mass was a retaining device built on the sloping surface to increase the level area at the back of the cave, and refuse had been filled in behind it in the leveling process. Over the surface was 25 to 35 cm of stone detritus that had come down from the roof after the cave was abandoned. The rooms were destroyed by fire and subsequently buried to a depth of 2.0 m by refuse and stone waste dumped down the slope from the level of Pit House 12. Many chalcedony flakes were present in the thin layer of sand that had accumulated on the floor prior to the fire. There were fragments of two wooden mosaic backs. One surface of each retained a layer of some adhesive substance, which at one time would have held a mosaic incrustation similar to those found, for example, in Canyon del Muerto (Morris 1925).

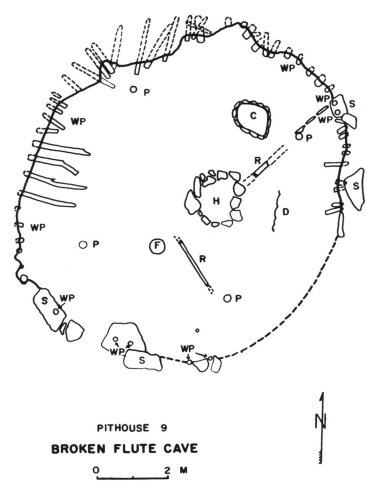

PITHOUSE 9

BROKEN FLUTE CAVE

0   2 M

N

Fig. 17.   Plan of Pit House 9, Broken Flute Cave.
C, Cist; D, deflector; F, floor pocket; H, hearth; P,
posthole; R, radial; S, sandstone block; WP, wall post.

Beneath floor. Less than 1 m in from the front of the
cave and about 0.75 m below the floor of Pit House 8A,
the Bernheimer Expedition found the mummy of a small
child wrapped in a rabbit-skin blanket and buried with
a cradle board of Basketmaker II type. The remains
were in a pothole dug into natural sand.

Pit House 9

Form. Pit House 9 (Fig. 17) was oval, its greatest
length 6.4 m. The excavation varied in depth from
0 to about 75 cm at the northeast corner. To provide a
level space for the floor, sandstone detritus had been
dug away until fairly solid substance was reached.

Bench. Along the north wall a small quantity of sand
had been placed on the floor to form a low and rather
narrow bench; it was badly collapsed.

Roof. Over the flat portion of the roof the mud coating had rested directly on the poles.

Floor. An uneven clay floor was spread over a mass of
fine stone chips and larger blocks. The tops of some of

the blocks had been beaten off to bring them to the
desired level. In many places the floor was 8 cm thick
and was laid in several coats.

Hearth. The fireplace was somewhat east of center.
Massive blocks in position must have made it difficult to
excavate the pit, which was 1 m in diameter at the top
and varied from 0.10 to 0.35 m in depth. The rim and
plaster on the stones were of mud.

Radials. South and slightly west of the fireplace a
radial log was embedded in the floor in line between the
south roof support and the center of the room. From the
northeast side of the hearth a thin curving partition
extended to the east wall. For the most part this had
broken down. A pole 15 cm in diameter, laid horizontally, extended toward the northeast roof support. An
upright slab was beside the roof support, and slabs, on
edge, 47 cm high, continued to the wall.

Deflector. About 70 cm east of the fireplace, the stubs
of a row of pine slabs were embedded in the floor. These
were burned off at floor level, but had once extended
above it. They appeared to have constituted the framework of a deflector, probably 90 cm in length. Presumably in line with the fireplace and the deflector there
would have been some sort of opening in the room wall,
comparable in position to the ventilators of pit houses
at other sites outside the Prayer Rock area; however,
erosion of the slope had removed this part of the house.
Exactly where the opening should have occurred, the
lower side of a metate set on edge, trough outward,
remained in position in the line of the wall; this stone
may have been set up temporarily to close the vent.

Cists. Between the forward pair of roof supports, a
slab socket and a post butt in line indicated that there
once had been a bin at least 55 cm square adjacent to
the west wall. Midway between the firepit and the east
wall was an oval mud-lined basin in the floor some
90 cm long. There was an irregular basin in the floor
45 cm north of the wing wall. It was 85 cm long and
44 cm deep, and made of slabs on edge joined together
with mud. The receptacle was filled with earth and the
floor of the room continued above it; its interior was
clean and unstained with smoke and there was nothing
to indicate its function.

Roof supports. The four roof supports were present
in their customary positions. The largest was 31 cm in
diameter.

Wall posts. The wall posts were set as conditions
would permit, some of them embedded a few centimeters
in earth and others resting upon natural blocks. Across
the southwest side where large solid blocks reached above
floor level, depressions up to 5 cm in depth had been
pecked into the stone to hold the lower ends of the
sloping timbers. These timbers varied from 15 to 17 cm
in diameter and were from 3 to 3.5 cm apart. The mud
at the edge of the floor had been smoothed upward and
filled in between the poles. On the sloping walls there was

a double layer of reeds against the poles, the second layer placed vertically against the horizontal one. These were lashed with withes placed between the layers. Where the wall base was buried below adjacent living surfaces, large stones had been leaned against the reeds and the outer mud plastering began at their upper edges. Along the east side juniper bark was laid outside of the reeds.

Fill. The room had burned with a number of artifacts in it. About 30 pottery vessels were scattered over the floor, but most of them were in the northern portion. They included a La Plata Black-on-white bowl, a seed jar and a wide-mouthed jar of Lino Gray, a narrow-mouthed jar and a wide-mouthed jar of plain gray pottery with mixed temper, a seed jar and a vessel with a lateral spout of plain gray pottery with unknown temper, and two fiber-tempered bowls. A wooden awl, 21 shouldered bone awls, and three tapered bone awls were scattered about. Also found were four coiled baskets; three of them were bowl-shaped and one was the bottom of a carrying basket. Along the north side there was a good deal of refuse on the floor. This refuse had probably fallen through the wall after the reeds had burned, but in time to prevent the total destruction of the articles on which it fell. From this area some relatively undamaged wooden implements, basket fragments, and sandals were recovered. There were the charred vestiges of two trays, the smaller one not more than 7.5 cm long and the larger one roughly oval, 20 cm long and 13.5 cm in greatest width; they were 1.7 and 1.2 cm thick, respectively. The material appeared to be cottonwood that had been neatly smoothed. Beside them was a large rough wooden slab, 60 cm long and 17 cm wide, narrowing down to 10 cm at one end; about half of its length had been smeared with red paint. Observed in the charcoal were many kinds of cordage of yucca fiber and human hair, at least three cordage aprons, a wooden feather box, and portions of digging stick blades. Portions of at least two animal skins were recognized. Charred bone and melted flesh were fused into a slag-like mass, indicating a few joints of meat may have been present. The charred layer varied from 10 to 40 cm in thickness.

The room had burned long before the abandonment of the cave. On top of the charred layer was a continuous deposit of refuse 20 to 50 cm thick, of a characteristic variety that accumulated in the open spaces of the caves. The bulk was composed of shredded vegetation such as reed leaves, corn husks and tassels, and occasional artifacts, which had been tramped upon until they were ground very fine. From top to bottom, turkey droppings were plentiful. Dust and sweepings were a minor element. A number of wood and clay figurines were found. Their localization in and above Pit House 9 may indicate that the structure or the area had some sort of ritual significance, and they may be linked to the presence of the deflector, which is absent in the open houses but present in later kivas. On the other hand, the structure had all of the usual domestic features and was exceptionally rich in artifacts.

Overlying the trash layer was clean sandy detritus from the cave roof that had accumulated since the cave was abandoned. It began without thickness over the southwest edge and reached a maximum of 30 cm at the northeast side. Four pottery pipes, one stone pipe and one stone pipe blank, three clay figurines, numerous flakes of implement stone, and a large notched point were found. There were also two clay effigies of carrying baskets, a large bone shaped like the celts of later times, and several bone spatulas. Notable among the textiles were two human hair leggings. There were a number of smooth flat cobblestones, highly polished from use and splintered into pieces by the heat; one was smeared with red paint. There were a cobblestone pestle and several manos; some of them showed a normal amount of wear, but one was new and thick. The manos had been used for grinding on only one surface. The upper surface of one mano had been used to grind paint; it was rubbed smooth in places and stained with pigments. There were two trough metates, a Utah-type metate, and a mortar. Additional artifacts from the fill included a hearth stick, a hearth and drill set, a large grooved stick, several worked sticks and cylinders, a number of miscellaneous fragments of cordage, pieces of red and yellow pigment, a corn cob with a stick in one end, a package of corn husks, fragments of two gourd vessels, a rodent-skin bag, a hide sack fragment, a bundle of feathers, a human scalp, about 50 juniper seed beads, a bundle of bark, two bone tubes, a bone bead, and an antler wrench.

Pit House 10

Form. Pit House 10 was situated immediately south of Pit House 9. It would appear that the two chambers were contemporaneous, since a large stone at their point of junction extended an equal distance into each chamber, and the mud that coated the wall of Pit House 9 was plastered directly on the rock. The south wall was gone. The chamber was nearly circular, 3.13 m in diameter.

Walls. What remained of the walls consisted of reinforced mud plastered between and against stones *in situ*.

Hearth. A central fireplace was gouged into the sandstone detritus. It was about circular, 1 m in diameter and 0.35 m deep.

Fill. Pit House 10 was abandoned before Pit House 9, and the fire that destroyed Pit House 9 did not spread to Pit House 10. It had been filled to a depth of at least 45 cm with clods and refuse. Artifacts found in the fill included 2 wooden awls, a foreshaft, 2 snare sticks, 6 yucca fiber aprons, some cordage and fiber bundles, 3 tump bands, a tobacco quid, 16 sandals, a human scalp lock, a shell pendant, a scrap of hide, 3 ears of corn, and an unfired effigy of a carrying basket.

Pit House 11

Form. The location of Pit House 11 (see Fig. 5) was indicated by a bowl-shaped hollow some 75 cm deep. The chamber was excavated deeply into the floor of the cave — down 0.70 m at the forward side and 1.80 m at the back. The pit had been dug larger than necessary so that after the wall was completed there was a ditch broad enough to walk in between it and the banks of the hole.

Walls. The back wall stood to a height of 1.25 m. The timbers of the forward wall appeared to have been taken out and the remaining portion of the wall had toppled inward upon the floor. Some details of wall construction were observed that were not seen in the other rooms. There were two very thick layers of reeds, the inner one horizontal and the outer vertical. The inner horizontal layer exhibited continuous thickness on the outside of the wall posts. The next, vertical groups of reeds, only the butts of which had been in evidence in the burned rooms, were present at 80 cm intervals. Outside of them were horizontal bands of withes, 65 cm from the base of the wall; these consisted either of one or two good large sticks or several smaller ones tied together to form a bundle and bound to the outer side of the vertical elements. They were completely covered with mud, heavily reinforced with shredded reed leaves and juniper bark and served as reinforcement for the wall. The mud was 16 cm thick at the base of the wall and thinned out to only 6 cm at the top of the pit house. At the bottom, the wall mud was spread out to form a flange over the floor of the ditch extending beyond it. Although the forward edge of the room lay 15 cm from the slope at the front of the cave, there was no indication of a ventilator or passage having passed through the ridge of natural substance that remained between the house excavation and the talus slope. The entry must have been through the roof.

Roof. In the debris above the north edge of a bin at the south side of the pit house, there were several fragments of reinforced mud that had framed a circular smoke vent about 40 cm in diameter. Whether this aperture had been present in the side wall or roof of Pit House 11, or whether the mud fragments were dumped in from elsewhere could not be determined.

Floor. The well-preserved floor curved up to join the plaster of the walls. It was level and was stained black from use. The surface consisted of clay about 1 cm thick.

Hearth. The fireplace was situated somewhat south of center. The interior diameter was 87 cm at the top and 63 cm at the bottom, and the depth was 65 cm. The lining consisted of thick flat sandstone slabs set on end. Some of these reached as much as 6 cm above the floor. Where they fell short, the space was filled out with rough stones laid in mud, and a rim 20 cm wide was formed, carefully rounded over the top.

Radials. A curving ridge of mud extended from the southwest side of the firepit to a junction with a bin built against the south wall. The beginning of a ridge at the southeast side of the hearth indicated that a similar radial had been present in that corner of the room.

Cists. There was a clay-lined stone bin outside of the room on the north side, in the space between the wall and the excavated pit. It was 1.95 m in greatest length and 1.10 m in width. It is probable that there was a small doorway from the room to the cist, and that the latter had served as a storage place. The floor was 20 cm above that of the larger chamber.

Fill. Pit House 11 was the only large dwelling chamber in Broken Flute Cave that had not burned. All the timbers had been torn out of it, leaving only a few broken pieces not suited for further use. It would appear that a great many of the reeds had also been salvaged, since the ones that remained over the central three-quarters of the floor area were short twisted pieces and detached leaves and chaff. There had been 3 to 5 cm of dust on the floor before the destruction of the room, and the clods from the roof had come directly down upon it. Subsequently the pit where the room stood had been filled with refuse, which reached a depth of about 60 cm at the center and sloped upward toward the edges of the pit. This deposit yielded many specimens, the most notable of which were two medicine pouches and their contents. Additional artifacts in the fill included two fire hearths, a hearth and drill set, three digging sticks, a basket, two aprons, some sandal fragments, a tump band, several miscellaneous fragments of cordage, a winter sandal, three shouldered bone awl fragments, some fiber-tempered sherds, and nondescript pieces of bark, gourd, and wood. Overlying the rubbish was some 20 to 30 cm of stone detritus from the cave roof.

Beneath floor. Under the floor west of the fireplace was a recess 45 cm deep. It was vaguely circular and walled with slabs sloping outward toward the top and sealed together with clay. The diameter was 1.15 m at the top and 85 cm at the bottom. On the side nearest the fireplace, 5 cm below floor level, a slender peeled juniper was laid across the edge of the pit, and another was comparably placed at the back cliffward side. The cavity was filled with earth and refuse, such as might have been gathered up anywhere in the cave, and the mud floor was plastered across it.

Pit House 12

Form. Pit House 12 (Figs. 18, 19) was 0.40 m deep at the forward side and about 1 m deep at the back. It was nearly circular, 6.50 m in the diameter parallel to the cliff and 6.26 m in diameter from front to back.

Benches. Around the northern and western boundaries of the room, an incline of clean sand comparable to a bench had been laid over the original mud flooring. At

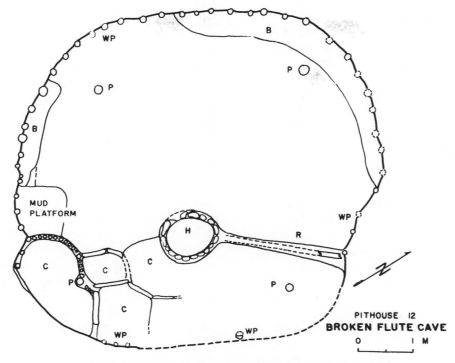

Fig. 18.   Plan of Pit House 12, Broken Flute Cave. B, Bench; C, cist;
H, hearth; P, posthole; R, radial; WP, wall post.

Fig. 19.   View of Pit House 12, Broken Flute Cave, looking across excavated floor toward
back of cave. Plastering extended between the sockets formed by the butts of the wall timbers.

the eastern end it was 25 cm wide, and it broadened to a width of 75 cm, with a height of 20 cm; the midportion had collapsed. Against the southwest wall there was a mud platform 10 cm in height and 1 m in length and breadth.

Floor. In the cliffward half of the room, points of large blocks jutting above the intended floor level had been beaten off to reduce them to the desired plane. Toward the margins, the floor turned upward to the walls.

Hearth. South of the center was an oval fireplace with greatest diameters of 80 cm at the top and 55 cm at the bottom, and a depth of 35 cm. It was lined with rough stones that reached at least 8 cm above the floor and it had been smoothed over with mud.

Radials. Between the fireplace and the northeast wall was a ridge of mud and stones 22 cm wide, at the top of which a radial pole 10 cm in diameter had been embedded. East of the radial the floor varied from 7 to 15 cm higher than the remainder of the floor. A second ridge of mud curved southward from the fireplace to the small bin nearby. The floor of the room was 7 cm higher on the east side of this ridge than on the west side.

Cists. The bin next to the mud platform on the southwest wall was 2 m long and 1 m wide. The south roof support stood just within a curve of its northern wall. The partition separating it from the rest of the room consisted of closely set round poles plastered over with clay. A second enclosure extended eastward from this bin for an unknown distance. Its remains were 1.28 m long and 1.05 m wide. The remainder of the partition between it and the previously mentioned bin consisted of a large sandstone slab set on edge. The front edge was of thinner slabs. Jutting northwest from the junction of these two bins was a smaller one 95 cm long and 60 cm wide, the front edges consisting of thin slabs broken down by the falling of the roof.

Roof supports. The four ceiling supports were juniper logs 15 to 18 cm in diameter.

Wall posts. The slanting wall timbers had burned out for a distance of about 4 m along the east side. Elsewhere there were poles 8 to 16 cm in diameter, spaced about 25 to 35 cm apart. Along the northeast side the butts had fallen forward, exposing the sockets. The timbers rested on natural earth, and the mud at the edge of the floor was brought to a height of 20 cm to fill the spaces between them (see Fig. 19). A horizontal layer of reeds was immediately outside the poles, tied in place with a meshwork of withes, and along the bottom portion of the wall, at least, a thick coat of juniper bark was placed against the reeds. A few sandstone blocks were leaning against the outside of the base of the wall.

Entry. There was evidence of an opening in the wall. The juniper bark laid horizontally outside the sloping timbers was turned backward upon itself and bound in this position, forming a smooth round end. This probably marked the west side of a ventilator opening or entrance.

Fill. Fire had destroyed the chamber, but apparently at a time when it was not in use, since the floor was almost free of artifacts. Two manos, three cobblestones, a slab pot lid, and portions of two vessels were the only articles found. Charred corn was present over the entire area, indicating the use of the structure for storage. Between the fireplace and the west wall there lay the charred remains of a pine slab that had been at least 1.5 m long, 25 cm wide, and 5 cm thick. It is possible that this was a shelf suspended from the ceiling. Some indication of an aperture comparable to a ventilator or entrance was expected, because the southeast edge of the chamber had not weathered away, but no such evidence was found. The room was only 25 cm deep on this side, so it may be that a ventilator had existed higher in the wall. Pit House 12 was probably one of the very last of the chambers to be occupied. The removal of its contents and the small amount of refuse above the charred remains of the roof would indicate that human occupation ended practically at the time the room was destroyed.

Pit House 13

Form. Pit House 13, situated almost 2 m higher than Pit House 11, was of relatively late construction. Toward the rear wall of the cave, natural blocks showed at the floor level, but the forward edge was built on trash. Only portions of the wall remained in position; the wall consisted of a row of rough sandstone blocks up to 46 cm tall, set on end and sealed together with mud. The chamber was 4.20 m long and 2.70 m wide.

Passage. From the west side of Pit House 13 an inclined passage led downward to Pit House 14. Two upright slabs in position midway along its length indicated a width of 35 cm and a height of at least 90 cm. The floor of the passage sloped downward some 65 cm over a distance of 1.50 m to the top of a wall at the northeast end of Pit House 14. This wall formed the north side of Pit House 14 and consisted of four upright slabs, their tops 67 cm above the floor. The floor of the passage outside of the upright slabs in the north wall consisted of flat slabs.

Floor. The floor was level and was surfaced with clay containing some vegetation. Beneath the east end of the room, extending partially under the wall, was an older cist lined with slabs and mud, 98 cm in diameter and 28 cm in depth. It had been filled with refuse and the floor of the pit house laid across it.

Hearth. The circular fireplace, situated somewhat west of center, was 58 cm in diameter and 18 cm in depth. It was lined with thin vertical slabs of stone.

Fill. Presumably the upper walls had been composed of crude masonry, since the fill contained nothing but small stones and clods; the cracks between them were filled with blown sand.

Fig. 20.   View of Pit House 14, Broken Flute Cave, looking across excavated floor.
View shows forked top of wooden roof support, and hearth and ashpit arrangement.

Pit House 14

Form. Pit House 14 (Fig. 20) was somewhat D-shaped and had been dug at least 1.5 m into sterile soil. Plaster had been applied directly to the banks of the excavation.

Walls. The north wall which abuts the passage to Pit House 13 was composed of four upright slabs, the tops 67 cm above the floor. The west wall consisted of cave earth sloping toward the pit house.

Roof. The larger horizontal roof timbers that had rested on the uprights had been removed from the room, but the smaller timbers that had spanned the spaces between them lay on the floor. These were round juniper sticks, 2.5 to 5.0 cm in diameter, and in some cases the bark had been left on. There had been a thick layer of juniper bark and then a final coating of mud. Judging from the roof support that was still standing, the horizontal supports could not have been more than 1.6 m from the floor. All the timbers in the interior of the room had been smoked black from use.

Floor. The floor was smoothly plastered.

Hearth. The fireplace was a basin 51 cm in diameter and 15 cm in depth; its mud rim reached 8 cm above the floor. The upper portion of the interior was baked but the bottom was clean and unstained, indicating that the cavity had been relined with mud but no fires were subsequently built in it.

Ashbin. Immediately east of the fireplace was a nearly square cavity, 37 cm across. The sides were of stones rising to the height of the fireplace and the corners were of mud. The interior was coated with ashes.

Partition. The room was divided almost in half by a ridge, the central part of which consisted of part of the fireplace rim. Two long stones set on edge formed the northeastern partition element; the southwestern ridge was of mud built over a round pole, and a flat slab of wood was embedded on the two-thirds nearest the wall (see Fig. 20). The average dimensions of these elements were 12 cm in width and 6 cm in height.

Cists. On either side of the fireplace, in the angles between it and the partitions, were circular holes 10 cm in diameter and 15 to 20 cm deep. The northeastern one was regular in contour, as if a post might have at one time stood in it. The southern one had been filled and sealed over with mud; in the sand fill beneath this coating were pumpkin seeds, grass stumps, a yucca pod with mature seeds, and the quills of a bouquetlike cluster of feathers, together with the cordage that had been attached to it. Across the partition from the southern hole was a third of similar diameter and depth (it can be seen clearly in Figure 20).

Roof supports. One roof support remained in place in the southeast corner. It was a peeled timber about 12 cm in diameter, set tip downward so that the flaring roots would provide anchorage for horizontal timbers (see Fig. 20). Wrapped around it, just above the floor, were many pieces of feather-wrapped cord. Holes in the floor in the other three corners indicated that posts had been present, and there was a fifth posthole adjacent to the partition at the center of the northeast side.

Fill. On the floor were a crude metate, two manos, some pecking stones, and a number of minor objects. From the fact that Pit House 14 was connected with Pit House 13 (see above, *Pit House 13: Passage*), and the fact that the timber work of the roof had not been entirely removed, it can be inferred that the chamber was of late origin.

Pit House 15

Form. Pit House 15, at the extreme southwestern tip of the cave, appeared to have been nearly circular, with a diameter of 7.25 m. A row of upright slabs 25 to 30 cm high marked the remaining edge. The northeast portion had weathered out completely.

Floor. The uneven stony surface had been leveled in preparation for the construction of the room, and a thin clay floor was spread over it.

Hearth. The fireplace had presumably been located slightly forward of the center. It was shallow, bowl-shaped, 87 cm in interior diameter, and 25 cm in depth. There was a raised rim of stones and mud averaging some 16 cm in width and 6 cm in height. The forward side of it was built against a natural block *in situ*. Ground into this block was a mortar hole 23 cm in diameter and 17 cm deep, coming to a sharp point at the bottom.

Roof supports. There was a burned off butt of a roof support 35 cm from the southwest side. Charred material behind the row of slabs indicated that the side timbers of the room had been used as in the previous rooms.

Fill. The room had burned at a time when it contained very few objects. Midway between the fireplace and the west side, a flat slab metate was lying directly on the floor. Two manos, several rubbing stones, sherds of two or three pots, and a few sherds of fiber-tempered bowls were the only artifacts recovered.

Pit House 16

Form. Pit House 16 lies mostly within the area occupied by the Great Kiva Circle. Its floor was 65 cm below the level of what would have been the floor of the Great Kiva Circle.

Hearth. The fireplace was situated at the center of the trench cut by the excavators from front to back of the cave (see Fig. 5). It was neatly constructed, with an inside diameter of 95 cm and a depth of 31 cm; the portion that extended into cave earth was lined with mud.

Rough stones hidden by plaster formed a neat round-topped rim, 10 to 12 cm in thickness and rising to an average of 10 cm above the floor.

Fill. A deposit of burned roof material immediately covering the floor was 10 to 20 cm thick. Two digging sticks, a foreshaft, a wooden needle, a basket, 2 miniature fiber-tempered bowls, a clay effigy of a carrying basket, and miscellaneous items of wood, stone, antler, and bone were found. In subfloor caches were four projectile points, a feather fan, two bone dice, scraps of hide sack, and two sinew bundles.

Great Kiva Circle

The Great Kiva Circle lay in the eastern section of Broken Flute Cave (see Fig. 5). The area had been brought to the desired level by dumping a mass of rock fragments on the burned remains of Pit House 16. The interstices in some places were open and in others were filled with sand, juniper bark, and other refuse. The upper 10 to 20 cm of this fill contained a greater proportion of earth and the surface consisted of tramped earth and dust. There was no evidence that a clay floor had been constructed for the Great Kiva, but the floor might have been tramped into oblivion in the centuries since it was built. The circle itself was constructed of a single row of sandstone slabs set upright. An indented corrugated jar was cached under the surface, probably after the Great Kiva Circle was built.

Two interrelated problems arise: Is the circle of sandstone slabs a great kiva? And is it contemporaneous with the Basketmaker occupation? In size, shape, and lack of features, it is not dissimilar to other early great kivas in neighboring areas. This class of architectural features is described in detail by Vivian and Reiter (1960). They list three Basketmaker III great kivas besides the one in Broken Flute Cave: those at Juniper Cove, near Kayenta; at Blue Mesa, near Durango; and at Shabik'eschee Village, in Chaco Canyon. Their distribution in Anasazi sites on three sides of the Prayer Rock district and their size, shape, and general lack of complex features supports the identification of the Broken Flute feature as a great kiva.

Pit House 16 in Broken Flute Cave was found under the Great Kiva Circle. No tree-ring dates are available for this pit house. Since there was no fired pottery among the rather diverse artifacts found cached beneath the floor, Pit House 16 may be a Basketmaker II room. The slab circle could therefore be assigned to any subsequent time. The presence of an intensive Basketmaker III occupation in the cave would favor the placement of the Great Kiva in that period. Later structures are present in small quantity, but they do not appear to have been habitations. Temporary brush structures might have accompanied them in association with an ephemeral Great Kiva, but no such temporary structures have been found, and a later dating of the Great Kiva does not seem likely.

The alternative explanation for the lack of pottery in Pit House 16 — that is, accident of deposition — could place the construction of the circle in late Basketmaker III times or later. However, other Basketmaker III pit houses in the cave had no pottery. The lack of architectural features and the position of the Great Kiva at the surface of the cave do not make a later temporal assignment any more likely than an assignment to Basketmaker III times.

So the case rests — evidence is not conclusive for either possibility, nor is the re-excavation of the slab-lined circle likely to clarify the situation. More complete knowledge of the character and distribution of Basketmaker III great kivas would perhaps help to resolve the problem.

Cists

Most of the 65 cists in Broken Flute Cave have been attributed to the Basketmaker occupation. The basis for this assignment was the nature of the mud used in the construction, rather than the position or the contents of the structures. The Basketmaker people reinforced the mud they used with a variety of vegetal substances; in the Pueblo periods this addition was not made.

Most of the cists had been emptied prior to the excavation of the cave and stood open; some were nearly full of fallen structural material and wind-blown sand. A few cists were filled with trash, and fewer still contained artifactual material that would appear to have been intentionally placed there. Cist 7 contained a burial and Cist 18 was a slab-lined hearth. Sherds of later vessels found within the cists indicate that some of them had been cleaned out and reused in prehistoric times.

The manner of construction and the size of the cists lacked regularity; the only standard involved was that of enclosing a space in some way. The forms were largely controlled by the nature of the chosen locations. Most of the cists were built contiguously along the back of the cave, many of them using the cliff for a wall or a floor. Rock material, logs, and vegetal-reinforced mud were used for the above-ground construction. Slabs and the natural earth of the cave floor were used for the subsurface cists. In many cases, the earth still showed the long gouging marks of the digging sticks used to excavate them. Most of the surface cists and some of the subsurface cists were plastered with a thin mud. Cists 33 and 34 were large enough and well enough constructed — with roofs and entrances — to serve as habitations; however, a hearth in Cist 34 was the only sign of occupation. Some cists were partitioned into two parts by an upright sandstone slab. Specific artifactual content of the various cists is itemized in E. A. Morris (1959b).

Remains of three kinds of roof structures were found.

Two involved the use of logs or sticks: one type had a cribbed roof, similar to that used in a modern Navajo hogan, and the other had timbers laid parallel across the opening with the ends resting on the tops of the walls. The third type of covering was merely a thin sandstone slab. The cists were circular, oval, triangular, rectangular, or irregular in plan, and they were bell-shaped, oval, rectangular, or irregular in section. Most were from 1 to 2.5 m long and 0.50 to 1.50 m wide, with a few falling outside of this range. Depths were difficult to determine because of the advanced state of ruin of many of the cists, but some were at least 2 m deep.

RAM'S HORN CAVE

Pit House 1

Form. Pit House 1 was 11.61 m from the north end of the cave. It extended from the talus slope back to a point 1.27 m distant from the cave wall.

Floor. The floor, all that remained of the structure, was an irregular semicircle. It was 12 cm below the surface along the front side and 34 cm deep at the back. It was covered with a film of dust at the northern end.

Wall. There were no timbers in the fill, but between the house and the cave wall lay a section of interlaced juniper-bark strips and thin reeds.

Fill. There were no artifacts and no signs of burning.

Pit House 2

Form. Pit House 2 was somewhat south of center in the cave. It had a semicircular floor 2.75 m in length and 0.92 m in greatest width. Its northern end adjoined two of the three cists in the cave, but apparently never included them. The long forward portion of this room did not exactly parallel the present talus, but faced due east.

Walls. No timbers or juniper bark were found, but chunks of mud plaster lay in the fill, which varied in depth from 5 to 13 cm.

Fill. No artifacts were found in the fill.

CAVE 1

The plan of Cave 1 is shown in Figure 7.

Pit House 1

Form. The rear edge of Pit House 1 had been dug at least 0.60 m into the cave floor. The room was 6 m long and the remaining floor was 3 m wide.

Bench. A slight slope had been left at the back of the pit and was smoothly plastered to form the forward edge of a bench of unknown width.

Wall posts. Charred remnants of the side poles that had risen from the back of the bench were present on the floor.

Fill. Part of a fiber-tempered bowl, part of a La Plata Black-on-white bowl, two or three plain gray seed jars, and two or three charred scallop-toed sandals were on the floor.

Pit House 2

Form. Pit House 2 was 6.10 m in length, and to judge from the curve of the wall, it had been nearly circular.

Bench. The bench along the remaining arc was 30 cm high and 60 cm wide.

Floor. The floor was so badly destroyed by moisture and settling that minor details were not discernible.

Roof supports. At the west side, 55 cm from the foot of the bench, was a hole beside an upright stone where the northwest ceiling support had stood.

Wall posts. Along the back edge of the bench was a slot in which the butts of the side posts had rested.

Fill. A seed jar and a few plain sherds were recovered from the floor.

Pit House 3

Form. A row of Pueblo I cists had been built against the back of the cave, entirely destroying the back side of Pit House 3. The chamber had been dug at least 55 cm into the cave floor. The forward edge of the room was outlined by the backs of natural blocks between which clay mud had been smoothed.

Floor. The floor was of mud spread thinly over the bottom of the excavation.

Hearth. The outer edge of the fireplace was 1.10 m from the center of the forward side. It was bowl-shaped, 60 cm in diameter, 15 cm in depth, and had been encircled by a thin ridge of mud that rose 5 to 8 cm above the floor.

Radials. From the forward edge of the fireplace extended two ridges of mud, one to the northeast wall and the other to the south wall.

Roof supports. Standing in the radial ridges were two of the four roof supports.

Wall posts. Some side poles had been inserted at floor level; others had rested back of the wall line, presumably at whatever was ground surface at the time of construction.

Fill. The room burned while it was occupied. Broken pottery vessels were scattered over the floor. Recognizable among them were plain gray seed jars, a narrow-mouthed jar, a small vessel with a lateral spout, a La Plata Black-on-white bowl, a polished red jar, and a fiber-tempered bowl. A considerable amount of this pottery had come from the roof; several of the vessels were found relatively high in the debris. Several manos, loaf-shaped rubbing stones, and good-sized cobblestones had been shattered by the heat. A few charred fragments of coiled baskets and two tapestry-weave sandals were seen in the burned layer, along with an axe and a dog skull.

Pueblo occupation of Cave 1 is described in Chapter 2 and further details of masonry and cist construction can be found in Morris (1959b).

CAVE 2

The plan of Cave 2 is shown in Figure 7.

Pit House 1

Form. The forward edge of Pit House 1 (Fig. 21) had weathered away. The enclosure was nearly circular, with a length of 5.65 m parallel to the cliff and a width of at least 5.30 m.

Bench. Across the rear side was a bench of red sand. It was 25 cm high and 40 cm in greatest width, and had been constructed after the floor was finished.

Floor. The floor consisted of a thin layer of mud spread over the irregular stony bottom of the pit. The mud had been plastered upward to fill the spaces between the butts of the wall poles. The level was the same on both sides of the partitions mentioned below.

Hearth. The fireplace was slightly forward of center, 95 cm in diameter and 28 cm in depth, with a plastered rim of mud 13 cm broad and 5 cm high.

Radials. Radial ridges extended from the forward edge of the hearth to the north and south walls. They consisted of mud for the 45 cm nearest the hearth and then became slab partitions. These partitions were 20 cm high; incorporated in each one was one of the front roof supports.

Cists. In the southeast corner of the chamber was a bin 0.32 m wide and at least 1.65 m in length; its western wall was an upright slab, and its northern wall consisted of posts set upright and enclosed in plaster.

Roof supports. The ceiling supports ranged up to 15 cm in diameter. The forward two were located in the radial ridges.

Wall posts. The side timbers varied from 9 to 15 cm in diameter and were spaced at intervals of about 25 cm. A layer of horizontal reeds had been piled against the sloping wall posts.

Fill. The fill varied in depth from nothing at the brink of the talus slope to 0.60 m at the back, which was about 1.5 m distant from the cliff wall. The house had burned while being occupied. Broken vessels were scattered all over. These included four fiber-tempered bowls; two La Plata Black-on-white bowls; a seed jar, a narrow-mouthed jar, and a wide-mouthed jar of Lino Gray; a seed jar and a trilobed bowl of Chapin Gray; a seed jar and a narrow-mouthed jar of plain gray with mixed temper; and two seed jars, two wide-mouthed jars, and a narrow-mouthed jar of plain gray with unknown temper. This is a total of at least 18 pots. Pine boards lay flat on the floor, several of them between the fireplace and the south wall and others near the north wall. These had been up to 1.35 m in length and 0.30 m in width,

Fig. 21. View of Pit House 1, Cave 2, looking southwest across excavated floor. Pit House 2 is in the background.

with an average thickness of 3 to 4 cm. There was nothing to indicate whether they had originally rested on the floor or had been suspended as shelves from the ceiling. Near one wall there was a large flat stone, which had been slightly used as a metate. Several manos, loaf-shaped rubbing stones, and large polished cobbles were scattered about. At least two trough metates had been on the roof. Charred remnants of a number of coiled baskets were on the floor. There were also portions of at least two twined tump bands and a great many sandals. Just south of the fireplace lay the cordage of a fur or feather string blanket. Additional artifacts from the fill included three stone pendants, eight stone beads, a stone drill, a fossil shell, lumps of red and yellow pigment, four shouldered bone awls and two perforated bone awls, and a large talon or claw.

Pit House 2

Form. Pit House 2 (Fig. 22) was dug about 65 cm more deeply into the cave floor than was Pit House 1, and its back wall was against the cave wall. The principal axis of the chamber was northwest-southeast. It was circular, its symmetry interrupted by a large block that jutted into the confines of the circle on the east side. The

dimensions of the room were 6.40 m by 5.80 m.

Bench. There was no indication of the usual sand bench. The surface of a sandstone block standing 25 cm above the floor was used as a bench. The side poles continued in a regular curve across the back of it.

Floor. The floor consisted of the tops of sandstone blocks and of spread mud.

Hearth. The fireplace, situated forward of center in the line of the principle axis, was 73 cm in diameter and 30 cm in depth, and had been bordered by a rim of mud.

Radials. Two radials extended from the fireplace to the walls. The southern one was indicated by a small timber laid on the floor; the eastern one was a low ridge of mud for 78 cm, beyond which a broken-down slab partition continued to the east side of the chamber.

Cist. There was a bin 95 cm square, its free edges composed of upright slabs of sandstone.

Roof supports. The butts of four unusually slender ceiling supports were excavated.

Wall posts. Where possible, the side timbers had been embedded in the floor; others were inserted in sockets pecked into the natural stone blocks of the floor. Horizontal reeds had been laid against the side timbers to support the reinforced mud shell of the room.

Fig. 22.   View of **Pit House 2, Cave 2**, looking across floor out of mouth of cave. Base of wingwall remains.

Entry. Directly in line with the principal axis of the room was a chamber 70 cm wide that opened into the main room. The southernmost corner of this enclosure remained standing to a distance of 75 cm out from the forward wall, but its size and shape could not be determined because of erosion. It had been at least 1.8 m wide and 1 m long. Up to the time that this room was excavated nothing had been found to indicate the presence of antechambers. This pit house showed what may have been the normal arrangement in this district. The opening between the pit house and the possible antechamber was 65 cm wide and the threshold was 50 cm above the floor. The door sill was of rounded mud.

Fill. Many pottery vessels, two fiber-tempered containers, baskets, sandals, tump bands, bone awls, and plaited matting had been in the room at the time of its burning. The ceramics included two fiber-tempered bowls, two La Plata Black-on-white bowls, a polished red bowl, a Lino Gray seed jar, two seed jars and a wide-mouthed jar of plain gray pottery with mixed temper, and a gray vessel with lateral spout and of unknown temper. Two or three metates and several vessels had come down from the roof. Scattered about the floor was an assortment of manos, rubbing stones, and cobbles polished by use. One round-toed sandal, one plaited, and many with scalloped toes were found. On the bench were a small vessel with a lateral spout, a number of burned

sandals, a tump band, and several cobblestones. Additional artifacts in the fill included a projectile point, a grooved axe, a grooved maul, four bone awls, and the tip of a digging stick.

Pit House 3

Form. The forward half of Pit House 3 was cut away by erosion. The chamber had been about 3.70 m in diameter.

Bench. A facing of thick sandstone slabs formed the forward edge of a bench 47 cm wide. The slabs were 65 cm tall and at the top sloped outward 15 cm from the vertical.

Hearth. A fireplace about 75 cm in diameter, lined with thin vertical sandstone slabs, jutted a short distance above the floor level, with its edge only 95 cm from the south wall of the room.

Wall posts. All of the timbers had been destroyed in this chamber, but along the undestroyed arc was some juniper bark that had been used instead of reeds to cover the side poles.

Pit House 4

Form. Pit House 4 was rectangular, with its principal axis parallel to the rear wall of the cave. The pit in which the room was constructed had been dug into the cave floor at least 0.50 m at the forward edge and 1.70 m

Fig. 23. View of Pit House 1, Pocket Cave, looking southwest across excavated floor. Notable are the mortar bin against the south wall, slabs at the base of the wall, and the lack of floor features.

next to the cliff. The outer edge of the pit had a slight overhang because of the inward-sloping face of a large natural block.

Walls. Along the east half of the north side, large slabs, flaring outward away from the floor, constituted the base of the wall; the western half consisted of the irregular faces of natural blocks.

Bench. Into the hard earth of the boundary at the back of the cave, a ledge averaging 36 cm in width and 58 cm in height had been cut to provide a bench. A mud rim was plastered along its edge. Along the south side, the natural blocks had been pecked down to form a slightly lower bench of irregular width.

Floor. The floor was irregular because of large stones encountered during excavation. South of the radial timbers the floor was considerably higher than in the main part of the room.

Hearth. The fireplace was D-shaped, flat across the south side, 80 cm in length and 75 cm in width. It was encircled by a low rim of mud.

Radials. Between the hearth and the west wall was a ridge of mud capped with a small timber. The southwest roof support stood in this ridge. From the opposite corner of the fireplace was the impression of a low ridge of mud that extended for 55 cm to the corner of a cist.

Cist. The outer boundary of the cist was the curve of the room wall, and its inner face was composed of verti-

cally-placed poles plastered over with clay.

Roof supports. The stubs of the four roof supports were in normal position. The southeast support stood where the radial touched the corner of the cist.

Wall posts. Across the south side, the stumps of the wall timbers lay as they had toppled forward. They were 13 to 18 cm apart.

Fill. The basal 45 cm of fill consisted of charred roof and wall materials. The room apparently had few contents at the time of the fire, but there had been a variety of objects on the roof. Among the chunks of roof clay were fragments of basketry, the remains of several sandals, manos, rubbing stones, and shattered metates. Additional artifacts found in the fill included five bone awls, an antler wrench, two chipped stone blades, an incomplete stone pendant, and a stone bead. Also found were a fiber-tempered seed jar, and a bowl and a vessel with lateral spout, both of plain gray pottery with unknown temper.

POCKET CAVE

The plan of Pocket Cave is shown in Figure 7.

Pit House 1

Form. Pit House 1 (Fig. 23) had been dug through refuse to a depth of 0.25 m at the south side, and 0.75 m at the north side. It was irregular in form, measuring

4 m from east to west and 4.2 m from north to south at floor level. At the back of the room, the slabs of the basal ring came within 0.65 m of the rear cliff wall. It is probable that when the walls were in place there was not sufficient room to pass between the chamber and the rear of the cave.

Walls. A row of thin slabs, 75 cm high and sloping outward at the top, lined the edge of the pit house. The walls had collapsed to the tops of the slabs on all but about one-third of the northeast arc, just north of the entry. Back of the bench was a row of upright slabs 60 cm high, plastered with a thin coat of clay. The wall southeast of the end of the bench was of clay plastered over the points of protruding natural blocks.

Bench. Portions of a bench began at the west end of the remaining portion of the northeast arc; it was 25 cm wide at the east end, widening to 45 cm over a length of 2 m.

Floor. The floor was the smooth sand of the pit bottom.

Hearth. The fireplace, situated slightly east of center, was 68 cm in diameter and 25 cm in depth. It was encircled by a low raised rim of mud.

Cists. Forty cm east of the fireplace was a mortar set into a slab-lined bin; the space between the slabs and the top of the mortar was sealed with mud. In the corner against the foot of the entry, between the mortar bin and the wall of the room, there was a small slab bin. In its northeast edge was the butt of a vertical timber 14 cm in diameter.

Roof supports. The four ceiling supports typically found in Basketmaker III living rooms were absent. Timbers for sustaining the roof were set into the basal ring of slabs. One was visible in the east wall and another was nearly opposite it on the west side. The post embedded in the side of the cist mentioned above may have served as a roof support.

Wall posts. Many smaller timbers, like the slanting wall poles of the typical chambers, had been set behind the tops of the slabs forming the basal ring, but their exact arrangement could not be determined.

Entry. A large flat stone 60 cm long, set on edge, joined the mortar bin to the room wall. At the top of this slab, 51 cm from the floor, was a rounded edge of mud which formed the inner edge of an antechamber floor 50 cm wide and 95 cm long. The northern wall had been a row of posts set vertically and plastered with mud. The southern wall had been a row of wooden slabs piercing the outer wall of the room. One would have expected this passage to be in a radial position to the circle of the chamber, but its orientation at a tangent may be explained by the fact that it pointed to the open front of the cave. If the passage had been placed with its end more toward the north, it would also have conflicted with Pit House 2.

Fill. The charred remains of the superstructure formed a layer of charcoal 6 to 14 cm thick over the entire floor. Recognizable in the burned layer was juniper bark that had been spread over the timbers. Scattered about over the room were several manos, loaf-shaped rubbing stones, and a number of smooth cobblestones. A few sherds of crude Basketmaker III cooking vessels were present in the charred layer, and a clay bottle stopper was also found in the fill. Additional observations concerning this room appear below in the *Comment* following the description of Pit House 2.

Pit House 2

Form. The floor of Pit House 2 was 45 cm above that of Pit House 1; its average diameter was 3.79 m at floor level. The excavation had been gouged down into the cave sand at the south side and against natural rocks at the north side.

Walls. The wall was faced with sloping slabs, except along the northern third, where it was made of natural stones and mortar spread against the bank of the excavation. The slabs rose to a height of 50 cm, sloping 25 cm outward over that distance. There was no bench along the north wall, which stood to a height of 1.4 m, but it could not be determined whether there had been one elsewhere in the chamber. At the north side, a pocket 1 m in depth and width had been gouged between natural blocks at a height of 50 cm above the floor. Immediately south of it was a platform 65 cm in length, slightly more than that in width, and 30 cm above the floor; its forward edge was faced with a rectangular slab of hard sandstone. It is possible that this platform was the floor of an antechamber passage similar to that described for Pit House 1, but here the outside opening must have been through the roof.

Floor. The floor of tramped sand, incorporating a sandstone block, was uneven — low toward the center and rising toward the sides.

Hearth. The location of the firepit could not be determined. Just inside the wall, and 30 cm from the south ceiling support, were the slabs of a sunken cist; they were blackened, but the discoloration could have occurred when the house burned.

Roof supports. Three roof supports were found set into the base of the wall; the fourth had eroded away.

Wall posts. The exact placement of the side timbers could not be determined, but their charred remains formed a deep layer of charcoal all over the floor. Juniper bark had been used as an intermediate layer between the poles and the final coating of mud.

Fill. Leaning against the northeast wall was a slab metate, the trough worn nearly through. Near the north side was a well-wrought mortar. Scattered about the floor were three manos, two loaf-shaped rubbing stones, a ball of red pigment, several cobbles, and a nearly

Fig. 24. View of Pit House 4, Pocket Cave, looking west across excavated floor.

cylindrical worked cobblestone that may have served as a pestle. There was also an unfired vessel with inward-sloping sides and a small mouth, and a large Obelisk Gray seed jar. The latter was set in a crude fiber-tempered mud bowl approximately 30 cm in diameter. Beside it was a seed jar equally crude in construction. The base was molded in a coiled basket and the thickness varied greatly; the finished object was more rough in appearance than many of the water-rolled clods seen in arroyo bottoms. Some fragments of sandals and cordage also were observed in the burned layer.

Comment on Pit Houses 1 and 2

After the fire, Pit Houses 1 and 2 were covered with a deposit containing a considerable amount of finely shredded vegetable refuse. Thereafter, a great mass of cave roof came down from above, covering the forward side of Pit House 1 and the entire area of Pit House 2, and shattering the contents. These chambers impressed the excavator as the crudest found in the area. They were merely lined cavities that had been roofed and provided with antechambers. The formal arrangement of a typical Prayer Rock Basketmaker dwelling was absent. Even the floors had not been plastered.

Pit House 3

Form. Pit House 3 was 6 m in diameter. Only a strip across the rear side was excavated. It was a Basketmaker III living room with a row of upright slabs, uniformly 40 cm tall, lining the excavation. The tops of the slabs were just visible before excavation was begun.

Floor. The floor sloped downward toward the center. It was of natural cave sand and had not been surfaced with mud.

Hearth. A hearth was present near the center of the room.

Roof supports. Apparently most of the timbers had been removed before the fire swept through the cave.

Fill. Immediately along the wall charred bark and small sticks were plentiful enough, but less than 1 m from the wall the composition of this material changed to refuse composed of dust, stone chips, and turkey droppings. Artifacts in the fill included a sandal-shaped board, a shouldered bone awl, a tapestry-weave sandal, a clay pipe, and a clay figurine fragment.

Pit House 4

Form. Pit House 4 (Fig. 24) was situated in the central portion of the cave floor and occupied the highest level available for building purposes. It was excavated 5 to 50 cm into the cave floor and was nearly circular, measuring 7.4 m long and 7 m wide.

Walls. The face of the cliff served as the back wall. At the southwestern side, three natural blocks were utilized as part of the boundary. Aside from these and the vertical area afforded by the cliff face, the basal ring was lined with slabs 68 cm high and sloping outward 25 cm from the vertical. The cracks between the slabs had been filled with vegetal-reinforced mud, and a coating of it had been spread over the rock faces. Reeds had covered the wall posts.

Bench. Whether or not a bench had existed along the tops of the wall slabs could not be determined; the side timbers had been torn away, and since the earth where they once stood had not been hardened by fire or moisture, most of it had weathered.

Roof. The mud on the central portion of the roof had come directly down on the floor. The smoke hole, which was intact, was 56 cm in diameter. The mud of the roof was 13 cm thick and had been smoothed by a patting motion of the hand; finger impressions were distinctly visible. Either the sheet of roof clay had slumped southwestward in falling, or the smoke vent had not been directly above the fireplace, since the southeast side of the vent lay 20 cm southwest of the southwestern edge of the hearth.

Floor. The floor had been surfaced with a thin layer of clay.

Hearth. The fireplace was southeast of center. It was circular, 90 cm in diameter and 22 cm in depth. A large stone had been encountered in the attempt to dig it, and a bowl had been hollowed into the rock as much as 10 cm deep in places; the surface showed the marks of the shaping tool. Rough pieces of sandstone had been set up as a lining for the sides and protruded somewhat above the floor; they were completely plastered over with a rim of mud.

Radials. There were four radial ridges on the floor. Three were symmetrically placed, dividing the floor area into a large northwest sector and two smaller sectors of equal size on the southeast. The fourth ridge, extending from the fireplace to a junction with the wall of a slab bin, divided the south sector in half. The floor ridges were about 17 cm wide and 8 cm high. Two of them were composed of a radial pole completely covered with mud; the other two were made of mud only.

Cists. A slab bin stood against the south side of the chamber (see Fig. 24). It was D-shaped, with the rounded side toward the room, 1.08 m long by 0.76 m wide. Mud was plastered between the slabs, giving the wall a maximum thickness of 10 cm. The highest remaining portion was 60 cm high.

Roof supports. The four ceiling supports were in the usual position away from the walls. These timbers and practically all of the other woodwork in the room had been torn out.

Fill. The room had not burned, and the floor was more intact than in some other houses. In the south sector, the clay was stained dark from long use and filth. Embedded in it were beans, grains of red and yellow corn, turkey feathers, human hair, rabbit fur, shredded yucca leaves and fiber, yucca cordage, part of the contents of a milkweed shell, and a great many minute flakes of chalcedony, evidently struck off as an arrow maker plied his trade. In addition there were a number of footprints of at least three sizes, ranging from those of a child to the large ones of an adult. The impressions of the forward ends of the two adult feet were immediately west of the radial ridge running southeastward from the fireplace. Evidently the individual had squatted with heels on this ridge, possibly for the purpose of washing his or her hair. About 50 cm in front of the footprints, a coiled basket had rested on the floor and may well have contained water for use in the cleansing process. Immediately beside the right footprint was a large handful of beaten yucca root, such as would have been used for shampoo. At the west side of the cist, adjacent to the south wall, there was a pile of five twined sandals, all of them worn. At the foot of the slabs bounding the southern sector of this cist, tucked beneath the mud, there was a tiny small-mouthed bottle covered with a red wash. The depth of the debris filling the room ranged from 40 to 70 cm. Additional artifacts in the fill included one plaited and one tapestry-weave sandal, an apron, pigment, a snare stick, a digging stick, a prayer stick, a shouldered bone awl, a bone tube, a clay figurine, a stone bowl, a La Plata Black-on-white bowl, and a Lino Gray narrow-mouthed jar.

CAVE 8

Pit Houses 1, 2, 3, 4

All of the pit houses had been burned and their inner sides, where the fill was deepest, were extremely wet. They were similar in every respect to the houses described above.

Form. The pit houses ranged in diameter from 3.75 to 6.50 m. They were vaguely circular and had been arranged to face the front of the cave.

Radials. In the northern three pit houses, radial divisions extended from either side of the fireplace to the walls, composed of poles embedded in ridges of mud. In the southernmost room the portion of the floor that would have borne these devices had weathered away.

Cists. In each of the northern three houses there was a slab bin where a radial pole approached the periphery. In the second from the south there was a series of four small slab bins side by side along the south wall.

Roof supports. Inside each house there had been four principal roof supports set out from the walls.

Wall posts. The slanting timbers of the side walls had been set either on cave earth at floor level or on jutting blocks where they were present. The covering of the side timbers had been of reeds, and one house had a layer of juniper bark between the reeds and the mud.

Fill. A large and typical series of Basketmaker III products was recovered from the rooms, all of which had burned during occupation. These included at least four seed jars, two wide-mouthed jars, and one globular vessel of Lino Gray; five seed jars, two narrow-mouthed jars, two wide-mouthed jars, and one deep bowl of Chapin Gray; and five seed jars, four wide-mouthed jars, and a deep bowl of plain gray pottery with mixed temper. There were also a few polished red pots, some La Plata Black-on-white bowls, and several unfired mud vessels. Some of these had been on the floors of the houses and some had been on the roofs, which collapsed during the burning. Human figurines and miniature carrying baskets of clay, many sandals, three fur and feather cord blankets tied into bundles, bits of hide, string and meat, bone awls, and wooden tools had been partially destroyed by the fire. Metates, manos, and cobblestones had been splintered in place by the heat. The greatest concentration of these materials was in the second pit house from the south. Notable in this structure was a tremendous quantity of charred foodstuffs. At least 13 coiled baskets and one plaited basket contained corn, seeds, and shelled and unshelled beans. More of these foods were found in a cist built at the end of the north radial timber of this house.

4. TREE-RING DATING

A large number of wood and charcoal specimens were collected by Earl Morris during the excavations and on at least one subsequent visit to the area. Some of these were submitted to Dr. A. E. Douglass of the Laboratory of Tree-Ring Research, University of Arizona (Douglass 1936). The remainder were sent to Gila Pueblo in Globe (Haury 1938). It was hoped that dendrochronological dates obtained from these two institutions would serve as checks on each other and would more firmly place the archaeological materials in time. Most of the latter group were subsequently checked by Douglass, and these and the Laboratory of Tree-Ring Research dates were published in Smiley's summary volume (1951).

More recently, the Southwestern Archaeological Project of the Tree-Ring Laboratory has re-examined all specimens from both collections and derived a new series of dates. These do not change the overall temporal placement of the sites, but they do add quantity and detail, and to a large extent they eliminate the problems encountered in dealing with dates from pieces of wood that originally came from a single timber (Bannister, Dean, and Gell 1966). It is this re-examination of the dates that has illuminated earlier portions of the occupancy in Broken Flute, Obelisk, and Pocket caves, dating to the decades just before and after A.D. 500. Unfortunately, there were few artifactual remains definitely associated with the early houses. Whether they are Basketmaker II houses or a very early manifestation of Basketmaker III is an unsolved problem.

The well-preserved Prayer Rock cave sites with their architectural pattern including pit houses with roof supports, walls, and ceilings built of datable species of wood, have provided an excellent series of dates (see Table 2). In interpreting these dates, several of the following situations, described by Bannister (1962), must be taken into consideration.

There is a clear case for the reuse of some timbers. Most specimens date from either before A.D. 508 or after A.D. 597. Several houses — for example Pit Houses 5 and 11 in Broken Flute Cave — provided mostly dates in the later period, with a timber or two dating in the earlier period. In a situation where the preservation of materials is such that the wood could be reused even today, it is easy to visualize the utilization of available prepared logs by a Basketmaker builder.

There is an almost equally clear case for the use of repair timbers. In some houses — for instance, Pit Houses 6 and 11 in Broken Flute Cave — the majority of the cutting dates cluster together, and then after a dateless gap of several years another date or two appears. It is likely that the latest dates represent repair of unsatisfactory timbers or remodeling of the structure, perhaps by adding shelves, a floor timber, or a storage bin. It is also possible that some of the late dates are from artifacts or hearth debris, although these types of materials would probably have been identified in the notes or during the course of analysis.

Table 2 shows that dates from a single house often occur over two consecutive years. Logs cut before the beginning of the spring growing season in a given year would have added their terminal year during the growing season of the previous year. Logs cut during or after the growing season of a particular year would bear a terminal ring from that year. In the semi-arid Southwest the spring growing season begins and ends abruptly and is short, occurring mostly during the months of May and June. Therefore, trees with cutting dates of, for example, A.D. 622–623, as found in Pit House 6 of Broken Flute Cave, could have been cut within two to ten months of each other. In all likelihood a house would have been built during, or at any rate soon after, the year in which all the materials were brought together.

In Broken Flute Cave, Pit Houses 5, 6, 7, 8, 9, 11, 12, and probably Pit Houses 4 and 14, were built between A.D. 620 and 630. Pit Houses 1, 2, 3, and 8A date just before and after A.D. 500. The dating on Pit Houses 1, 2, and 3 is open to some question because of the small number of dates available for each structure. However, the number of dates from Pit House 8A and its undeniable stratigraphic position underneath Pit House 8 — solidly dated in the 620s — leave little doubt as to its relative age. As much of its architecture as may be seen is similar to that of the later structures. If it is indeed early, then those traits are early too. If it was built later, but still before Pit House 8, and entirely of used timbers, then we are unfortunately deceived in obtaining five early dates.

The dating of the pit houses in Cave 2 shows clearly that they were built about A.D. 660–670. Although the dates are not so numerous or so localized from specific pit houses, the indications are that Caves 1, 3, 6, 7, and 8 had an occupation of similar age. The dates from Pocket and Obelisk caves correspond to those of the early occupation in Broken Flute Cave.

All of the Prayer Rock caves containing Basketmaker occupations provided 178 dates between A.D. 325 and 676. The 122 cutting dates and all except three widely distributed early noncutting dates are between A.D. 430 and 676. There were no cutting dates and only four noncutting dates between A.D. 508 and 597, which indicates a hiatus in construction. However, no corresponding break in stratigraphic deposits or artifactual typology was noted. The artifacts found in the earlier houses were few in number and seemed quite consistent both in kind and manufacture with those from later houses. If those early houses were cleaned out prehistorically, then the artifacts found in them are actually later trash deposits. Also, the dates for the "early" houses, in at least some cases, may be entirely from reused timbers.

It is possible, of course, that Basketmaker III development might turn out to be dated as early as A.D. 500 and before, thus including all of the Prayer Rock remains. To decide this clearly, however, carefully excavated sites representing only the fifth and sixth centuries are needed.

TABLE 2
Tree-Ring Dates from Prayer Rock Caves

Site	Tree-Ring Dates (A.D.)
Broken Flute Cave	
Pit House 1	501*, 508*
Pit House 2	468, 499*
Pit House 3	505
Pit House 4	491*, 628*
Pit House 5	457*, 609, 628, 629* (2)
Pit House 6	602, 606, 613, 622, 622* (3), 623 (3), 623* (5), 627*
Pit House 7	623*, 624*, 625 (2), 625* (3), 626*
Pit House 8	618, 624 (2), 625, 625*, 627*
Pit House 8A	469, 469*, 470*, 493, 494*
Pit House 9	515, 611*, 613, 623* (4), 624* (7)
Pit House 11	491, 568, 574, 619, 621*, 625*, 635*
Pit House 12	621*, 623 (2), 623* (3)
Pit House 14	627
Pit House 17	489*, 505*, 605*
General	354, 378, 430*, 437, 474, 474*, 597*, 612*, 622*, 623* (2), 624*, 625* (2), 637*, 652
Cave 1	
Pit House 1	657
Pit House 3	658
Cave 2	
Pit House 1	626*, 655, 657, 666* (2), 667 (3), 667*, 668, 668*, 669 (7), 669* (3)
Pit House 2	667 (2), 668, 669 (6), 676* (2)
Pit House 4	642, 645, 654 (2), 655, 656*, 657, 658 (4), 660 (2), 663, 665*, 668, 670*
West Ledge deposit	644*, 656, 657
Cave 3	646
Cave 6	556, 636, 660, 661*, 674 (3), 674* (4)
Cave 7	666, 666*, 674
Cave 8	668
Obelisk Cave	
Burned room east center	325, 438, 480*
General	446*, 478*, 479* (2), 480 (2), 484, 484*, 486*, 489*
Pocket Cave	438

*Cutting date. Dates listed represent one specimen unless followed by a number in parentheses indicating multiple specimens. A date is presented as a cutting date if the specimen has one of the following criteria present: bark, beetle galleries, surface patination that develops under bark, or a continuous outer ring; dates for all other specimens are presented as noncutting dates. For further details, and for varying degrees of confidence in cutting dates, see Bannister, Dean, and Gell (1966).

5. BURIALS

A small number of mummies and skeletons were discovered during the excavation of the Prayer Rock caves. They had been placed in crevices next to the cliff or in trash-filled cracks between rocks. The human remains that were uncovered were replaced in their graves by the excavator, who provided the descriptions below. Cave 4 appeared to have been specifically a burial cave; no architecture was found there, but burials were scattered over the surface, apparently from disturbances in later times. The use of caves for burial only is probably a continuation of the practice noted in DuPont Cave and other Basketmaker II caves where burial cists were the predominant prehistoric remains (for example, see Pepper 1902: 4). The placement of the graves in a specific area and the erosion of the trash deposits at the cave mouths partially account for the fact that so few burials were found in the dwelling areas.

BROKEN FLUTE CAVE

Burial 1

In a crevice between sandstone blocks lay the disturbed skeleton of a child. It had lain on the right side, flexed, with head toward the west. A good deal of hair, raggedly cut to a length of about 5 cm, adhered to the skull, which was long and slightly asymmetrical on the right side of the back. The forward end of a scallop-toed sandal was in questionable association.

Burial 2

Burial 2 was in Cist 7, dug into compact sandy earth against the back wall of the cliff. The cist measured 1.75 m by 1.25 m and had been deeper than 1.15 m. The hole sloped forward at an angle of about 45 degrees to the rear side of the excavation. The front bank was undercut so that most of the body lay beneath the overhang at a depth of 1.10 m below the cave floor. The body was that of an adult male, fairly tall, lying on his back with head turned to the right, pointing slightly south of west. The left arm was straight, with the hand resting over the head of the left femur. The right arm was straight by the side to the elbow, then bent so that the hand covered the left groin. The legs were closely flexed, with the heels almost touching the buttocks and the knees leaning to the right, forming an angle of about 90 degrees with the trunk.

Above and below the body was a thick bed of juniper bark. The body was wrapped in two blankets, one of fur cloth and the other of feather cloth; both were badly decayed. Across the right wrist lay fragments of two disintegrated sandals. A severed bead cord remained in place in the left ear. On the legs, hands, chest, and left side of the face most of the skin was present. The hair was closely clipped around the hairline, but was several inches long at the crown of the head. About half of it was distinctly gray. Apparently the individual was killed by a heavy blow on the upper side of the head, which was crushed over an area 8 cm in diameter.

Clean sand and large slabs of stone that had been used in cist walls formed a covering over the burial. On top of this stone layer, scattered over the western half of the cist and crushed by the weight of some overlying stones, were fragments of two flutes, a long digging stick with a blade at one end, and two finely wrought dartlike implements similar to atlatl shafts, but lacking either pit or notch at the blunt end and bearing no positive proof of having been feathered.

Burials 3, 4, and 5

Three burials were in the rock slide at the east end of the cave. Shredded bark, cordage, strings of a blanket, and an occasional human bone were found in the fill.

Burial 3 was a very small child on its back with knees drawn up and head toward the northwest. It was lying about one meter deep, next to two large stones. The legs had been bound in a flexed position by a strand of yucca fiber passed around the thighs and the middle of the calves. The body had been placed on sand and covered with a small amount of juniper bark.

Burial 4 was another child about the same size, buried at the same level. The body was on its back with legs slightly bent. A rabbit skin blanket reaching from the head to the middle of the thighs was adhering to the flesh.

Burial 5 was the skeleton of an adult male, lying 1 m north of the first child and 45 cm below it. He was on his back with legs flexed and knees vertically elevated. The head was tilted upward and forward, facing toward the east. The remains had been wrapped in a feather string blanket caught together above the body with strands of yucca fiber. Some of the same fiber and a small quantity of juniper bark had been spread directly over the blanket. Above the bark and fiber lay two digging sticks, one across and one lengthwise over the trunk. Over these and lengthwise on the grave was a peeled pole thought to be a piece of roofing material, and then a great mass of greasewood brush piled in layers, the tip ends at the center of the mass and the stalks pointing outward from it.

A quantity of hair cut to a length of 10 cm adhered to the blanket where it covered the skull. The arms were slightly bent at the elbows and the hands were together over the pelvis. On the left wrist was a bracelet of twelve *Olivella* shells strung on a yucca cord with a large shell bangle in the center of the outward side. The teeth were mature but little worn. The right side of the forehead had at one time been crushed over an area of 3 cm by 8 cm. This blow had shattered and broadened the entire right side of the nose. Despite the fact that the bone was pressed in to a depth of at least 7 mm, it had completely healed. The long bones showed evidence of advanced disease; they were pitted and in some places greatly enlarged. The stature of the individual was estimated to be about 1.72 m. Just above the skull was the plaited portion of a large yucca basket; it did not appear to be a burial accompaniment.

Burial 6

About 2 m south of the center of the Great Kiva Circle, at a depth of about 40 cm, lay the remains of an infant. It was partially flexed, placed on its back with its head to the south. The body was wrapped in yucca fiber, and above it was spread a small feather string blanket in a perfect state of preservation. A shallow pit for the remains had been scooped into the natural earth of the cave floor, and the earth removed had been used as fill.

Burial 7

The scattered bones of a child were found against the cliff 3 m south of Pit House 2, about 50 cm beneath the surface.

Burial 8

Less than 1 m from the edge of the talus slope and about 75 cm below the floor of Pit House 8A, the Bernheimer Expedition found the mummy of a small child wrapped in a rabbit skin blanket and buried with a cradle board of Basketmaker II type. The remains were in a hole dug into natural sand.

CAVE 2

Burial 1

At the extreme northeastern end of the remaining portion of the cave floor were found the skull and a few bones of a child. The skull was extremely short and excessively deformed at the back; it may represent a Pueblo burial.

CAVE 4

Numerous human bones and juniper bark were visible in the southern portion of the shelter. Excavation revealed that a number of interments had been made in the crannies between the large blocks that formed most of the natural deposit. At least eight adults and four children had been buried in this cave, and it is presumed that even more burials had once been placed here. With one exception, the graves had been looted in ancient times, presumably in a search for beads and ornaments. The skeletons had been ripped out of their rough pits and the bones and wrappings scattered. The baskets that had accompanied them had been thrown out on the surface and were tramped to pieces.

The pits were lined with long strips of juniper bark and a covering of the same material had been spread above each body. Cordage of both fur and feather string blankets was observed, and there were quantities of prepared yucca fiber. In other localities, this fiber was often used as an inner wrapping for bodies, and twists of the same material were placed with them as offerings.

Burial 1

The tightly flexed burial of a mature woman less than 5 ft tall was found in a pit. The arms were by the sides with hands between the thighs and knees brought up against the chest. The remains had been wedged back downward into the pit, and the forcing of the body into the restricted space had tipped the head forward; to judge from the angle of the neck vertebrae, the skull had been between the knees. The bead hunters had dug down to the body, twisted off the head, and thrown it out of the pit.

Burial 2

About 40 cm distant from Burial 1 was an undisturbed infant burial, in a pit about 35 cm wide and 60 cm long. The tiny body was closely flexed on its back with its head toward the east. Along one side were a quantity of large piñon nuts and at least three ears of corn. Resting partly against the bark lining of the pit and partly on the right side of the skull was a tiny unfired mud bowl. Covering the head was an inverted coiled basket, and above it and the folded legs lay another basket. The skull, the only one found in this cave, was particularly long and was undeformed.

The perishable objects were badly decayed, but the beads worn by the baby indicated that the ancient looters were well rewarded for their efforts in the rest of the cave. On the left wrist was a bracelet of *Olivella* shells, with a single bangle of abalone, and around the neck was a long strand of disk-shaped beads, about 1.5 cm in diameter, made of pink and white stone.

POCKET CAVE

Three infant burials were found in Pocket Cave. Perishable objects in all three of the burials were decayed almost beyond recognition. The skulls of the first two infants were crushed so that the form was not evident, but it was plain that the backs of the skulls had not been deformed. The third skull was removed entirely; it was totally without deformation and quite long.

At the east end of Pocket Cave, between a cist and the cliff wall, were the jaw and a few large bones of an adult.

Burial 1

Near the south end of the cave, 3 m from the back wall, a mass of juniper bark was visible in the sloping hardpan layer. It proved to be the covering of an infant that had been buried in a pothole some 50 cm in diameter. The body was closely flexed, with head toward the south. The remains had been wrapped in some sort of string blanket, and a small coiled basket had been inverted over the skull.

Burial 2

The body of a second infant was 0.75 m farther forward and 1.5 m up the slope from the first. It also was in a small pothole in the hardpan and completely enveloped in juniper bark. The body was flexed, lying on its back with its head toward the west. Four coiled baskets had been laid on top of the burial bundle, which had been wrapped first in prepared yucca fiber and then in a string blanket. Around the neck was a strand of *Olivella* shells and white disk beads.

Burial 3

A third infant was similarly buried, 1.5 m closer to the cliff than Burial 2. It was tightly folded, back downward, with head to north of west. Over the face there had been an inverted basket. On the left wrist was a bracelet of *Olivella* and white shell beads, and around the neck was a string of *Olivella* and white disk beads.

6. CERAMICS

The excavator recovered 211 whole and restorable vessels from the floors and the fill of the pit houses, and thousands of sherds from the trash. Most of these date from the Basketmaker III occupation, although the ceramic contents of some cists and a portion of the surface finds are one of the significant indicators of later Pueblo visitors. The nature of the pottery collected from the original excavation, which consists mostly of restorable vessels and of sherds other than plain wares, as well as small samples of plain gray sherds found beside each excavation unit when I visited the caves in 1958, indicate that a certain amount of selection was made in the field. Probably most or all of the whole and restorable vessels, and all of the smudged, fugitive red, polished red, and decorated sherds were retained and were available for this study.

PUEBLO POTTERY

The late sherds consist mostly of types in use in the Kayenta and Mesa Verde branches during Pueblo times. In some instances most of a single vessel was found in a cist, in others a few sherds of diverse types were found scattered on the surface in a cave. The types present are indicated in Table 3. The wide range of types, representing a number of later time periods, and the presence of small storerooms in some of the caves provide indications of the nature of the Pueblo occupation. Probably the valley floors were farmed by people who lived in permanent villages not far away, and who came to this locality where arable land and a water supply were present during the growing season. The easily accessible caves could have provided shelter for them and their harvested crops.

BASKETMAKER POTTERY

The Basketmaker III ceramic remains consisted, for the most part, of plain gray ware, with a small but persistent admixture of Basketmaker III decorated pots and a few gray smudged, fugitive red, and polished red types. Unfired fiber-tempered specimens, mostly bowls, were in association with fired vessels, mostly jars, in many pit houses.

Anna O. Shepard of the Carnegie Institution of Washington examined some sherds from the Mesa Verde sites excavated by O'Bryan. In her description, as quoted in

TABLE 3
Pueblo Pottery Found in Prayer Rock Caves

Pottery	No. of Specimens	Provenience
Kana-a Gray (Colton and Hargrave 1937: 195; Abel 1955)	1 jar	Cave 6
Moccasin Gray (Abel 1955)	1 jar	Broken Flute Cave, Cist 50
	1 jar	Cave 1
Mancos Gray (Abel 1955)	1 sherd	Cave 1
Pueblo II-III Indented Corrugated	1 jar, 1 sherd	Broken Flute Cave
Kana-a Black-on-white (Colton and Hargrave 1937: 205; Colton 1955)	5 sherds	Cave 1
Mancos Black-on-white (Colton and Hargrave 1937: 230; Abel 1955)	7 sherds	Cave 5
Mesa Verde Black-on-white (Colton and Hargrave 1937: 231; Abel 1955)	1 bowl	Broken Flute Cave, Cist 50
	4 sherds	Cave 5
Kayenta Black-on-white (Colton and Hargrave 1937: 217; Colton 1955)	1 sherd	Broken Flute Cave
Unknown Black-on-white	1 sherd	Broken Flute Cave
	4 sherds	Cave 1
	1 jar	Cave 5
San Juan Red Ware (Abel 1955)	3 sherds	Broken Flute Cave
Deadmans Black-on-red (Colton and Hargrave 1937: 71)	2 bowls	Cave 1
Tusayan Black-on-red (Colton and Hargrave 1937: 74)	1 bowl	Cave 12
Zuni Pueblo V Polychrome	5 sherds	Broken Flute Cave

his report (O'Bryan 1950), a comparison is made between these sherds and other Basketmaker III pottery assemblages of which the Prayer Rock complex is one. Her remarks indicate the kinds of problems that exist in the definition of types in the Mesa Verde branch, and of the type of analysis that will be needed to order the confusion:

A small series of sherds from early deposits was examined with the binocular microscope in order to ascertain the proportion of rock-tempered pottery. The samples were too small for statistical summary by type, but the following outline will indicate the frequency of the two main tempering materials:

Site 145, Pit II, B.M. III, dates 664. Lino Gray, Twin Trees Polished, La Plata Black-on-white.

Temper: Rock 27
　　　　　Sand 6

The small sample of B.M. III and P. I pottery which I examined was distinctly heterogeneous in appearance. Igneous rock could be obtained from the Mesa Verde from pebbles in an ancient gravel deposit, but this fact does not in itself dispose of the problems of intrusives. It may be of interest therefore, to compare the paste of B.M. III Black-on-gray from neighboring regions:

	Temper	
Region	Rock	Sand
La Plata District		
Paint: 33 iron oxide		
67 organic	99	1
Red Rock (Prayer Rock)		
Paint: 27 iron oxide		
1 organic	25	3
Durango, four sites		
Paint: 2 iron oxide		
34 lead glaze		
5 organic	11	30
Shabik'eschee Village		
Paint: 18 iron oxide		
1 organic	1	18

In the two regions having a strong preponderance of rock tempered pottery, rock was available locally, in the La Plata Valley as drift boulders, and in the Red Rock District as cobbles from the Carrizo Mountain in the bed of the Red Wash. To complete the record, it may be noted that plain ware in the La Plata corresponds in paste to the painted ware; but that in the Red Rock District plain ware is mainly sand-tempered. A possible explanation is that the production of painted ware in the latter district was restricted to the settlements near the Red Wash, and plain pottery was made throughout the region.

More discussion on temper is followed by a statement on paint.

The distribution of paint types in the area under consideration can be roughly sketched. The La Plata Valley is divided, with organic paint characteristic of the section north of the state line where most of the B.M. III sites are located and iron oxide paint preponderating in the south. The latter paint is typical of the Mesa Verde on the north, Red Rock to the west and Chaco Canyon on the south. [O'Bryan 1950: 89–91].

The above findings agree roughly with my less intensive analysis of the sherds and whole vessels from the Prayer Rock district. One hundred sherds from Broken Flute Cave, the same number from Cave 2, and three lots of 100 sherds each from the site assemblage in general were analyzed and counted to determine the relative quantity of temper types present. The results, listed in Table 4, were fairly consistent.

TABLE 4
Temper Analysis of 500 Selected Sherds from Prayer Rock Sites

Site	Sherds with quartz sand temper	Sherds with mixed temper	Sherds with crushed rock temper	Total Sherds
Broken Flute Cave	59	21	20	100
Cave 2	44	28	28	100
Provenience Unknown: Sample A	61	24	15	100
Sample B	57	30	13	100
Sample C	50	31	19	100
Average	54	27	19	

It was noted that a restorable wide-mouthed jar and several isolated sherds had tiny particles of shells included in the paste. In some cases, these appeared to be minute snail shells and in others they were fragments of shells. These sherds were given to Robert J. Drake, then with the Department of Zoology, University of Arizona for analysis. His findings (1958) were as follows:

The molluscan material remains were seen to be almost whole shells of small freshwater snails which had been entombed in the matrix of the pots. The genus of this type of shell is *Gyraulus*. *Gyraulus* is in the family Planorbidea, it can be known as 'small planorbid.' From the small amount of *Gyraulus* material, 5 or 6 fragmentary shells, a specific identification cannot be made.

There are some plates of shell with ridges on them. These are about 1 mm by 2 mm by ⅓ mm and, I think, came from larger snails of the succineid groups (family Succineidae) which are almost amphibious although generally known as landshells that live in damp situations around small pools and inland beaches.

In addition to these two types, there are remains of small discoid snails which may or may not be remains of land forms. These are about 2 mm across. They may only be smaller and more fragile *Gyraulus*.

All of the forms discussed here very probably are now living in the Prayer Rock area. The enclosure of the shells and shell fragments is thought to be accidental.

Thus it would seem that the shell material was an accidental inclusion in the clay or in the tempering material. The shells are so small and delicate that their collection would have been a difficult task, and any subsequent treatment would have resulted in crushing them to powder. Probably the Basketmaker people did not know they were there. Besides the shell fragments, the tempering material in these few sherds is crushed rock.

An examination of the literature reveals that the status of Basketmaker III plain and decorated types in the Mesa Verde area is in a state of taxonomic fluctuation. Sherds may be roughly placed in time according to the Pecos system, with a fair degree of accuracy. That there are internal variations within these categories becomes apparent upon an examination of any sample, or upon the comparison of two or more assemblages. The studies by Miss Shepard (O'Bryan 1950) document this in detail. Several ordering systems have been suggested to categorize these differences into units with temporal or geographical distribution and cultural significance (Colton and Hargrave 1937; O'Bryan 1950; Abel 1955).

The contribution of Abel (1955) was the most detailed study available at the time this original manuscript was written. The sherd sample from the Prayer Rock district changes some aspects of his described distributions, but basically the attributes of the vessels fit the published definitions. It is in the significance of the tempering materials and the geographic distributions that questions arise (for more current information see Breternitz, Rohn, and Morris 1974).

The Basketmaker III vessels recovered are listed by ceramic type and by vessel form in Table 5. The shapes exhibit a limited range of variability with a close correlation to type. Plain types are listed according to Abel's classification on the basis of tempering differences.

Plain Gray Ceramics

With the exception of Obelisk Gray, all of the plain gray vessels (Figs. 25, 26, 27*e-k*, 28) were similar in size, shape, rim form, and surface treatment. Most of them were spherical or nearly spherical jars with various kinds of mouths and neck openings. They were somewhat smoothed without being polished. The Obelisk Gray vessels were highly polished and differed from the others slightly in shape. The unpolished plain gray specimens were divided into three categories on the basis of tempering material; two of these categories are defined types, and the other is transitional between them. A fourth category was established for the whole vessels whose temper could not be seen well enough to classify.

Lino Gray

About half of the plain gray sherds were Lino Gray (Colton and Hargrave 1937: 191–92; Colton 1955). However, the presence of a large number of sherds that could not be sorted obscured the relative amounts of different temper ingredients. The type was distinguished on the basis of its quartz sand temper.

Chapin Gray

Somewhat less than a fourth of the plain gray vessels had crushed rock temper and no quartz sand. This is the basis for the differentiation of Chapin Gray from Lino

Gray (Abel 1955). Abel states that there is distinct geographic distribution. Mesa Verde Gray Ware (Abel 1955) is distinguished from Tusayan Gray Ware on the basis of containing crushed rock instead of quartz sand as tempering material, and on the basis of distribution of the types of Mesa Verde Gray Ware north of the San Juan River and the types of Tusayan Gray Ware south of the river. The Prayer Rock caves are south of this boundary and contain substantial quantities of Chapin Gray. Several hypotheses have been suggested, but the current evidence does not definitively support any of them. First, the Chapin Gray vessels may have been imported to the Prayer Rock Valley from north of the San Juan River. Second, since the sites under discussion occupy an area near the boundary between the two distributions, the presence of the two types and an intermediate type might indicate that tempering material was a choice made by each potter and that both kinds of material were available. Third, it is possible the San Juan River only approximates the boundary and is not to be taken as the border at this particular spot.

Plain Gray with Mixed Temper

This category should probably be included with Chapin Gray, but its intermediate position between Lino Gray and Chapin Gray may shed light on the nature of the definition and distribution of these types. These vessels had crushed rock and quartz sand temper. The sample included 39 vessels of this type.

Plain Gray Ware with Unknown Temper

The tempering material could not be observed in 36 vessels, and they were therefore assigned to this category.

Obelisk Gray

Obelisk Gray (Fig. 29 *f–i*; Abel 1955) is a highly polished Lino Gray with the same tempering material. It differs from Lino Gray in shape range, including mostly elongated shouldered seed jars and a large deep bowl. These vessels constituted the collection from which the type was named.

Decorated Ceramics

Lino Fugitive Red

Lino Fugitive Red (Fig. 30 *c*; Colton and Hargrave 1937: 193–94; Colton 1955) is like Lino Gray with an unfired red wash added to the exterior.

Lino Smudged

Lino Smudged (Fig. 30 *a, b, d*; Haury 1940: 84) has not been defined. The three bowls that constitute the sample are unusual — they were found in a site containing mostly plain ware jars. They were not quite so deep as the plain or decorated bowls, the rims were thinner and more pointed, and the interiors were smoothed and

TABLE 5
Vessel Forms of Basketmaker Pottery from Prayer Rock Caves

Vessel Form	Lino Gray	Chapin Gray	Plain Gray, mixed temper	Plain Gray, unknown temper	Obelisk Gray	Lino Fugitive Red	Lino Smudged	La Plata Black-on-white	La Plata Black-on-white, fugitive red exterior	Lino Black-on-gray	Unknown Red-on-gray	Unknown Polychrome	Polished Red Ware	Unfired, untempered mud vessels	Unfired fiber-tempered ware
Seed jars	8	9	15	8											3
Seed jars, shouldered	1		1	1											1
Seed jars, elongated		3	2	1											
Seed jars, elongated, shouldered					5										
Seed jars, elongated, vertically pierced lugs				1											
Seed jars, elongated, horizontally perforated lugs	1														
Seed jars, shouldered, vertically perforated lugs	2														
Seed jars, vertically perforated lugs								1				1			
Seed jars, basket-impressed															1
Narrow-mouthed jars						1									
Narrow-mouthed jars, straight neck	5		2	5											
Narrow-mouthed jars, flaring neck	1				1										
Narrow-mouthed jars, straight neck, strap handle		2													
Narrow-mouthed jars, neck sloping inward		1													
Narrow-mouthed jars, straight neck, vertically perforated lugs			1												
Wide-mouthed jars, straight neck	3		9	1											
Wide-mouthed jars, flaring neck	6	2	5	7										1	
Wide-mouthed jars, recurved neck	1														
Wide-mouthed jars, recurved rim		1		1											
Wide-mouthed jars, sloping neck			1												
Wide-mouthed jars, neck gradually sloping inward			1	1											
Wide-mouthed jars, recurved rim, strap handle				1											
Wide-mouthed jars, straight neck, horizontally perforated lugs				1											
Wide-mouthed jars, recurved rim, vertically pierced lugs													3		
Globular jars, probably with large recurved neck	1														
Globular vessel with lateral spout				4											
Globular vessel with lateral opening				1											
Deep bowls	2			1	1	1	3	29	1	1	1		7		1
Shallow bowl															8
Shallow bowl, lugs															1
Shallow bowl, basket-impressed															4
Shallow bowl, basket-impressed, lugs															5
Shallow bowl, basket-impressed, loop handles															1
Shallow bowl, partitioned into three(?) parts		1													
Partitioned bowl, two parts				1											
Quadrilobate jar			1												
Effigy head in side of bulbous jar neck			1												
Shape of vessels undeterminable	2			1										1	
TOTALS	33	19	39	36	7	2	3	30	1	1	1	1	10	2	25

had a more or less shiny surface. The type that most resembles these vessels is Forestdale Smudged, a brown smudged ware from the Mogollon area.

Black-on-white Ceramics

With a single exception, the iron paint black-on-white vessels were deep bowls, and the design had frequently turned brownish in color at the time of firing. One vessel, with a typical design on the interior, was a seed jar. The execution of the design must have been a difficult procedure, since the painter's hand would have filled the opening. With the jar half filled, the pattern would have been obscured.

Fig. 25.   Wide-mouthed, straight-necked plain gray jars. *d*, with horizontally perforated lugs; *f*, clay jar stopper in place. Height of *g*, 31 cm.

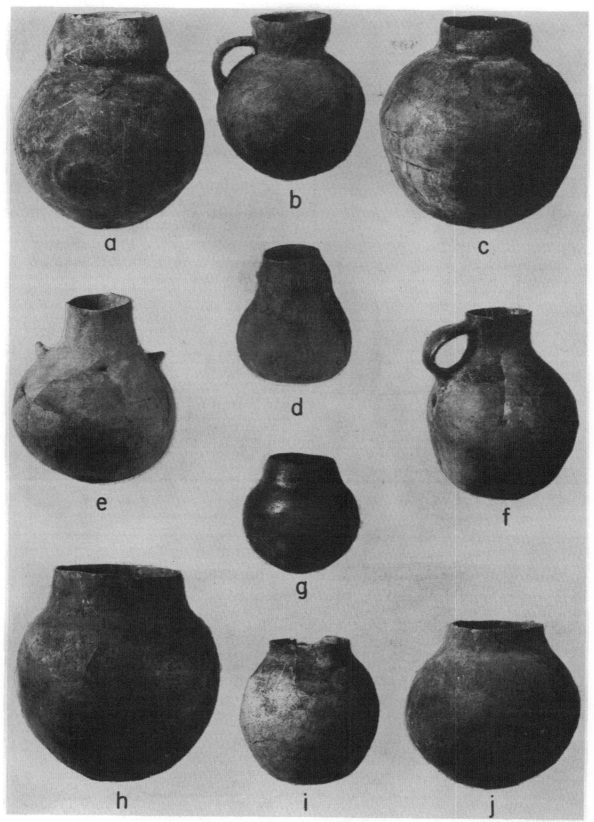

Fig. 26.   Plain gray vessels. *a–d*, wide-mouthed, recurved rim jars;
e–j, wide-mouthed, sloping-necked jars; *b*, *f*, with strap handles;
e, with vertically perforated lugs. Height of *a*, 28 cm.

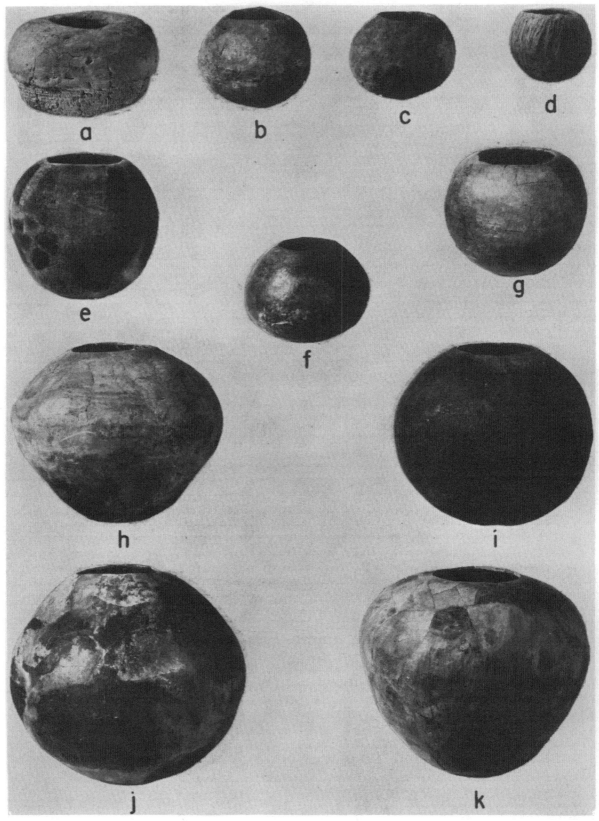

Fig. 27.   Unfired seed jars and plain gray vessels. *a–d*, unfired fiber-
tempered seed jars; *e*, *g*, elongated seed jars; *f*, *i*, round seed jars;
h, *j*, *k*, elongated shouldered seed jars. Height of *k*, 25 cm.

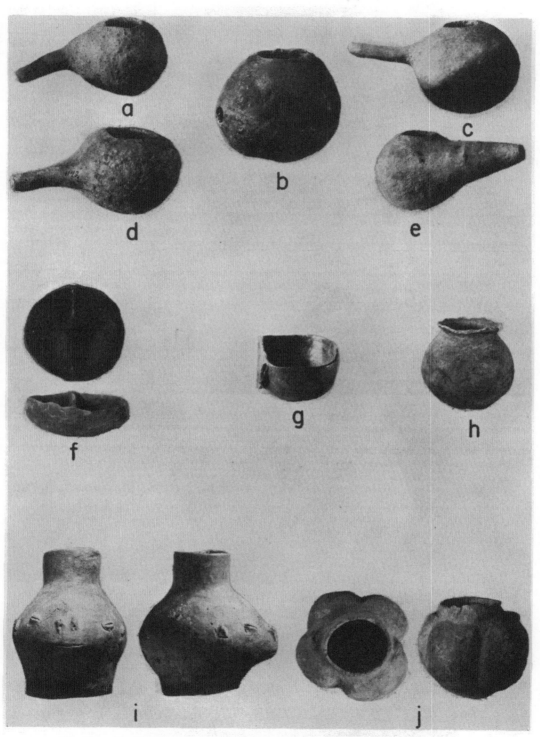

Fig. 28. Various forms of plain gray vessels. *a–e*, vessels with lateral spouts; *f*, *g*, partitioned bowls; *h*, round jar with widely flaring neck (?); *i*, effigy head on neck of broken vessel; *j*, quadrilobate jar. Height of *i*, 12 cm.

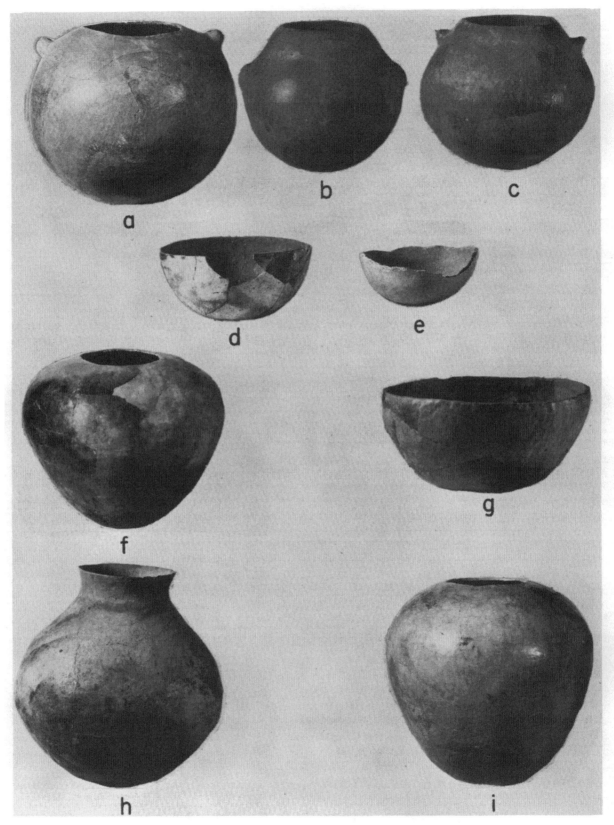

Fig. 29.   Polished red and Obelisk Gray vessels. *a–e*, polished red; *a–c*, with vertically pierced lugs; *b, c*, with recurved rims; *f–i*, Obelisk Gray Ware; *f, i*, elongated shouldered seed jars; *g*, deep bowl; *h*, narrow-mouthed jar, flaring rim. Height of *i*, 29 cm.

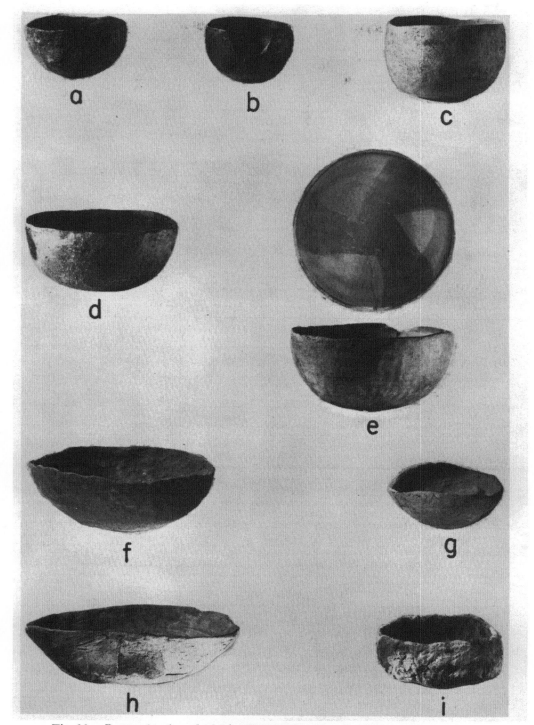

Fig. 30. Pottery bowls. *a, b, d,* Lino Smudged; *c,* Lino Fugitive Red; *e,* unknown red-on-gray; *f–i,* unfired fiber-tempered bowls. Height of *e,* 10 cm.

These vessels correspond to the type La Plata Black-on-white as defined by Hawley (1936: 23) to include all kinds of tempering material. Abel (1955) distinguishes the iron paint La Plata Black-on-white with quartz sand temper, from a new type, the iron paint Chapin Black-on-white with crushed rock temper. The distributions parallel those of the plain wares, and are respectively north and south of the San Juan River. The Prayer Rock district is south of the river, and the decorated vessels are tempered with crushed rock. Since the

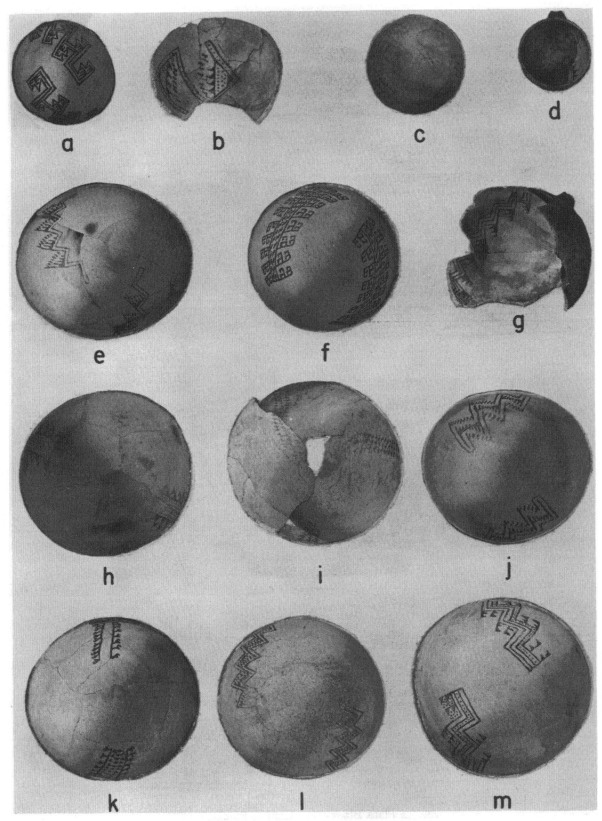

Fig. 31.   La Plata Black-on-white vessels. *a–f*, *h–m*, deep bowls; *g*, seed jar painted on interior; *b*, with fugitive red exterior. Diameter of *m*, 25 cm.

distributional importance of tempering material is yet to be clarified, the more general term La Plata Black-on-white will be used here.

La Plata Black-on-white

The La Plata Black-on-white (Hawley 1936: 23) vessels were decorated with two, three, or four design elements spotted at random on the interior (Fig. 31 *a*, *c–m*). They were probably derived from the types and placement of patterns on the baskets (Morris 1927).

La Plata Black-on-white, Fugitive Red Exterior

The presence of black-on-white pottery with fugitive red exterior (Fig. 31 *b*) is predictable in an area where a fugitive slip was added to the plain gray bowls. One sherd was found in addition to the vessel representing the type.

Lino Black-on-gray

The vessel of Lino Black-on-gray (Colton and Hargrave 1937: 191; Colton 1955) was tempered with quartz sand and decorated with a carbon paint design similar to that used on the Chapin Black-on-white (Abel 1955) vessels. Its center of distribution is in the Kayenta branch, and must therefore be considered intrusive into the Prayer Rock district.

Unknown Red-on-gray

The single vessel in this class (Fig. 30 *e*) may be a misfired black-on-gray or red-on-orange, but its color does not resemble the typical brownish appearance of the iron black paint, and the design layout is quite distinctive. The ceramic affiliations are closest to San Juan Red Ware (Abel 1955). The paste and temper closely resembled that used in the Lino Gray vessels. The design layout and composition were reminiscent of some of those used at an early time in the Mogollon area to the south.

Unknown Polychrome

A large sherd of a vessel with a red design bordered in black was found in a pit house. Superficially it resembled Tusayan Polychrome (Colton and Hargrave 1937: 96). It was tempered with a mixture of quartz sand and crushed rock. The position of this seed jar in Basketmaker III context is difficult to explain. It may be a rare prototype of later polychrome wares, or it may be intrusive.

Polished Red Ware

Polished Red Ware was named by the Awatovi Expedition. A few polished sherds have come from almost every site representing the Basketmaker III time horizon in the Anasazi area, and there are regional variations within the polished red distribution (Lino Red or Tallahogan Red, Wendorf 1953: 114; Tallahogan Red,

Daifuku 1961: 49). The Prayer Rock sample of three jars and several bowls (Fig. 29 *a–e*) is larger than most. Anna O. Shepard examined these specimens for evidence of southern manufacture but found none.

Unfired Vessels

Fiber-tempered Ware

A large number of unfired fiber-tempered vessels were found (Figs. 27 *a–d*; 30 *f–i*; 32, 33). Summarily, it would seem that fiber-tempered vessels occurred occasionally in Basketmaker II sites, that they may have occurred with fired pottery in certain Basketmaker III sites, and that after A.D. 700 they became very rare. They were described in detail by E. H. Morris (1927), who postulated that the unfired vessels constituted the prototype of independently invented fired plain ware. Now, with the information available from the Mogollon area where the manufacture of plain pottery began in the first centuries A.D., this hypothesis seems rather unlikely.

A probable explanation for the occurrence of the fiber-tempered pots is that they were locally made copies of true pottery vessels known from the area to the south. In other words, the idea of clay containers may have diffused northward before the knowledge of the manufacturing process. The presence of fired and unfired vessels together in the Prayer Rock pit houses dates the overlapping period of the two concepts between about A.D. 600–650. It is probably significant that most of the unfired vessels are bowls, while most of the fired vessels are jars.

These fiber-tempered vessels were molded of clay and decomposed sandstone mud heavily reinforced with a variety of vegetable materials. Some of them were formed with apparent forethought and care; others were built in a haphazard fashion that is reflected in the lumpy finished product. Most of the vessels were constructed by adding thick coils of clay to the existing rim and flattening them somewhat between the hands; this produced a varying thickness from one part of the vessel to another. The finished rim was typically very irregular in shape, height, and thickness. Nearly half of the bowls were started by pressing the clay into a coiled or plaited basket, as indicated by the impressions of the weave on the bottom exterior. Tabular lugs projected from two opposed sides of a number of the vessels, and the largest bowl had two loop handles similar to those seen in later Mesa Verde jars.

Untempered Mud Vessels

Two vessels were molded from lumps of mud made up of the decomposed bedrock in which the caves were formed, rather than from the clay that was utilized in true fired pottery. They may have been the efforts of children.

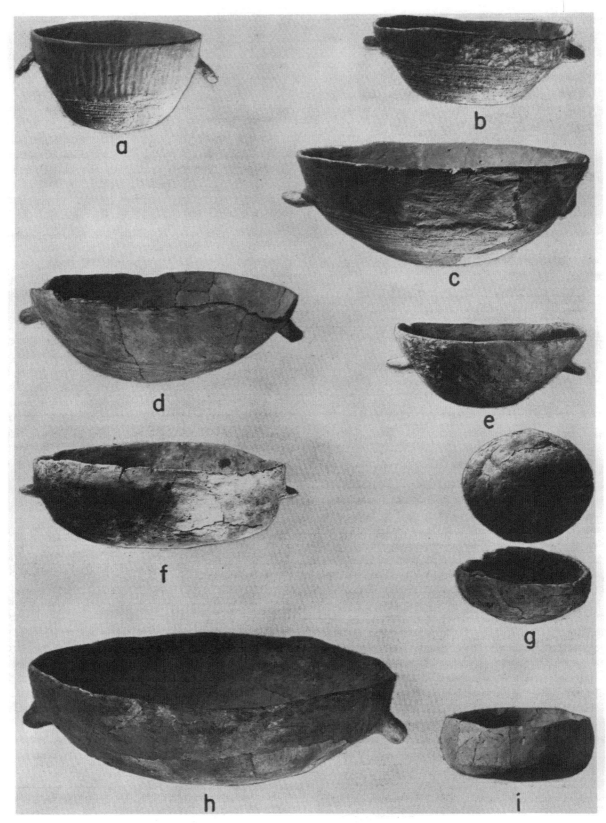

Fig. 32. Unfired fiber-tempered vessels. *a–e*, basket-impressed. Diameter of *h*, 50 cm.

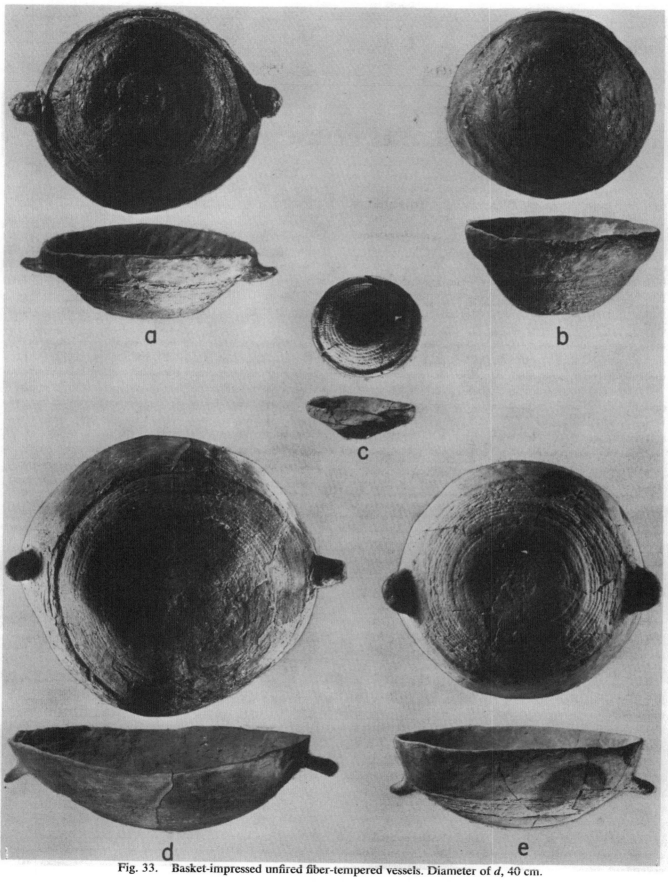

Fig. 33. Basket-impressed unfired fiber-tempered vessels. Diameter of *d*, 40 cm.

7. ARTIFACT DESCRIPTION

The artifacts are categorized by material. This organization, based on the physical and chemical properties of the specimens, minimizes the possibility of variation in interpretation. The material groups are subdivided into functional categories based largely on the morphology of the individual specimens and their inferred use in the lives of the people. The functional categories are divided into classes on the basis of manufacturing technique or minor differences in morphology. In some cases, the classes are further subdivided. The numbers of specimens are listed for each class or type, and the proveniences are given. For a number of the larger pieces, the dimensions have been rounded off to the nearest 5 cm.

The assemblage as a whole is similar to the materials obtained in other Basketmaker caves in northern Arizona (Guernsey and Kidder 1921; Guernsey 1931; Kidder and Guernsey 1919; Nusbaum, Kidder, and Guernsey 1922). Artifact distribution within the pit houses is discussed in the Introduction.

STONE

The stone artifacts include both specimens in the excavated collections and artifacts that because of their size, quantity, or weight were listed in the field notes and left in the various caves. I collected data on these latter specimens in 1958. Because of the limited time available in the field, only the biggest caves were visited, and without doubt there are unenumerated stone artifacts remaining in the smaller, more remote caves. It seems likely, however, that the uncatalogued pieces would fit into the rather tightly defined categories of the current classification.

The artifacts include eight specimens made of the local red sandstone forming the caves, and 344 specimens of materials not available in the immediate vicinity. The latter materials include the following (numbers of specimens given in parentheses): white, gray, and variegated sandstone (36); chalcedony (46); quartzite (21); petrified wood (2); lignite (3); turquoise (2); minerals and fossils (40); fine-grained igneous rock (85); coarse-grained igneous rock (3); and other stone materials (106).

To a large extent, specific materials were used for certain types of tools. For example, most chipped stone specimens listed as being of "other" material are of chalcedony, and most metates of "other" material are of white or gray sandstone.

Most specimens have been modified by chipping, grinding, and pecking techniques or through use. Those that have not had their original condition altered by these techniques are classified as artifacts on the basis of their material or on the basis of the context in which they were found. The lithic terminology used by Woodbury (1954) has been followed unless otherwise indicated.

The lack of waste products from stone working activities — particularly from the flaking of chipped stone tools — is notable, with the exception of numerous tiny flakes embedded in the floor of one pit house. It is possible that this material was lost when the brinks of the talus slopes weathered away. It is also possible that it was bypassed as insignificant during the excavation and the compilation of the field catalogue. However, it is considered more likely that the by-products of tool manufacture (except for those from the locally derived sandstone) were left at the various sources of material or at intermediate manufacturing areas.

Chipped Stone

Stone artifacts with intentional or use chipping on all or some surfaces and edges are included in this category. In most instances, artifacts of similar shape and manufacture are classed together regardless of size or material. In other cases, the nature of the size distribution warrants the establishment of subgroupings based on size.

Drills

Class A (4 whole; Fig. 34 *b*, *c*). Triangular shafted, with some specimens slightly flanged at base, sides gradually tapering to tip, base straight or slightly convex, biconvex to triangular in section. Suggestion of long straight-sided stem may be accidental on one specimen. Pressure flaked all over both surfaces, with secondary retouching along edges. Chalcedony, fine-grained igneous rock.

Length, 3.5–6.3 cm; width, 1.0–1.7 cm; thickness 0.3–0.7 cm. Provenience: Broken Flute Cave (General, 2); Pocket Cave (General, 1); General (1).

Class B (2 whole; Fig. 34 *a*). Flanged base, long slender shaft tapering to tip, biconvex in section. Pres-

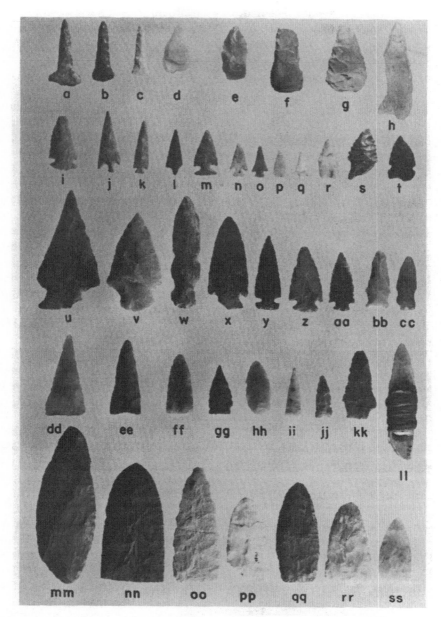

Fig. 34. Drills, flakes, projectile points, and blades. Drills: *a,* flanged base; *b, c,* slightly flanged base and straight sided; *d,* random flake. Flakes: *e–h.* Projectile points: *i, m, y,* side notched, base flaring and flat, sides straight, blade long; *j, l, v,* diagonal notched, shoulder of stem wider than base, straight sides; *k, x,* diagonal notched, slightly expanding stem, edges convex; *n, z, aa,* diagonal notched, expanding stem, concave sides; *o,* deep diagonal notched, expanding stem, edges concave; *p,* double notched, straight base; *q,* diagonal notched, straight stem, downraking barbs; *r, s,* corner notched, straight stem; *t,* side notched, asymmetrical stem; *u,* side notched, flat flaring base; *w, cc,* broad side notches, crudely flaked; *bb,* wide side notches, concave base; *kk,* diagonal notched, shoulder of stem wider than base, edges irregular. Blades: *dd, ee, gg, ii, jj,* sides straight tapering to tip, base straight; *ff, ll, nn, oo, pp, qq, rr, ss,* sides convex, base straight; *hh, mm,* sides convex, pointed at each end. Length of *mm,* 11.7 cm.

sure flaked all over both sides, with secondary retouching along both edges. Chalcedony.

Length, 2.7 cm, 5.1 cm; width, 1.5 cm, 2.2 cm; thickness, 0.5 cm, 0.6 cm. Provenience: Cave 2 (Pit House 1, 1); General (1).

Class C (2 whole; Fig. 34 *d*). Random flakes, tapering to point from wide base, wedge-shaped in section. Tip smoothed by grinding. One has a shaft of cane with

the drill inserted in one end and tied in place with yucca cordage. Chalcedony.

Length, 1.5 cm, 3.5 cm; width, 1.2 cm, 2.1 cm; thickness, 0.6 cm. Provenience: General (2).

Projectile Points and Blades

Class A (9 whole; Figs. 34 *ff, ll, nn–ss;* 51 *a*). Stemless, wide blade, sides straight or slightly convex, tapering variously to tip, base straight or slightly indented, biconvex in section. Pressure flaking all over both surfaces, with some retouching along edges. One specimen is a hafted knife. Chalcedony, fine-grained igneous rock.

Length, 4.4–8.9 cm; width, 2.2–4.8 cm; thickness, 0.3–0.8 cm. Provenience: Broken Flute Cave (General, 1; Pit House 16, 3); Pocket Cave (General, 2); Cave 2 (General, 2); General (1).

Class B (6 whole; Fig. 34 *dd, ee, gg, ii, jj*). Stemless, triangular shape, straight sides tapering to tip, straight base, biconvex section. Pressure flaking all over both surfaces, secondary retouching along edges. Chalcedony, petrified wood.

Three specimens: length, 2.6–3.8 cm; width, 1.8–2.3 cm; thickness, 0.3–0.8 cm. Three specimens: length, 4.7–6.1 cm; width, 2.4–2.9 cm; thickness, 0.4–0.8 cm. Provenience: Broken Flute Cave (General, 2); Pocket Cave (General, 3); General (1).

Class C (7 whole; Fig. 34 *hh, mm*). Stemless, leaf-shaped, sides convex tapering to tip at each end, one point slightly sharper than the other. Rough retouching along edges, crude pressure flaking on most surfaces. Chalcedony, quartzite, fine-grained igneous rock.

Six specimens: length, 3.0–4.3 cm; width, 1.4–2.0 cm; thickness, 0.8–1.6 cm. One specimen: length, 11.7 cm; width, 4.5 cm; thickness, 1.3 cm. Provenience: Broken Flute Cave (General, 3); Obelisk Cave (General, 1); General (3).

Class D (2 whole; Fig. 34 *r, s*). Corner-notched, triangular in shape, straight stem, concave base, straight sides tapering to tip. One specimen has slightly notched edges. Pressure flaking all over both surfaces and some retouching along edges. Chalcedony.

Length, 3.0 cm, 4.0 cm; width, 1.8 cm, 2.3 cm; thickness, 0.6 cm, 1.0 cm. Provenience: Broken Flute Cave (General, 1); General (1).

Class E (1 whole; Fig. 34 *q*). Diagonal-notched, triangular in shape, straight stem, flat base, downraking barbs, edges straight sloping to tip. Pressure flaking all over both surfaces with retouching along the edges. Chalcedony.

Length, 1.9 cm; width, 1.3 cm; thickness, 0.3 cm. Provenience: Broken Flute Cave (General).

Class F (1 whole; Fig. 34 *kk*). Diagonal-notched, shoulder of stem wider than base, long and triangular in shape, edges irregular, one edge irregularly notched, biconvex in section. Pressure flaking all over both surfaces and edges. Chalcedony.

Length, 5.1 cm; width, 2.6 cm; thickness, 0.4 cm. Provenience: Broken Flute Cave (General).

Class G (5 whole; Fig. 34 *j, l, v*). Diagonal-notched, narrow stem with shoulder as wide as or slightly wider than the base, long and triangular in shape, straight sides sloping to tip, biconvex in section. Pressure flaking all over both sides and secondary chipping along edges. Chalcedony, quartzite, fine-grained igneous rock.

Length, 3.0–4.6 cm; width, 1.4–2.4 cm; thickness, 0.3–0.6 cm. Provenience: Broken Flute Cave (General, 1); Pocket Cave (General, 1); Cave 2 (General, 1); General (2).

Class H (4 whole; Figs. 34 *x*, 50 *m*). Diagonal-notched, slightly expanding stem, slightly convex base, triangular in shape, edges straight sloping toward tip, biconvex in section. Pressure flaking over most surfaces and some retouching along edges. Chalcedony, quartzite.

Three specimens: length, 2.1–3.3 cm; width, 1.2–4.1 cm; thickness, 0.3–0.8 cm. One specimen: length, 7.3 cm; width, 4.1 cm; thickness, 1.5 cm. Provenience: Broken Flute Cave (General, 1; Pit House 16, 1); General (2).

Class I (3 whole; Fig. 34 *n, z, aa*). Diagonal-notched, expanding stem, triangular in shape, slightly convex base, edges straight to slightly concave sloping to tip. Biconvex in section. Pressure flaking on all surfaces and along all edges. Chalcedony, fine-grained basalt.

Length, 2.2–7.1 cm; width, 1.3–3.0 cm; thickness, 0.3–0.9 cm. Provenience: Broken Flute Cave (Pit House 9, 2); General (1).

Class J (3 whole; Fig. 34 *o*). Deep diagonal-notched, triangular in shape, expanding stem, straight base, edges slightly concave toward tip, biconvex in section. Pressure flaking all over both surfaces and secondary retouching on edges.

Two specimens: Length, 3.6 cm, 4.8 cm; width, 2.7 cm; thickness, 0.5 cm, 0.8 cm. One specimen: length, 7.0 cm; width, 3.0 cm; thickness, 0.6 cm. Provenience: Broken Flute Cave (General, 1); Obelisk Cave (General, 1); Cave 2 (Pit House 4, 1).

Class K (5 whole; Fig. 34 *k*). Diagonal-notched, expanding stem, straight or convex base; blade triangular in shape, edges slightly convex, biconvex in section. Pressure flaking on both surfaces and secondary retouching on edges. Chalcedony, fine-grained rock.

Length, 3.3–5.0 cm; width, 1.3–2.8 cm; thickness, 0.3–0.6 cm. Provenience: Broken Flute Cave (General, 4; Pit House 9, 1).

Class L (1 whole; Fig. 34 *p*). Double-notched, corner and lateral notches present on both sides, base straight; blade triangular in shape, edges straight sloping to tip; biconvex in section. Pressure flaking on both surfaces and secondary retouching on edges. Chalcedony.

Length, 2.0 cm; width, 1.2 cm; thickness, 0.2 cm. Provenience: General.

Class M (1 whole; Fig. 34 *u*). Side-notched, notches shallow, base flaring and flat, sides slightly convex; biconvex in section. Pressure flaking all over both surfaces and retouching along edges. Material unknown.

Length, 3.8 cm; width, 1.9 cm; thickness, 0.6 cm. Provenience: Broken Flute Cave (General).

Class N (2 whole; Fig. 34 *t*). Side-notched, asymmetrical stem, base slightly concave in off-center position, blades short and triangular in shape, sides slightly convex. Pressure flaking all over both surfaces and along edges. Chalcedony, fine-grained rock.

Length, 3.3 cm; width, 2.0 cm, 2.1 cm; thickness, 0.6 cm, 0.8 cm. Provenience: Broken Flute Cave (General, 1); General (1).

Class O (5 whole; Fig. 34 *i, m, y*). Side-notched, bases flaring and slightly convex, blades long and triangular in shape, edges straight and tapering to point, biconvex in section. Pressure flaking on all surfaces, secondary retouching along edges. Chalcedony, quartzite, fine-grained rock.

Length, 2.2–5.5 cm; width, 1.5–2.1 cm; thickness, 0.5–0.8 cm. Provenience: Broken Flute Cave (Pit House 9, 1); Cave 2 (Pit House 2, 1); General (3).

Class P (4 whole; Fig. 34 *w, cc*). Side-notched, broad shallow notches; one specimen has double notches. Bases thick and slightly convex, blades leaf-shaped, edges convex tapering to tip. Intermittent pressure flaking on surfaces. Specimens generally thick and crude. Chalcedony.

Three specimens: length, 3.6–4.0 cm; width, 1.4–1.7 cm; thickness, 0.6–1.8 cm. One specimen: length, 8.2 cm; width, 2.2 cm; thickness, 1.3 cm. Provenience: Broken Flute Cave (General, 2); Obelisk Cave (General, 1); General (1).

Class Q (2 whole; Fig. 34 *bb*). Side-notched, broad shallow notches, concave base, blade roughly leaf-shaped, edges roughly straight sloping to tip, biconvex in section. Pressure flaking on all surfaces and some retouching along edges. Chalcedony. Measurements unavailable; proveniences unknown.

Class R (5 whole). Tip fragments, undiagnostic as to form. One looks like a tip of a Class A specimen; one is a hafted knife from a cache under the floor of Pit House 9, Broken Flute Cave. Other proveniences not recorded.

Flakes

Class A (8 whole and fragmentary; Fig. 34 *e–h*). Unshaped oblong to irregular flakes with one or, rarely, two edges pressure chipped to form cutting edge, plano-convex or biconvex in section. One is the blade of a scarifier (Fig. 87 *f*); one was found wrapped in a hide bundle. Chalcedony, fine-grained rock.

Length, 1.9–7.2 cm; width, 1.7–3.3 cm; thickness, 0.4–1.3 cm. Provenience: Broken Flute Cave (General, 1; Pit House 6, 1; Cist 54, 1); Cave 8 (2); General (3).

Scrapers

Class A (5 whole). Thick random flakes, irregular in shape, plano-convex to irregular in section. A few rough spalls have been knocked off one or both sides by percussion techniques to produce crude cutting edges. Some secondary chipping through use on the edges. Chalcedony, jasper, quartzite.

Length, 5.2–8.7 cm; width, 4.5–8.0 cm; thickness, 1.0–3.9 cm. Provenience: Broken Flute Cave (Surface, 2; Cist 54, 3).

Choppers

Class A (7 whole). Large thick angular core implements, irregular in shape, plano-convex or biconvex in section. Shaped by percussion flaking on some edges and on one or both sides. Secondary chipping and battering through use on edges. Chalcedony, fine-grained rock.

Length, 8.0–14.0 cm; width, 7.3–12.0 cm; thickness, 4.0–7.6 cm. Provenience: Broken Flute Cave (Surface, 6; Cist 54, 1).

Fragments

Class A (6 specimens). Miscellaneous chips of rock, one smeared with blue paint. Chalcedony, petrified wood, coarse-grained rock.

No dimensions taken. Provenience: Broken Flute Cave (Pit House 6, 5; Pit House 4, 1).

Ground Stone

All stone artifacts exhibiting evidence of grinding through manufacture or use are included in this section.

Metates

Following Woodbury (1954: 50), metates are distinguished from grinding slabs; metates are made of standardized shaped stones, exhibiting a shaped grinding surface with indications of a reciprocal grinding motion.

Class A (9 whole and fragmentary; Fig. 35 *c*). Trough metates, open at one end. Made of oval to rectangular slabs with rounded edges and corners, partially shaped by pecking. Grinding surface rectangular in shape, occupying less than full surface, contiguous with one end. Working surface slightly convex along both axes, often flat except near edges. Specimens show pecking on grinding surface, presumably done to roughen it for more effective use. Gray sandstone.

Length, 53–61 cm; width, 38–42 cm; thickness, 4–12 cm. Provenience: Broken Flute Cave (Surface, 6; Pit House 6, 1; Pit House 7, 1); General (1).

Class B (1 whole; Fig. 35 *d*). Trough metate, open at one end, depression in shelf at other end (Utah type). Rectangular in shape, with rounded corners shaped by pecking. Grinding surface roughly rectangular, contiguous with one end, slightly convex along both axes. Small depression on closed end of metate, possibly to serve as rest for mano. The depression is 13 cm long, 8 cm wide, and 1 cm deep. Gray sandstone.

Length, 47 cm; width, 33 cm; thickness, 9 cm. Size of working surface: length, 30 cm; width, 33 cm; depth, 5 cm. Provenience: Broken Flute Cave (Pit House 9).

Class C (1 whole; Fig. 35 *a*). Basin metate. Woodbury classifies specimens of this type in a grinding-stone category, but in this assemblage, the size and general shape resemble the trough metate (other grinding slabs are different in size and shape); therefore this artifact is described separately. Roughly rectangular in shape,

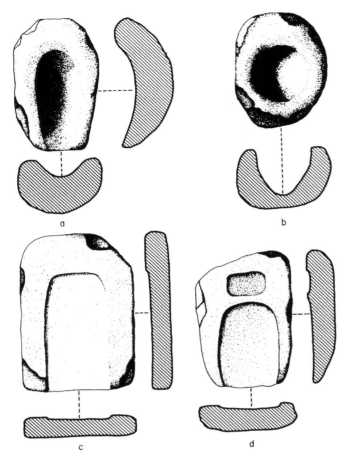

Fig. 35.   Metates and mortars. *a*, basin metate; *b*, mortar; *c*, open end trough metate; *d*, open end trough metate, Utah type. Length of *c*, 60 cm.

made on an unshaped slab. Working surface deeply concave along both axes; the greatest depression is in the center of the area. Grinding surfaces roughened by pecking. Gray sandstone.

Length, 47 cm; width, 29 cm; thickness 19 cm. Size of working surface: length, 35 cm; width, 17 cm; depth, 6 cm. Provenience: Broken Flute Cave (Surface).

Grinding Slabs

This category includes those specimens with concave grinding surfaces that do not fit the formalized metate type, and are larger than the better-shaped flat palettes; these tools probably reflect a more generalized use.

Class A (5 whole and fragmentary). The specimens are made on unshaped or slightly shaped oval to rectangular slabs with rectangular sections. Working surfaces vary; some are shallow and occupy the whole surface of the stone, and others have one or more small depres-

sions scattered over the surface. Use striations are uniformly along the long axis of the working surface. Sandstone, coarse-grained rock.

Length, 16.5–30.5 cm; width, 10–24 cm; thickness, 3.5–8.0 cm. Size range of working surfaces: length 18 cm; width, 9–12 cm; depth, 0.2–1.5 cm. Provenience: Broken Flute Cave (Surface, 1; General, 4).

Mortars

Class A (2 whole; Fig. 35 *b*). Made in oval to round boulders, roughly shaped by percussion techniques. Deep grinding concavity, conical in shape, with slightly rounded sides. Working surface roughened by pecking. Red sandstone.

Length, 39 cm, 48 cm; width, 28 cm, 31 cm; thickness, 20 cm, 21 cm. Size range of working surface: length, 17 cm, 20 cm; width, 28 cm, 31 cm; depth, 15 cm, 17 cm. Provenience: Broken Flute Cave (Pit House 6, 1; Pit House 9, 1).

Miniature Mortar

Class A (1 whole). Square in shape, rectangular in section, with rounded edges and corners. Grinding surface conical with rounded bottom. Red sandstone.

Length, 12.8 cm; width, 11.9 cm; thickness, 6 cm. Provenience: Broken Flute Cave (Surface).

Bowls

Class A (1 whole; Fig. 36 *a*). Oval in shape, hemispherical in section, interior and exterior surfaces ground smooth. Short stubby handle on one end, a slight encircling groove separating it from body, walls thick, rim flat. Surface painted white. Diagonal black line running from rim toward center on one side of interior is all that remains of a design. Fine-grained red sandstone.

Length, 18.6 cm; width, 15.5 cm; thickness, 8 cm. Size of working surface: length, 11.4 cm; width, 12.1 cm; depth, 5 cm. Provenience: Broken Flute Cave (Pit House 6).

Class B (1 whole; Fig. 36 *b*). Oval in shape, rectangular in section, straight sides, flat bottom. Exterior and flat rim shaped all over by pecking, interior shaped by grinding. Interior oval in shape and hemispherical in section. Red sandstone.

Length, 18.6 cm; width, 15.6 cm; thickness, 8 cm. Size of working surface: length, 16.0 cm; width, 11.5 cm; depth, 5.5 cm. Provenience: Pocket Cave (Pit House 4).

Cooking Slabs

Class A (10 whole and fragmentary; Fig. 37). Round to rectangular in shape, shaped by pecking and grinding. Extremely thin, one surface frequently showing fire-blackening and organic material occasionally adhering

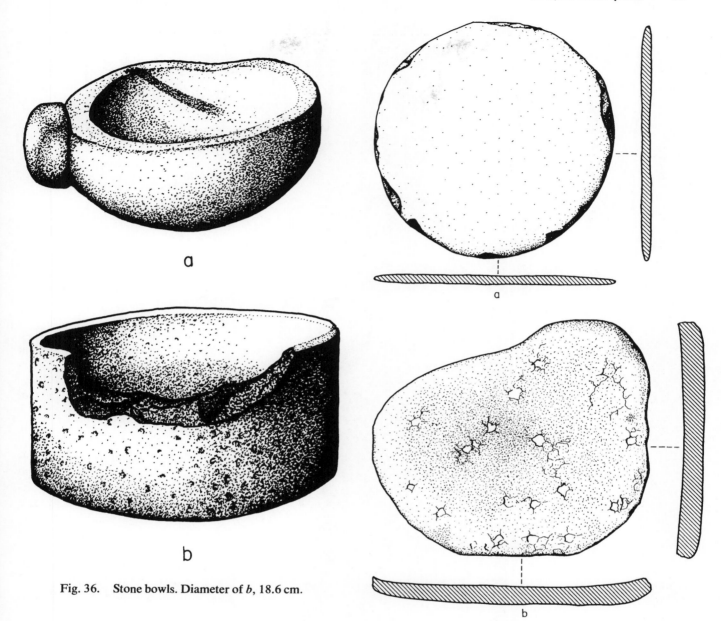

Fig. 36.   Stone bowls. Diameter of *b*, 18.6 cm.

Fig. 37.   Stone cooking slabs. Length of *b*, 30 cm.

to the other. One surface may be slightly smoothed and concave. White sandstone.

Length, 28–55 cm; width, 27–53 cm; thickness, 0.9–7.0 cm. Provenience: Broken Flute Cave (Surface, 9; Pit House 7, 1).

Flat Palettes

Class A (8 whole and fragmentary). Rectangular to round in shape, rectangular in section, thin flat-surfaced slabs, shaped all over by pecking and grinding. One or two working surfaces; fine-grained specimens show striations running in all directions. Four specimens show spots of color derived from natural pigments, two red and two yellow. Sandstone, fine-grained rock.

Length, 8–15 cm; width, 4.7–9.8 cm; thickness, 0.5–1.4 cm. Provenience: Broken Flute Cave (General, 1); Obelisk Cave (General, 4); General (3).

Hammerstones

Class A (4 whole and fragmentary). Roughly round stones showing chipping and battering over whole surface through use. Quartzite, fine-grained rock.

Length, 7.8–8.3 cm; width, 6.5–7.8 cm; thickness, 4.6–6.2 cm. Provenience: Broken Flute Cave (General, 4).

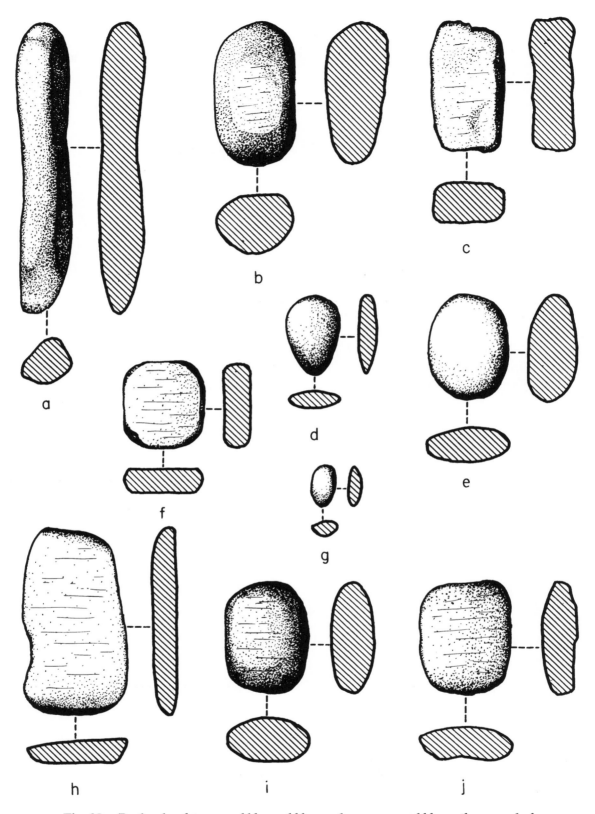

Fig. 38.   Pestles, handstones, pebbles, cobbles, and manos. *a*, cobble pestle, unworked, ends battered; *b*, shaped pestle, ends battered, sides smoothed by grinding; *c*, handstone; *d*, unworked cobble; *e*, worked cobble; *f*, one-hand bifaced mano; *g*, polishing pebble; *h*, rectangular uniface mano, ends sharply curved; *i*, rectangular, uniface manos, corners rounded; *j*, rectangular, uniface mano. Length of *a*, 26 cm.

Pestles

Class A (3 whole and fragmentary; Fig. 38 *a*). Natural stream-worn cobbles, long and thin, rectangular to round in section. One end slightly pointed, showing battering through use. Fine-grained rock.

Length, 15–26 cm; width, 6–10 cm; thickness, 4–7 cm. Provenience: Broken Flute Cave (Surface, 2; Pit House 9, 1)'.

Class B (4 whole and fragmentary; Fig. 38 *b*). Oblong in shape, round in section, shaped all over by grinding and pecking. Two sides flattened by grinding, striations parallel to short axis. Ends battered and flattened through use. White sandstone, fine-grained rock.

Length, 13–16 cm; width, 7.9 cm; thickness, 6–8 cm. Provenience: Broken Flute Cave (Surface, 4).

Grinding Pebbles and Cobbles

Class A (10 whole, 1 fragmentary). Flat stream-worn pebbles. Oblong in shape and section. On most specimens, striations formed irregularly in all directions through use. No specimens had been used long enough to alter the original shape. Two specimens were much larger than the rest. Fine-grained rocks.

Length, 7.6–30 cm; width, 4.8–11.8 cm; thickness, 1.3–3.0 cm. Provenience: Broken Flute Cave (Surface, 5; Pit House 6, 1); Obelisk Cave (General, 4); General (1).

Unworked Pebbles and Cobbles

Class A (17 whole; Fig. 38 *d, g*). Unworked(?) stream-worn pebbles and cobbles, exhibiting flat surfaces and rounded edges with a high polish, oval and oblong in section. No indications of use except that one specimen had a large spot of red pigment on one side and a spot of blue pigment on the other. Smaller specimens may have been polishing pebbles. Quartzite, fine-grained rock.

Length, 3.6–15 cm; width, 2.8–10.3 cm; thickness, 1.3–6.8 cm. Provenience: Broken Flute Cave (Surface, 6; Pit House 6, 1; Pit House 7, 5; Cist 16, 3); Obelisk Cave (General, 2).

Worked Cobbles

Class A (35 whole and fragmentary; Fig. 38 *e*). Stream cobbles, oval to irregular in shape, oval in section. Surfaces flattened through use, exhibiting polish and/or striations. Four show yellow or red paint on working surface. Quartzite, fine-grained rock.

Length, 8.3–15 cm; width, 6.6–12 cm; thickness, 2.7–7.0 cm. Provenience: Broken Flute Cave (Surface, 21; Pit House 6, 1; Pit House 9, 1); General (12).

Handstone

Class A (1 whole; Fig. 38 *c*). Rectangular in shape and section, made on rectangular two-hand mano. Working surface made on upper surface of mano, smeared with yellow paint. Sandstone.

Length, 13 cm; width, 10 cm; thickness, 4.4 cm. Provenience: Broken Flute Cave (General).

Manos

This category is divided into two general types, one-hand manos and manos considered to have been used on trough metates. As Woodbury (1954: 67) indicates, this is not a satisfactory grouping, but a more adequate system has yet to be established.

Class A (2 whole; Fig. 38 *f*). One-hand manos, two working surfaces. Nearly round with flattened sides, rectangular in section, shaped by pecking and grinding. Working surface originally pecked, well smoothed through use. Both are straight along both axes, no striations present. Sandstone, fine-grained rock.

Length, 9.5 cm, 10.0 cm; width, 9.5 cm, 9.6 cm; thickness, 2.7 cm, 4.6 cm. Provenience: Broken Flute Cave (General, 1; Pit House 6, 1).

Class B (7 whole). One-hand manos, two working surfaces. Oblong to rectangular in shape, oval in section, shaped by pecking and grinding. Working surfaces slightly concave along both axes, striations (where present) parallel to short axis. White sandstone.

Length, 11.1–17.5 cm; width, 8.5–10.0 cm; thickness, 3.4–8.0 cm. Provenience: Broken Flute Cave (Surface, 7).

Class C (10 whole and fragmentary; Fig. 38 *j*). Rectangular to oblong in shape, rectangular with rounded corners in section, shaped by grinding and pecking. Working surfaces slightly convex along both axes. Working surface intentionally roughened by pecking. One is made on a broken metate. White sandstone, fine-grained rock.

Length, 14.7–22.0 cm; width, 8.3 cm; thickness, 2.3–6.0 cm. Provenience: Broken Flute Cave (General, 10).

Class D (1 whole; Fig. 38 *h*). Rectangular with rounded corners in shape, plano-convex in section. Edges shaped by grinding. One working surface, well worn through use, intentionally roughened by pecking, flat along short axis, slightly concave along long axis with ends sharply curved and well worn. White sandstone.

Length, 22.5 cm; width, 10.9 cm; thickness, 2.6 cm. Provenience: Broken Flute Cave (Surface).

Class E (4 whole and fragmentary; Fig. 38 *i*). Rectangular with rounded corners in plan and section, edges shaped by grinding and pecking. One working surface, straight along both axes. One specimen smeared with iron oxide. Sandstone, fine-grained rock.

Length, 17.5–26.0 cm; width, 8.7–11.0 cm; thickness, 3.0–6.2 cm. Provenience: Broken Flute Cave (Surface, 3; Pit House 6, 1).

Fig. 39.   Full grooved mauls. *a, b,* round section,
ends battered; *c,* round section, ridge on either side
of groove; *d,* rectangular section, broken haft.
Length of *d,* 21 cm.

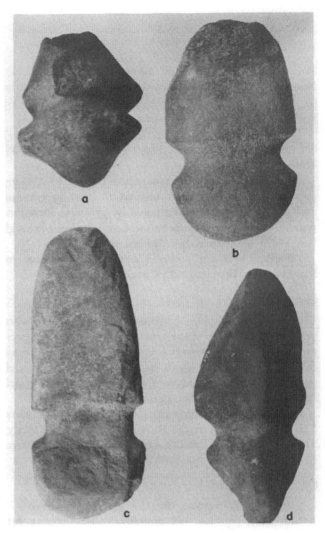

Fig. 40.   Full grooved axes. *a, d,* made on angular cobbles; *b, c,* made on oval cobbles.
Length of *c,* 22 cm.

Mauls

Class A (4 whole; Fig. 39 *a–c*). Full grooved, made
on a cobble, shaped by pecking and grinding. Oval in
shape and section, groove centrally located or nearly
centrally located. Groove about 2.0 cm wide, 0.5–1.5
cm deep, formed by pecking. One specimen (Fig. 39 *c*)
has slight ridge on each side of groove. Fine-grained
rock.

Length, 13.5–16.0 cm; width, 9.0–11.7 cm; thickness, 7.1–9.5 cm. Provenience: Broken Flute Cave
(General, 1); Cave 2 (Pit House 2, 1); Cave 8 (General, 1); General (1).

Class B (1 whole; Fig. 39 *d*). Edge notched, rectangular in shape and section. Shaped all over by pecking.
Notches centrally located, V-shaped in section, 1.5 cm
wide, 0.7 cm deep. Ends battered through use. Wooden
haft is present, portion that passed around head is
broken, stone fastened to haft by piece of cord. Coarse-
grained rock.

Length, 21 cm; width, 8 cm; thickness, 6.5 cm. Provenience: Broken Flute Cave (General).

Axes

Class A (2 whole; Fig. 40 *a, d*). Full grooved, angular
in shape and section. Poll unworked, bit well ground to
narrow cutting edge, almost a point, striations parallel
or diagonal to short axis. Groove formed by pecking,
0.5 to 2.5 cm deep, 1.5 cm wide. Tools apparently made
on fortuitously shaped pebbles. Fine-grained rock.

Provenience: General (2).

Class B (1 whole). Full grooved, angular shape and
section. Poll unworked, bit well ground to sharp cutting
edge. Groove formed by pecking, about 2 cm wide and
0.5 to 1.5 cm deep. Tool made on cobble. Hafted by
wrapping a slender stick around stone twice and wrapping this with strips of bark; handle missing. Fine-grained
rock.

Length, 14.6 cm; width 7.8 cm; thickness, 5.0 cm.
Provenience: Cave 6 (General).

Class C (2 whole; Fig. 40 *b, c*). Full grooved, oblong
in shape and section, slightly worked by pecking and
grinding. Groove about 2 cm wide and 0.5 to 1.5 cm
deep, missing on one face of one specimen. Bit rounded

and battered through use, made on fortuitously shaped cobbles. Fine-grained rock.

One specimen: length, 16.6 cm; width, 9.8 cm; thickness, 4.6 cm. Provenience: Broken Flute Cave (General, 1); General (1).

Pipes

Tobacco (*Nicotiana* sp.) was identified chemically and microscopically in five Prayer Rock pipes by chemists in the research and development department of Philip Morris, Inc. (Johnson, Gager, and Holmes 1959). This was the first time that such an analysis had been made on Anasazi specimens. The problems involved in the identification of tobacco (a complicated procedure) and in its prehistoric usage are discussed by Dixon and Stetson (1922), Jones (1944), and Gell and Jones (1962). Other plants were also utilized.

In addition to the tobacco remains in the pipes, unused tobacco plant parts were found in a pottery jar, and tobacco was identified as constituting part of the contents of some of the yucca fiber quids. These multiple occurrences in clear contextual situations provide a detailed picture of the place of tobacco in Basketmaker life.

Class A (4 whole; Figs. 41 *a*, *b*; 42 *c*). Tapered cylinders with slightly convex walls, round in section, outward edge ground off flat, proximal end squared off with edges flat and sharp. Bore biconical where observable. Two specimens have wooden bits, cylindrical in shape, bored through center, inserted into mouth end of pipe and secured with dark brown substance, probably pitch. Dottle remains in three specimens. Fine-grained rock.

Length, 4.7–6.0 cm; diameter, 2.1–3.1 cm; length of bit, 1.8–2.8 cm; diameter of bit, 0.8–1.2 cm. Provenience: Broken Flute Cave (Pit House 9, 1; General, 1); Obelisk Cave (General, 1); Cave 6 (General, 1).

Class B (1 whole; Fig. 41 *f*). Tapered cylinder with almost straight walls, section round, distal edge ground off flat; proximal end has flat thin edge, slightly notched at regular intervals. Bore probably biconical. Dottle remains in pipe. An irregularly trending groove about 0.1 cm deep had been carved around barrel, possibly to hold a cord. Fine-grained laminated sandstone.

Length, 6.2 cm; diameter, 2.8 cm; depth of bowl, unknown; diameter of bowl, 1.6 cm. Provenience: Pocket Cave (General).

Class C (1 whole; Figs. 41 *c*, 42 *a*). Cylinder with concave walls, round in section, ends ground off flat, bore conical with rapidly flaring sides abruptly changing to small cylindrical hole. Bone bit joined to pipe by being inserted over wood sleeve inserted in mouth end of pipe. Both pieces highly polished. Lignite and bone.

Length, 4 cm; diameter, 2 cm; length of bit, 2.6 cm; diameter of bit, 1.5 cm; depth of bowl, 1.5 cm; diameter of bowl, 1.7 cm. Provenience: Broken Flute Cave (General).

Class D (3 whole; Figs. 41 *d*, *e*, *h*; 42 *b*, *d*). Tapered cylinders with slightly convex walls, section round to oval. Ends ground off flat. Bore conical with straight walls. Trace of dottle remains. Fine-grained rock.

Length, 4.8–6.9 cm; diameter, 2.2–3.0 cm; depth of bowl, unknown; diameter of bowl, 1.2–1.8 cm. Provenience: Broken Flute Cave (General, 1); Obelisk Cave (General, 1); Cave 8 (General, 1).

Pipe Blanks

Class A (3 whole; Fig. 42 *e*, *h*). Rectangular in shape and section with rounded corners. Holes drilled along long axis from one end, shape conical with rounded bottom, 1–4 cm deep, 1–2 cm wide. Exterior of stone shaped by pecking and grinding. These specimens are probably unfinished pipes. Sandstone, fine-grained rock.

Length, 8–13 cm; width, 4.0–7.6 cm; thickness, 3–7 cm. Provenience: Broken Flute Cave (Pit House 9, 1); Cave 3 (General, 1); General (1).

Pigments, Minerals, and Fossils

Most of the pigments and mineral specimens (see Table 6) were found loose in trash, and some were cached in bundles of several sorts within the house structures. Two of the white amorphous lumps (Fig. 44 *b*) react with hydrochloric acid and may be lime; red amorphous lumps may be hematite. The yellow amorphous lumps are not sulphur. Fossil shells occurred in limestone deposits.

Pendants

Class A (14 whole and fragmentary; Figs. 43 *a–f*, 50 *l*). Differentiated from beads by having perforations nearer one end than the other, and general rectangular or oblong shape. Smoothed pieces of fine-grained stone, perforated by biconical drilling. Shape oblong to rectangular with rounded edges and corners. Section oval to rectangular with rounded corners. Selenite, turquoise, fine-grained rock.

Length, 1.1–6.2 cm; width, 0.7–1.3 cm; thickness, 0.1–1.6 cm; diameter of perforation, 0.1–0.6 cm. Provenience: Broken Flute Cave (General, 7; Pit House 8, 1); Pocket Cave (General, 1); Cave 2 (Pit House 1, 5).

Beads

Class A (6 whole; Fig. 43 *i*). Round, rectangular, and oval in shape, single biconical perforation, shaped all over by grinding. Lignite, fine-grained rock.

Length, 0.6–2.8 cm; width, 0.6–1.0 cm; thickness, 0.1–1.1 cm; diameter of perforation, 0.2–0.4 cm. Provenience: Broken Flute Cave (General, 2); Cave 2 (Pit House 1, 3; Pit House 4, 1).

Class B (1 whole; Fig. 43 *h*). Oval in shape, rectangular in section, double biconical perforation. Shaped all over by grinding. Specimen may be of the "figure eight" bead class. Fine-grained rock.

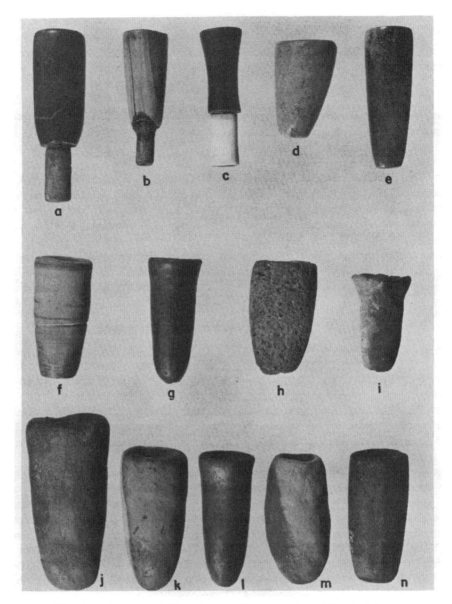

Fig. 41.   Stone and clay pipes. *a, b*, stone pipes, biconical bore, wooden bit; *c*, lignite pipe with bone bit, shallow bowl; *d, h*, stone pipes, flaring bore; *e*, stone pipe, gradually tapering bore; *f*, striped sandstone pipe, groove carved around barrel, gradually tapering bore (?); *g, i–n*, clay pipes. Length of *j*, 8.5 cm.

Length, 1.2 cm; width, 0.7 cm; thickness, 0.3 cm; diameter of perforation, 0.3 cm. Provenience: Cave 2 (Pit House 1).

Class C (2 whole). Cylindrical in shape, one specimen slightly tapered. Bored biconically through long axis. All surfaces smoothed by grinding. These specimens look like copies of shell beads with the point of greatest width off center. Fine-grained rock.

Length, 2.3 cm, 2.6 cm; width, 0.9 cm, 1.2 cm; thickness, 0.9 cm, 1.1 cm; diameter of perforation, 0.3 cm. Provenience: Cave 2 (Pit House 1, 2).

Class D (6, and one lot of 70; Fig. 43 *k*). Rounded in shape, bored biconically, all surfaces smoothed by grinding. Red and white variegated stone, turquoise.

Diameter, 0.5–1.7 cm; thickness, 0.1–0.7 cm. Provenience: Broken Flute Cave (General, 6); Cave 4 (Burial 2, lot of 70).

Effigy or Fetish

Class A (1 whole; Fig. 92 *d*). Natural iron concretion consisting of contiguous semi-hemispherical nodules. Bottom ground off smooth. Resembles a generalized life

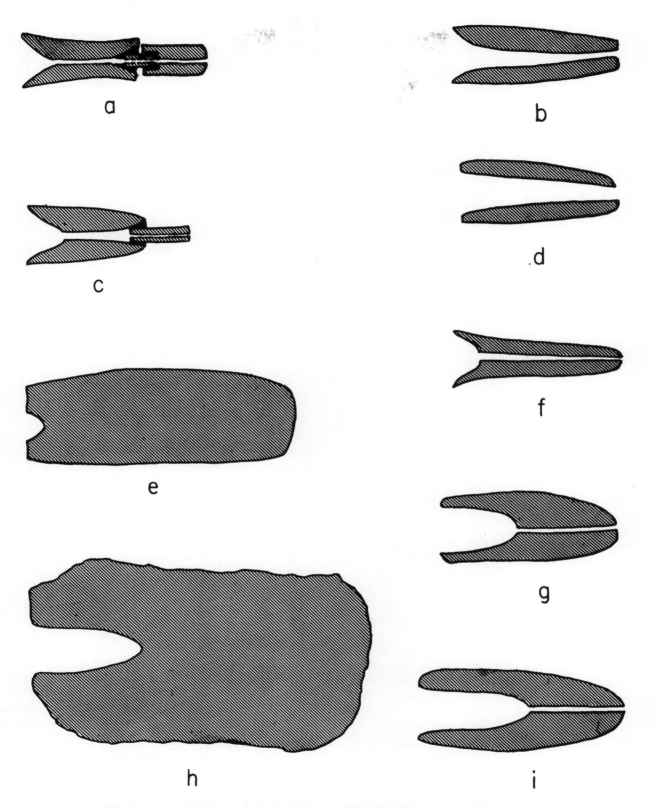

Fig. 42.   Sections of stone and ceramic pipes and pipe blanks. *a*, lignite pipe with bone bit, shallow bowl; *b, d*, stone pipes, gradually tapering bore; *c*, stone pipe, wooden bit, biconical bore; *e*, stone pipe blank, bore incomplete, exterior smoothed by grinding; *f*, stone pipe, flaring bore; *g, i*, ceramic pipes, flaring bores; *h*, stone pipe blank, bore incomplete, exterior shaped by pecking. Length of *h*, 13 cm.

TABLE 6
Pigments and Minerals from Prayer Rock Caves

	Kaolin lumps	White amorphous lumps	Hematite lumps	Red amorphous lumps	Blue amorphous lump	Yellow amorphous lumps	Brown amorphous lumps	Black metallic crystalline lumps
General			3, faceted by use		1			2
Broken Flute Cave								
General	1	3	3			4		
Pit House 6			1 ball					
Pit House 7		1						
Pit House 9				1, semi-metallic		1		2, faceted by use
Cist 54			1					
Cave 2, Pit House 1			1			1		
Pocket Cave, Pit House 2				1 ball				
Cave 8, General		5, in pots						
Cave 10, General		1, in fiber bundle						
Obelisk Cave, General	1						2, in hide sack	

form. Shell bead with lignite center stuck in pitchy substance on one side of back. Pitchy material extends to other side and probably there was originally a bead there also. Iron concretion.

Length, 2.7 cm; width, 1.9 cm; thickness, 1.7 cm. Provenience: Broken Flute Cave (Pit House 8).

Disks

Class A (3 whole; Figs. 43 *g, j,* 44 *g*). Unperforated, biconvex in section, edges rounded by grinding. Surfaces smooth to highly polished. Fine-grained sandstone, lignite.

Diameter, 4.7 cm, 5.4 cm, 10.5 cm; thickness, 0.5–1.0 cm. Provenience: Broken Flute Cave (Pit House 16, 1; Cist 20, 1); General (1).

Class B (2 whole; Figs. 43 *l,* 44 *d*). Perforated disks, round in shape, biconvex with rounded corners in section. Smooth to highly polished surfaces and edges. Specular hematite (Fig. 43 *l*), fine-grained white stone or shell.

Fig. 43 *l,* diameter, 2.7 cm; thickness, 0.9 cm; diameter of perforation, 0.2 cm. Provenience: Broken Flute Cave (Cist 20, 1); Cave 8 (General, 1).

Cylinders

Class A (1 whole; Fig. 43 *q*). Rectangular in shape, round in section, smoothed all over by grinding. Surface slightly faceted by grinding. Red sandstone.

Length, 11.3 cm; diameter, 3.1 cm. Provenience: Cave 3 (General).

Miscellaneous Worked Stone

Class A (5 whole; Fig. 43 *m–p*). Rectangular pieces of worked stone of unknown use. Rectangular to oblong in shape, rectangular in section, with edges and corners smoothed slightly by grinding. Few striations on surfaces, probably a result of manufacturing process. Some of these may be pendant blanks or atlatl weights (Kidder and Guernsey 1919: 180). Red sandstone, soapstone, chalcedony, fine-grained rock.

Length, 3.1–7.2 cm; width, 1.6–2.9 cm; thickness, 0.3–1.4 cm. Provenience: Broken Flute Cave (General, 4); Cave 2 (Pit House 4, 1).

BONE

With some exceptions the tools in this category are made from the leg bones of deer, antelope, and other animals. Most of the specimens use the unaltered shape of the bone with a carefully worked tip, blade, or edge. Many of them exhibit a high polish resulting from manufacture or use. Bone does not seem to have been an important tool material.

A similar situation was noted in the Forestdale Valley (Haury 1940: 113; Haury and Sayles 1947: 79) and at Point of Pines (Wheat 1954: 157). However, at the Basketmaker II sites north of Durango bone constituted a major portion of the artifactual inventory (Morris 1954: 60). This difference is probably attributable to the location of the Durango villages in an area where hunting may have predominated over agriculture.

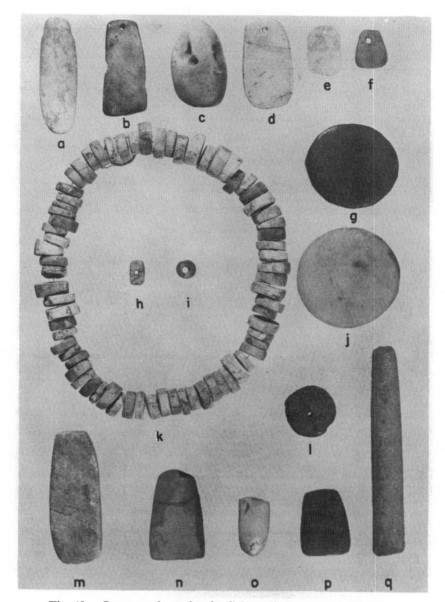

Fig. 43. Stone pendants, beads, disks, cylinder, and small pieces of worked stone. *a–f*, pendants; *g, j*, disks; *h*, bead, may be of 'figure eight' type; *i*, bead, cylindrical biconical bore; *k*, red and white beads found in Burial 2, Cave 4; *l*, perforated disk; *m–p*, small pieces of worked stone; *q*, cylinder. Length of *q*, 11.3 cm.

Awls

Most of the Prayer Rock bone awls are shouldered, exhibiting a sharp tapering of the shaft near the tip. The sides of the shaft are unaltered or slightly smoothed, and the sides of the tip are extensively ground down to produce a short, sharp, needlelike point. In many cases this tip is centrally located; in a few cases it is off center or at an edge. A few awls have tapered points with a gradual change in thickness from shaft to tip. The shafts, tips, and to a lesser extent the heads are frequently polished through use. Sharpening striations diagonal to the long axis are often present near the tip. Many of the specimens were made much shorter than the original length of the bones, or were repeatedly resharpened. No notched awls characteristic of those found in the Mogollon area were found.

With a few exceptions the tools are made from the long bones of deer or antelope, which had been killed after the epiphyseal union had closed. The distal end of the metapodial bone was by far the most common portion used, followed in frequency by the distal end of the tibia.

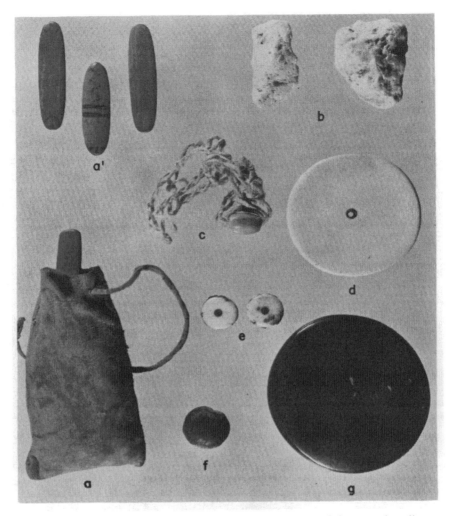

Fig. 44.   Contents of small basket. *a*, hide sack containing wooden dice set (*a'*) and wooden pellet (*f*); *b*, two lumps of kaolin; *c*, wooden bead; *d*, perforated stone disk; *e*, shell disks; *g*, stone disk. Length of *a*, 7.0 cm.

Some of the awls made on split long bones are smoothed by grinding to the extent that the indications of manufacturing technique are completely obliterated. Others show distinct marks of the cutting of a groove on each side of the shaft along the long axis of the bone; the two portions were then broken apart.

The classification is derived from Kidder (1932: 205) and is based on the method of altering the head of the bone. Additional groups are based on unusual shape, size, or treatment of the material. The measurements of the diameter of the bones were not considered to be a cultural manifestation and are not included below.

Class A (1 whole; Fig. 45 *a*). Shouldered, head of bone unaltered.

Length, 13.5 cm. Provenience: Broken Flute Cave (Pit House 9).

Class B (8 whole; Fig. 45 *b*). Shouldered, head of bone split and unsmoothed. Split by cutting deeply along central groove and breaking.

Length, 6.9–9.4 cm. Provenience: Broken Flute Cave (Pit House 7, 1; Pit House 8, 2); Obelisk Cave (General, 1); Pocket Cave (Pit House 4, 1); Cave 2 (General, 1); Cave 8 (General, 1); General (1).

Class C (84 whole; Fig. 45 *d–f*). Shouldered, head of bone split by cutting along central groove, then smoothed. Some specimens with very sharp points and some rounded and dulled, probably from use — perhaps a reflection of difference in sharpness for sewing hides or baskets.

Length, 5–16 cm. Size distribution: 5.0–6.9 cm, 26; 7.0–8.9 cm, 25; 9.0–10.9 cm, 21; 11.0–12.9 cm, 10; 13.0–14.9 cm, 1; 15.0–16.9 cm, 1. Provenience: Broken

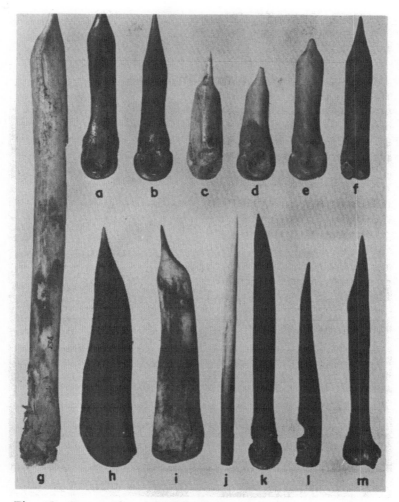

Fig. 45. Bone awls. *a*, shouldered, head unaltered; *b*, shouldered, head split, unsmoothed; *c*, shouldered, head split and smoothed, tip inset from all faces; *d–f*, shouldered, head split and smoothed; *g*, shouldered, head split, unsmoothed, long shaft; *h*, shouldered, head removed by grinding, shaft flat; *i*, shouldered, head removed by grinding, shaft thick and angular; *j*, tapered, splinter of long bone; *k*, tapered, head split and smoothed by grinding; *l*, *m*, tapered, head intact. Length of *g*, 27.1 cm.

Flute Cave (General, 7; Pit House 6, 5; Pit House 7, 3; Pit House 8, 12; Pit House 11, 2; Pit House 15, 15; Cist 20, 1; Cist 54, 1); Obelisk Cave (General, 12); Pocket Cave (General, 5; Pit House 3, 1; Pit House 4, 1); Cave 2 (General, 2; Pit House 2, 3); Cave 3 (General, 7); Cave 8 (General, 4); Cave 10 (General, 1); General (2).

Class D (1 whole; Fig. 45 *g*). Shouldered, head of bone split and unsmoothed, very long shaft. Cutting grooves prominent on split edges.

Length, 27.1 cm. Provenience: Obelisk Cave (General).

Class E (1 whole). Shouldered, head of bone split and smoothed, shaft grooved by grinding through use on two faces near tip, at slight angle to short axis of specimen.

Length, 9.1 cm. Provenience: Broken Flute Cave (Pit House 6).

Class F (1 whole; Fig. 45 *c*). Shouldered, head of bone split and smoothed, tip inset from all faces, shoulder continuous around shaft.

Length, 7.5 cm. Provenience: Broken Flute Cave (General).

Class G (19 whole; Fig. 45 *h*, *i*). Shouldered, head of bone wholly or partially removed by splitting and grinding, shafts broad and flat or round to angular.

Length, 6.3–13.9 cm. Provenience: Broken Flute Cave (General, 1; Pit House 7, 1; Pit House 8, 3; Pit House 9, 1; Cist 54, 1); Obelisk Cave (General, 2); Cave 2 (General, 2; Pit House 1, 2; Pit House 2, 1); Cave 8 (General, 1); General (4).

Class H (4 whole, 1 fragmentary). Shouldered splinter awls, made of long bone fragments, edges and most surfaces smoothed by grinding on all except one specimen.

Length, 5.2–13.7 cm. Provenience: Broken Flute Cave (Pit House 9, 1; Cist 46, 1); Obelisk Cave (General, 1); Cave 2 (Pit House 1, 1); Cave 8 (General, 1).

Class I (1 whole). Shouldered splinter awl, tip on each end. Entire surface smoothed by grinding.

Length, 8.5 cm. Provenience: Broken Flute Cave (Pit House 9).

Class J (12 fragmentary). Shouldered tip fragments, nature of shaft and head indiscernible.

Provenience: Broken Flute Cave (Pit House 6, 1; Pit House 7, 1; Pit House 8, 2; Pit House 9, 2; Cist 54, 1); Obelisk Cave (General, 2); Pocket Cave (General, 1); Cave 2 (General, 1); General (1).

Class K (1 whole; Fig. 45 *m*). Tapered awl, head intact, smoothed by grinding, made of deer or antelope ulna.

Length, 12 cm. Provenience: Broken Flute Cave (Pit House 3).

Class L (1 whole; Fig. 45 *k, l*). Tapered awl, head split and smoothed by grinding.

Length, 14.8 cm. Provenience: Broken Flute Cave (Pit House 9).

Class M (2 whole; Fig. 45 *j*). Tapered awl, made of splinters of long bone, smoothed on all surfaces by grinding.

Length, 7.6 cm, 14.7 cm. Provenience: Broken Flute Cave (Pit House 8, 1; Pit House 9, 1).

Class N (1 fragmentary). Tapered awl, tip fragment, shaft decorated by set of continuous zigzag grooves.

Length, 9.9 cm. Provenience: Cave 2 (Pit House 2).

Class O (4 fragmentary). Tapered tip fragments, nature of shaft and head indiscernible.

Length not taken. Provenience: Broken Flute Cave (Pit House 7, 1; Pit House 9, 1); Obelisk Cave (General, 1); Cave 2 (General, 1).

Perforated Awls

Class A (4 whole; Fig. 46 *a, d*). Shouldered awls made of splinters of long bone, all surfaces smoothed by grinding. Perforated near end opposite tip by biconical drilling.

Length, 6.8–9.4 cm. Provenience: Cave 2 (Pit House 1, 2; Pit House 2, 2).

Class B (2 whole; Fig. 46 *b, c*). Tapered awls, made of splinter of long bone, all surfaces smoothed by grinding. One specimen perforated centrally by biconical drilling. One specimen with incomplete perforation at base.

Length, 8 cm. Provenience: Broken Flute Cave (Cist 47, 1); General (1).

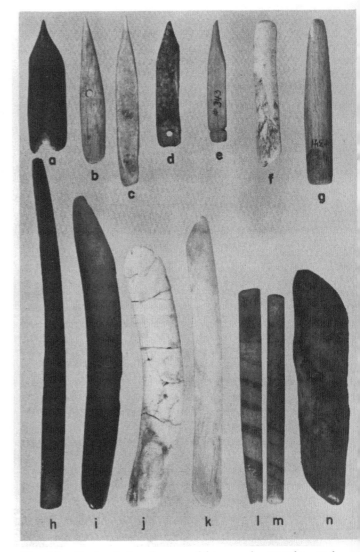

Fig. 46.   Perforated and grooved bone awls, spatulas, and scrapers. *a, d,* shouldered awl, perforated base; *b,* tapered awl, centrally perforated; *c,* tapered awl, incomplete perforation at base; *e,* shouldered awl, grooved base; *f, h–k, n,* rounded tip spatulas; *g,* spatula, both ends worked; *l, m,* spatulas, both ends worked, diagonal parallel stripes on shaft. Length of *h,* 19.5 cm.

Grooved Awls

Class A (2 whole; Fig. 46 *e*). Tapered or slightly shouldered awls, made of splinters of long bone, all surfaces smoothed. Groove at base end.

Length, 7.0 cm, 22.5 cm. Provenience: Broken Flute Cave (Pit House 8, 1; Pit House 9, 1).

End Scrapers

Class A (1 whole; Fig. 47 *h*). Humerus of deer, cut diagonally to long axis, leaving wide rounded working edge near proximal end. Edge ground thin by abrasion and polished through use.

Length, 16.8 cm. Provenience unknown.

Class B (1 whole; Fig. 47 *f*). Long bone of elk or bison, split and ground smooth on all surfaces, head missing. Working edge across wide diagonally cut end, sharpened by grinding on inner side of shaft.

Length, 24.1 cm; width, 5.2 cm; thickness, 1.5 cm. Provenience: Broken Flute Cave (Pit House 9).

Class C (3 whole; Figs. 47 *g*, 48 *c*). Long bones split and ground smooth on all surfaces. Working edge across one end, rectanguloid in shape, wider and thinner than shaft, prepared by grinding on inner side of shaft. One specimen shaped like a beamer, some wear on cut edges.

Length, 18–24 cm; width, 3.1–3.8 cm; thickness, 0.6–1.8 cm. Provenience: Broken Flute Cave (Pit House 6, 1); Cave 8 (General, 1); General (1).

Class D (1 whole; Fig. 47 *j*). Long bone split and ground smooth on all surfaces, straight working edge across one end same width as shaft, sharpened by grinding on inner surface.

Length, 17.4 cm; width, 3.0 cm; thickness, 2.0 cm. Provenience: Broken Flute Cave (Pit House 9).

Spatulas

Class A (1 whole; Fig. 46 *g*). Long thin implement, smoothed on all surfaces by grinding. Both ends are prepared; one has a thin flat rectangular blade, sharpened by grinding on one surface; the other has a sinuous edge, formed by grinding near opposite edges on each side, and slightly worn off.

Length, 19.6 cm; width, 1.2 cm; thickness, 1 cm. Provenience: Broken Flute Cave (Pit House 9).

Class B (2 whole; Fig. 46 *l*, *m*). Long thin implements smoothed on all surfaces by grinding. Both ends have thin rectangular cutting edges shaped by grinding on both surfaces. Both have six thin painted stripes running diagonally from left to right.

Length, 11.7 cm, 12.3 cm; width, 1.0 cm, 1.2 cm; thickness, 0.3 cm. Provenience: Cave 3 (General, 1); unknown (1).

Class C (2 whole; Fig. 46 *n*). Split long bones smoothed on all surfaces by grinding. Working end rectanguloid with rounded corners, sharpened by grinding on one surface. Edges polished from use.

Length, 8 cm, 9 cm; width, 1.2 cm, 1.5 cm; thickness, 0.6 cm, 1.0 cm. Provenience: Broken Flute Cave (Pit House 9, 1); Obelisk Cave (General, 1).

Class D (1 whole). Shaft fragment, made from splinter, smoothed on all sides by grinding. Tip missing.

Length not taken. Provenience unknown.

Class E (5 whole; Fig. 46 *f*, *i–k*, *n*). Rounded tip spatulas, made of split pieces of long bone, smoothed all over by grinding, surfaces polished. Tips, thinner than shafts, sharpened by grinding on lower surfaces.

Length, 14.5–25.0 cm; width, 1.7–3.2 cm; thickness, 1.0–1.7 cm. Provenience: Broken Flute Cave (Pit House 9, 1); Obelisk Cave (General, 1); Pocket Cave (General, 1); Cave 2 (Pit House 2, 1); unknown (1).

Class F (2 whole; Fig. 48 *e*, *f*). Reworked awls, heads split and smoothed by grinding, tips rounded and blunt, somewhat thinned by grinding on all surfaces.

Length, 6.4 cm, 10.2 cm. Provenience: General (2).

Tubes

Class A (2 whole; Fig. 47 *i*). Long bone tubes, ends cut off square and smoothed by grinding. Surfaces somewhat polished from use. These may be similar to the type of specimen described in Guernsey and Kidder (1921: 105). One specimen has wide cut almost severing it.

Length, 11.4 cm, 14.4 cm; diameter, 1.5 cm, 1.8 cm. Provenience: Broken Flute Cave (Pit House 9, 1); Pocket Cave (Pit House 4, 1).

Class B (4 whole; Figs. 47 *b*, 50 *m*). Bird bone tubes, ends cut off square. Ends and surfaces smoothed by grinding.

Length, 3.0–6.1 cm; diameter, 0.4–0.9 cm. Provenience: Pocket Cave (General, 1); unknown (3).

Class C (1 whole; Fig. 47 *e*). Short thick perforated cylinder, surface and perforation oval in shape. Smoothed all over by polishing.

Length, 2.6 cm; width, 2.0 cm; thickness, 0.9 cm. Provenience: Broken Flute Cave (Pit House 9).

Whistle

Class A (1 whole). Long thin tube of bird bone, perforated near one end with small drilled hole. Ends and surfaces smoothed by grinding.

Length, 3.1 cm; diameter, 1.4 cm. Provenience: Broken Flute Cave (General).

Pendants

Class A (1 fragmentary; Fig. 48 *a*). Thin wide piece of bone, perforated by two biconically drilled holes at center of one end. Shape oval with a long straight side; edges, corners, and surfaces ground smooth and polished. One side slightly concave along both axes and showing higher polish.

Length, 9.2 cm; width, 5.3 cm; thickness, 0.4 cm. Provenience: Cave 3 (General).

Class B (1 whole; Fig. 47 *c*). Mandible of canine, most of teeth remaining. Broken off just in front of ramus, ends ground off smooth. Buccal sides of corpus perforated near break and natural cavity on end reamed out to provide opening for suspension from a string. Some fleshy material remained on the bone.

Length, 6.2 cm; width, 2.5 cm; thickness, 1.6 cm. Provenience: Broken Flute Cave (General).

Dice

Class A (2 whole; Fig. 47 *a*). Pieces of long bone shaft, oval in shape. Ground smooth on edges and convex surface, concavities on inner surface left rough, and

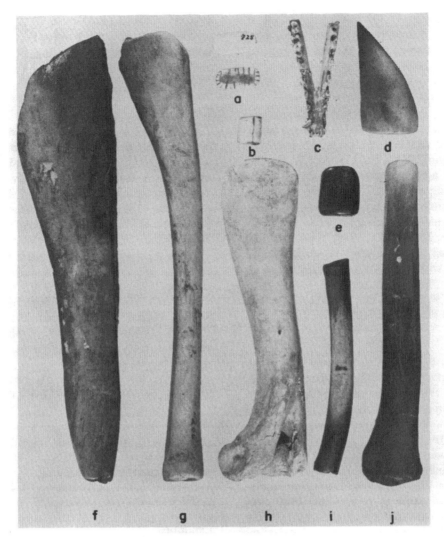

Fig. 47. Miscellaneous artifacts of bone. *a*, die (both sides); *b*, thin cut bird bone; *c*, perforated mandible pendant; *d*, thin slab, rounded edges; *e*, short thick perforated cylinder; *f*, large scraper, broad diagonal blade; *g*, end scraper, wide thin working edge; *h*, humerus end scraper; *i*, thin-walled tube, wide cut on one side; *j*, end scraper, thin straight working edge. Length of *f*, 24.1 cm.

edges irregularly scored with short grooves formed by cutting.

Length, 2.2 cm; width, 1.1 cm; thickness, 0.2 cm. Provenience: Broken Flute Cave (Pit House 16, 2).

Slab

Class A (1 whole; Fig. 47 *d*). Piece of thin flat bone, triangular with a rounded side. One surface and edges highly polished. May be a reworked pendant fragment.

Length, 6.4 cm; width, 2.9 cm; thickness, 0.2 cm. Provenience: Broken Flute Cave (Pit House 16).

Mandible Fragment

Class A (1 whole; Fig. 48 *d*). Posterior portion of one corpus and anterior portion of ramus of a deer. Teeth broken off, portions of roots remaining. Broken edges roughly smoothed by grinding. Main portion of tool shows some polishing from use.

Length, 16.3 cm; width, 4.4 cm; thickness, 1.3 cm. Provenience: Obelisk Cave (General).

Splinters

Class A (4 fragmentary). Broken splinters of long bone, some with slightly ground points. One (Fig. 87 *g*) is the blade of a scarifier, with the following dimensions.

Length, 6.0 cm; width, 0.9 cm; thickness, 0.4 cm. Provenience: Obelisk Cave (General, 1); General (3).

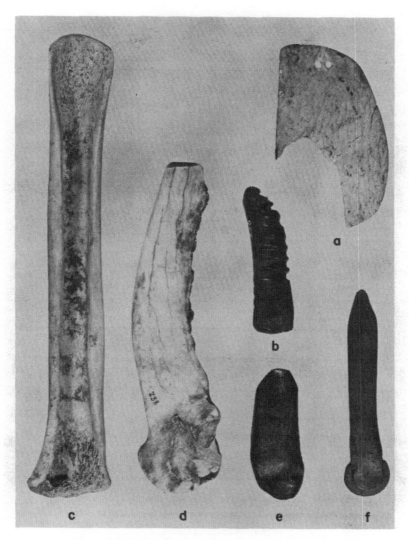

Fig. 48. Miscellaneous artifacts of bone. *a*, perforated pendant; *b*, grooved cylinder; *c*, end scraper, rectangular working edge; *d*, worked mandible fragment; *e*, *f*, awls reworked as spatulas, heads split and smoothed, tips rounded by grinding. Length of *c*, 22.1 cm.

Grooved Cylinder

Class A (1 whole; Fig. 48 *b*). Shaft of long bone, smoothed on sides and ends. Three sides deeply scored with wide, flat-bottomed, nearly parallel grooves worn by abrasion. Remaining end has a shallow conical depression. Direct resemblance to a large class of wooden cylinders.

Length, 14.1 cm; diameter, 2.0 cm. Provenience: Broken Flute Cave (Pit House 7).

ANTLER

Artifacts made from antler were rare. It is an intriguing possibility that the large number of deer from which bone and hide artifacts were derived were killed after their antlers had fallen. A number of factors may have been involved, however, including cultural preference.

Wrench

Class A (1 whole). Made from basal part of an unusually large antler, possibly elk, ends smoothed by grinding. Tine broken off one side and scar smoothed by grinding. Oval perforation near center, symmetrical in form with rounded edges.

Length, 19 cm; width, 4.6 cm; thickness, 4 cm. Provenience: Broken Flute Cave (Pit House 9).

Spatula

Class A (1 whole). Fragment of tine, probably from a deer, square end as wide as shaft. Surface smoothed all over by grinding on both sides, ends somewhat roughened and squared off from use.

Length, 7.7 cm; width, 1.2 cm; thickness, 1.2 cm. Provenience: Obelisk Cave (General).

Fig. 49.   Artifacts of feathers and horn. *a*, perforated horn spoon;
b, f, horn cylinders; *c*, bundle of feathers wrapped in juniper bark;
d, feather fan with pitch handle; *e*, feather fan of loosely suspended
feathers; *g*, mountain sheep horn wrench. Length of *d*, 34 cm.

Flaker

Class A (1 whole). Tip of tine faceted through use. No other data available.

HORN

Some of the mountain sheep horns were cut from the skull. Others were not sufficiently preserved to determine whether they had been found on the ground or cut off a dead animal.

Wrench

Class A (2 whole; Fig. 49 *g*). Mountain sheep horns, tips and basal portions missing. Perforated centrally with oval holes.

Length, 23.7 cm, 27.7 cm; width, 6.6 cm, 6.7 cm; thickness, 2.3 cm, 3.7 cm; perforation length, 2.3 cm; perforation width, 1.8 cm. Provenience: Ram's Horn Cave (General, 2).

Cut Horn

Class A (1 whole). Mountain sheep horn, cut off on sides of base, center separated by breaking. Tip rounded naturally.

Length, 17.3 cm; width, 3.4 cm; thickness, 1.9 cm. Provenience: Cave 3 (General).

Cylinders

Class A (Set of 11; Fig. 49 *b, f*). Rough cylinders made from mountain sheep horn. Some have a flat side or a slightly conical shape. Ends and sides are crudely rounded by grinding. These may be flakers (Guernsey 1931: Plate 4), although some are small.

Length, 3.1–10.4 cm; diameter, 0.6–1.5 cm. Provenience: Obelisk Cave (General, 11).

Spoons

Class A (3 fragmentary; Fig. 49 *a*). Made from mountain sheep horn slab ground very thin. One specimen oval in shape, concave along both axes; edges and surfaces carefully smoothed by grinding; two rows of perforations are parallel to the short axis. Two fragments are flat and covered with pitch.

Length, 8.5–16.8 cm; width, 2.7–5.6 cm; thickness, 0.3–0.4 cm. Provenience: Cave 3 (General, 2); Obelisk Cave (General, 1).

Fragment

Class A. Piece of large horn, one side and end smoothed by grinding.

Length, 10.5 cm; width, 5.6 cm. Provenience: Broken Flute Cave (Pit House 16).

SHELL

The specimens composed of shell were divided into three major categories — pendants, beads, and worked shell. The shell identifications were supplied by Robert J. Drake, then of the Department of Zoology, University of Arizona.

The shells are *Haliotis* (abalone) from the southern California coast; *Agaronis testacea* (L.), *Spondylus* (red spiny oyster), *Conus*, *Pyrene*, *Turritella*, and *Glycymeris* from the Gulf of California. All the *Oliva* and *Olivella* specimens appear to be from the Gulf of California rather than the Pacific coast.

Pendants

Specimens with a perforation at one end or side are classified as pendants.

Class A (1 whole; Fig. 50 *e*). Small *Glycymeris* with natural shape altered by polishing on all surfaces. Perforated by grinding off the beak.

Diameter, 2.8 cm; thickness, 0.8 cm. Provenience unknown.

Class B (1 whole; Fig. 50 *h*). *Glycymeris* circle, beak rounded and perforated for suspension.

Diameter, 7 cm; thickness, 0.8 cm. Provenience unknown.

Class C (1 whole; Fig. 50 *a*). *Turritella*, first convolution of head removed, tip removed, surface and edges smoothed by grinding. A portion of the convolution next to the head has been removed by grinding, forming a perforation.

Length, 6.5 cm; diameter, 1.9 cm. Provenience unknown.

Class D (7 lots; Figs. 50 *b, d, l*; 72 *a*). Fragments of larger shells, shaped on all sides by grinding, round or oblong in shape. Perforation drilled through one end. One specimen has two perforations close together.

Length, 1.3–4.9 cm; width, 1.0–2.8 cm; thickness, 0.1–0.6 cm. Provenience: Broken Flute Cave (General, 4; Pit House 10, 1); Pocket Cave (General, 1); Cave 4 (General, 1).

Class E (1 whole; Fig. 50 *c*). Fragments of *Haliotis fulgens* (Phillippi), original shape completely altered, edges smoothed and polished. Ground to a trapezoidal shape, concave in section, two perforations near short parallel side, long parallel side notched at regular intervals.

Length, 4.2 cm; width, 3.4 cm; thickness, 1.0 cm. Provenience unknown.

Beads

Class A (3 lots; Fig. 50 *i, m*). Short cylindrical beads, centrally perforated, shaped all over by grinding.

Diameter, 0.2–1.5 cm; thickness, 0.1–0.6 cm; perforation, 0.1–0.7 cm. Provenience: Atahonez (General, 12 *Olivella*); Pocket Cave (Surface, 540 *Olivella*); unknown (2 *Spondylus*).

Class B (9 lots; Figs. 50 *f*, 72 *b*). Oval or conical shells, perforated by grinding off the ends. Almost all are worn thin through use.

Length, 0.7–2.5 cm; diameter, 0.4–1.3 cm. Provenience: Broken Flute Cave (General, 1 *Conus*, 1 *Oliva*, 6 unspecified); Cave 4 (86 *Olivella*); unknown (1 *Conus*, 75 *Olivella* and *Haliotis*, 6 *Olivella* and *Agaronis testacea*, 2 unspecified).

Worked Shell

Class A (1 whole; Fig. 50 *g*). *Conus*, worked all over by grinding and polishing.

Length, 3.0 cm; diameter, 1.6 cm. Provenience unknown.

Class B (2 whole; Figs. 44 *e*, 50 *k*). Disks, round to oval in shape, surfaces and edges well smoothed.

Diameter, 1.2 cm, 1.4 cm; thickness, 0.3 cm, 0.1 cm. Provenience: Broken Flute Cave (Pit House 8, 1 gastropod); Obelisk Cave (General, 1 *Haliotis*).

Class C (1 whole; Fig. 50 *j*). Section of *Glycymeris* shell with edges polished.

Length, 6.5 cm; thickness, 0.5 cm. Provenience unknown.

FEATHERS

All feathers not otherwise specified by species or color are turkey. The identifications were provided by J. T. Marshall, Department of Zoology, University of Arizona.

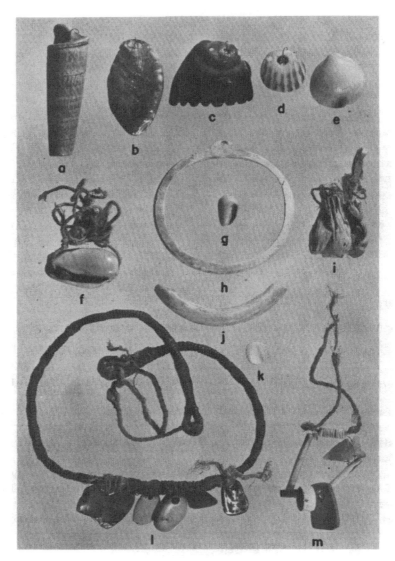

Fig. 50.   Artifacts of shell. *a, Turritella* pendant; *b, d,* pendants; *c,* abalone pendant; *e,* small whole perforated *Glycymeris; f,* conical shell perforated by grinding off both ends; *g,* polished *Conus; h, Glycymeris* pendant; *i,* two cylindrical beads on string wrapped with corn husks; *j,* worked fragment of *Glycymeris; k,* shell disk; *l,* necklace with shell and turquoise pendants; *m* (clockwise from top), short cylindrical beads, stone projectile point, tubular bone bead, perforated sherd, shell disk bead, stone disk bead, tubular bone bead. Length of *a,* 6.5 cm.

Fans

Class A (1 whole; Fig. 49 *d;* Guernsey 1931: Plate 49). Seven feathers, ends wrapped in bundle of juniper bark, covered with hide, and sewn with yucca fiber cord to form handle. Feathers were laid side by side with webs overlapping.

Length, 34 cm; width, 6 cm; thickness, 2 cm. Provenience: Obelisk Cave (General).

Class B (1 whole; Fig. 49 *e;* Nusbaum, Kidder, and Guernsey 1922: 84; Guernsey 1931: Plate 49; Guernsey and Kidder 1921: Plates 18, 39). Bundles of small black

and white feathers are tied to ends of several pieces of cordage; red and blue feathers are inserted in the tie. The lengths of cordage are then tied in a small bundle, a piece of hide is included in the wrap, and two strings with the ends tied together serve as a small carrying loop.

Length, 16 cm; width, 3.4 cm; thickness, 2 cm. Provenience: Broken Flute Cave (Pit House 16).

Pieces of Cut Quill

Class A. Five short segments of large quill, strung side by side on yucca fiber cordage. Each end of string passes through each quill and doubles back through the next. Ends of string tied in square knot close to last quill.

L. L. Hargrave of the Southwest Archaeological Center of the National Park Service examined this specimen. His comments are as follows:

I am amazed at the accuracy of these primitive people in close-measuring since we found the lengths of these five sections are from 23.8 to 24.2 mm, much less than 1 mm difference! Moreover, it puzzles me how they cut the quills so cleanly. With a sharp knife we had difficulty in cutting feathers for study. A minimum of three feathers were used. The circumference of the quills falls within the range of the size of the flight feathers (primaries) of an adult turkey. However, diagnostic structural characters of the shaft of the turkey quill differs from those exhibited by the tubes, and the walls of the turkey quills are translucent. Measurements of a flight quill from an adult female Golden Eagle gives the same size range as the archaeological tubes. However the eagle quill is not translucent but has a dense creamy case, as do all five of the Basketmaker tubes. Quill sections Nos. 1, 2, and 3 could be from an Eagle (species?). Quill sections Nos. 4 and 5 are not from an eagle but might have been made from sections of the primaries of a Pelican, a Wood Ibis, or a Swan.

Kenneth Stager of the Los Angeles County Museum examined the specimen and thought that the largest quill might be from a Trumpeter Swan, *Olor cf. buccinator*, but the identification could not be definite.

Length, 4.4 cm; width, 2.4 cm; thickness, 0.6 cm. Provenience: Broken Flute Cave (General).

Bundles of Feathers

Class A (10 whole and fragmentary and 1 lot; Fig. 49 *c*). Bundles of from 2 to 20 feathers wrapped with bark, yucca leaves, yucca fiber, or yucca fiber cordage. Feathers sorted roughly for size and color. These were probably wrapped this way to protect the webs. One bundle consisted of plucked tufts just as taken from the turkey.

Provenience: Broken Flute Cave (General, 4; Pit House 9, 1; Pit House 16, 2 and 1 lot); Cave 3 (General, 1); Cave 11 (General, 1); General (1).

Split Feathers with Notched Quills

Class A (1 lot). Split feathers with remaining portions of quills notched at regular intervals, presumably as preparation for being wrapped around cord in feather-cord blankets.

Provenience: Broken Flute Cave (General).

Feathers Used on Prayer Sticks and Ceremonial Objects

Class A (5 specimens). These feathers were so poorly preserved that only their occurrence could be noted. One was stuck into the pith of a corn cob, three were stuck into a ball of mud with a flat bottom to rest on, and one was tied to the end of a stick with a yucca leaf.

Provenience: Broken Flute Cave (General, 5).

HIDE

The hide of animals that were killed was the single natural substitute for cloth. The remains that were found probably give only a suggestion of its great utility.

Sacks Made from Whole Skins

Class A (4 whole, 2 fragmentary; Fig. 51 *a, l*). Small rodent skins with the feet left on or the legs tied up with string, heads absent. The neck opening served as an aperture, closed by wrapping with cordage. The skins were turned inside out and were so thin that probably no tanning process was necessary to keep them pliable. Tail of one twisted on itself, forming long hard handle(?). One skin had fur intact, both ends open, yucca fiber cord running through one eye hole and out of the other end of the bag.

Length, 17–33 cm; width, 5–8 cm. Provenience: Broken Flute Cave (General, 1 with shell and talons and 1 with turkey beards; Pit House 6, 1 empty; Pit House 9, 1); Obelisk Cave (General, 1 with brown paint); unknown (1 with hafted knife).

Sacks Made from Leather

Class A (2 whole; Fig. 44 *a*). Cylinders of leather. One specimen, empty when found, sewn up one side, ends closed by wrapping with yucca and soft fiber cordage. Seam on inside, sewn with over-under stitch with yucca fiber cord. One specimen (illustrated), sewn across bottom and up side, contained wooden dice set and was tied with leather cord.

Empty specimen: Length, 24 cm; width, 8 cm. Provenience: Obelisk Cave (General).

Class B (1 whole). Round-bottomed, straight-topped bag, carrying straps attached to each corner of top, opening in one corner below strap. Seam on inside, sewn with over-under stitch with yucca fiber cord. Straps are long tubes of leather sewn on the outside with an over-under stitch of yucca fiber cord. Several holes were patched in prehistoric times by putting pieces of leather on the inside and sewing around the edges with yucca fiber cordage. This sack was empty.

Length, 60 cm; width, about 12 cm. Provenience: Broken Flute Cave (Pit House 6).

Class C (3 fragmentary). Pieces of hide sacks, too fragmentary to describe. Two specimens show a seam where two pieces were joined by an over-under stitch running from one to the other; the sewing material was yucca fiber cord. Another is a cylindrical piece of hide with the fur remaining.

Provenience: Broken Flute Cave (Pit House 9, 1; Pit House 16, 2).

Fig. 51. Whole animal hide sacks and contents. *a*, hide sack, containing: *b*, projectile point; *c*, two shell pendants and one bead on a string; *d*, two galena crystals wrapped in fiber; *e*, shell and lion-claw necklace; *f*, shell disk; *g*, stone disk, and *h–k*, four small sinew-wrapped leather bundles containing a piece of metallic ore, a powdered red-orange mineral and two unknown powders, three tiny sinew bundles with shell and turquoise cylindrical beads tied to them, and four tiny sinew-wrapped bundles that once had feathers tied to them. *l*, sack containing turkey beards. Length of *a*, 28.5 cm.

Wrappings

Class A (6 whole and fragmentary). Small pieces of hide used as wrappings for minerals, beads, and foodstuffs. These packages are tied shut with cordage or a piece of leather thong.

Length, 2.5–9.0 cm; diameter, 1.5–2.3 cm. Provenience: Broken Flute Cave (General, 2; Pit House 6, 1); Obelisk Cave (General, 1); General (2).

Human Scalp Lock

Class A (1 fragmentary). Piece of thin charred hide with human hair attached. Bound up with a piece of yucca fiber cordage.

Provenience: Broken Flute Cave (General).

Pieces of Hide

Class A (10 whole and fragmentary). Most are irregularly shaped scraps of tanned hide; two are long thin rolls tied up with string. Hair remains on some of them. One whole badger hide, cut off just in front of hind legs, turned inside out, scraped but untanned; yucca fiber cordage strung through slits cut in hide that covered nose and chin, as if for suspension.

Provenience: Broken Flute Cave (General, 3; Pit House 9, 1; Pit House 10, 1); Obelisk Cave (General, 2); Cave 9 (General, 3).

Cordage

Class A (3 pieces). Narrow strips of hide and fur twisted upon themselves to form cordage. One is a two-yarn S-twist strand, one is a 6-ply round braid, and one is a 3-yarn Z-twist strand.

Length, 22–45 cm; diameter, 0.35–0.6 cm. Provenience: Broken Flute Cave (General, 1); Cave 11 (General, 1); General (1).

Sandals

Class A (1 whole, 2 fragmentary). Roughly rectangular pieces of hide. Whole specimen has a yucca fiber cordage toe loop. One fragment has a loop of yucca fiber cordage at one end that might have been a toe loop or a heel strap. The other fragment has edge loops of yucca fiber cordage on two adjacent edges, shape undetermined.

Length, 13–22 cm; width, 8.5–11.0 cm. Provenience: Broken Flute Cave (General, 2); Cave 3 (General, 1).

SINEW

Bundles

Class A (2 whole; Fig. 82 *a*). Bundles of sinew, pieces folded back on themselves and wrapped after the addition of each strip. A number of additional pieces have been added to bundles by laying the increments parallel and wrapping them around the mid portion.

Length, 6.5 cm, 14.0 cm; diameter, 0.8 cm, 3.8 cm. Provenience: Broken Flute Cave (Pit House 16, 2).

Cordage

Class A. Numerous short pieces of sinew were used as cordage to tie or wrap parts of other artifacts.

DOG HAIR

Some textiles were found that were made from dog hair cordage. Notable among these were two caches of intricately made sashes. Tufts of dog hair were also found stored in a small jar. With a few exceptions, the animal fiber in the artifactual inventory was hair from the Basketmakers themselves or from their dogs. It is interesting to note that both types of hair were utilized for rather specialized articles of clothing. Hough (1914: 75) reports a dog hair sash found around the waist of a mummy in Tularosa Cave; it is very similar to the sashes described below in Class B.

Sashes

Class A (6 whole; Fig. 52). The analysis of this group of sashes, which is summarized in Table 7, was done by employees of the Carnegie Institution of Washington under the direction of Earl H. Morris.

Six finely woven sashes were found tied in a bundle in Obelisk Cave (Fig. 52 *a–f*). Each sash is a wide flat braid with a braided fringe at each end. The end of each fringe is lashed, leaving a yarn tassel protruding. Two sashes are white, two are brown, and two are white with brown woven decorations. One of these has a narrow zigzag line along each edge; the other has narrow brown lines crisscrossing the whole width of the sash. The sashes range in total length from 147 to 270 cm and in total width from 2.2 to 7.3 cm. The bundle of sashes was wrapped with a cord of the same material (see Fig. 53 and *Cordage*, Class D).

Flat braids involving 25 to 119 threads compose the main portion of the sashes. The threads are plaited in an over-2, under-2 weave with an odd number of threads being used in each plait. This is best seen in the left and right pitch of the threads at the corresponding edges of the sash. If the plaiting had been done with an even number of threads, the threads on the right side would strike from left to right. The plaiting is done alternately from each side of the plait to the center. The method is particularly well illustrated in sash *d* (Fig. 52), where the zigzag lines along the borders and the great width resulted in considerable confusion in the weaving and a number of irregularities and errors in the center portion. The flat braided portions of the sashes range from 78 to 170 cm in length. In sash *d*, there is indication of where the plaiting was begun. About 20 cm from one end the greatest number of warp threads is present. Weaving is presumed to have proceeded toward the farther end, because the number of threads gradually diminishes, the brown pattern is finished in a neat symmetrical fashion, and a thread has been inserted near the farther end with both ends going toward that end. After that end was completed, the weaver finished the other end, dropping only a few threads, and without taking care in the construction of the brown design.

In sash *d*, on either side of the plait the brown thread zigzag pattern makes a border about 0.65 cm wide and 0.65 cm from the edge. The border is composed of four adjacent threads of brown fiber, woven in an over-2, under-2 fashion. The zigzag pattern is made possible by a manipulation of the threads in which a thread from the left and a thread from the right are looped and interchanged (Fig. 54). In sash *e*, the crisscross pattern is produced by plaiting some brown threads in with white ones and manipulating them in the same manner as the others, carrying them from one side to the other and back with an over-2, under-2 movement (Fig. 55).

Fig. 52.   Dog hair sashes. *a–f*, sashes found in a bundle cached in Obelisk Cave; *g*, dog hair cord used to tie bundle. Length of *a*, 270 cm.

The braided fringe elements (Fig. 56) are extensions of the threads used in the flat braids. Out of a total of 141 fringe elements, 107 have 8-thread braids. In one specimen, a 4-thread braid is typical. The remainder range between 4 and 12 threads per fringe element. Errors occur occasionally in the braiding of most fringe elements, as threads were used out of their proper turn. Fringe elements range from 26.7 to 56.6 cm in length. There is considerable variation among elements of a single sash.

There are lashings at the ends of the braided fringe elements to prevent their unraveling. Ten variations in the method of lashing were noted (Fig. 57). All but a few fringe elements on each sash were finished with a single type of lashing. The deviations were probably unintentional. Sash *b* has a shell strung on each of the braided fringes (Fig. 53 *c*).

The tassel threads at the ends of the braided fringe elements are very irregular in length. Some are as long as 12 cm, the average length being about 7.5 cm (Fig. 53 *a*).

The length of the individual threads on each sash was determined by computing the length before and after braiding. The major variables considered were the slope of the thread as it was woven diagonally across the sash and the amount of length taken up by the over-under movement of a given element. The figures derived are presented in Table 7.

Class B (2 whole). Two other sashes were found cached beneath the floor of Pit House 6, Broken Flute Cave. They correspond to those described in the previous class in material and general manufacture, but lack the size and precision of weave so characteristic of the former class. Both are made of 14 2-ply, S-twist threads, about

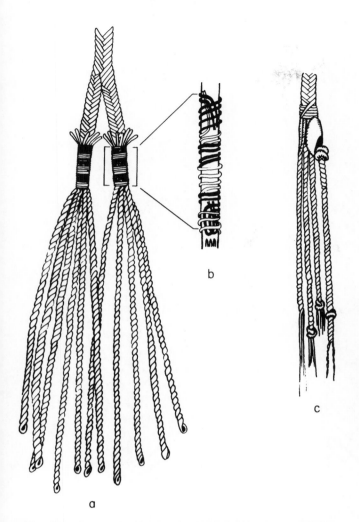

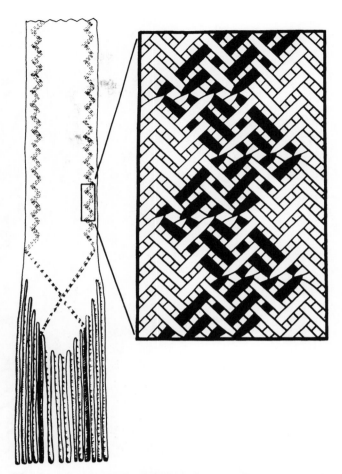

Fig. 54. Detail of pattern formation in dog hair sash shown in Figure 52d.

Fig. 53. Fringe and lashing techniques on dog hair sashes. a, detail of fringe and tassel on tie cord shown in Figure 52g; b, detail of lashing on fringe a (black indicates brown, white indicates yellow); c, detail of fringe on sash shown in Figure 52b.

0.1 cm in diameter. Both sashes are about 130 cm long and 1.5 cm wide, and both are made from white dog hair. The body of the sashes is made with an over-1, under-1 technique with some irregularities. Short tassels of varying lengths were left at each end. One end of each specimen is lashed by wrapping the base of the tassel threads with one of their number, which is fastened at the end with a knot.

Cordage

Class A (1 fragmentary). Piece of 12-ply square braid made of 2-yarn, Z-twist strands.

Provenience: Broken Flute Cave (General).

Class B (3 fragmentary). Three pieces of multi-ply round braid used as apron strings. Condition of preservation so poor that twist cannot be determined.

Provenience: Broken Flute Cave (General, 3).

Fig. 55. Detail of pattern formation in dog hair sash shown in Figure 52e.

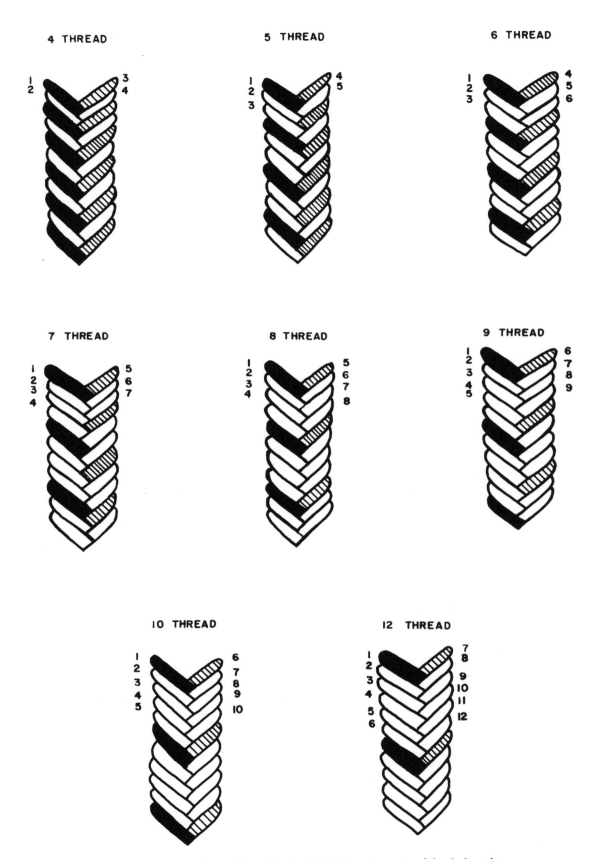

Fig. 56.   Disposition of threads in braided fringe elements of dog hair sashes.

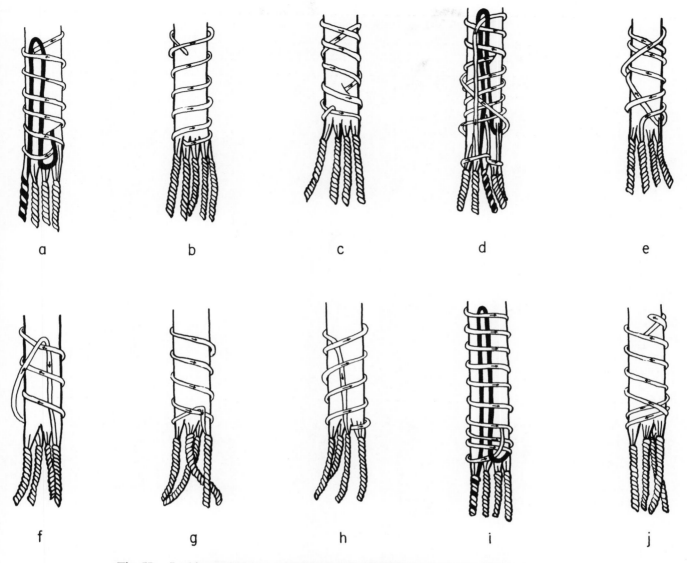

a b c d e

f g h i j

Fig. 57. Lashing techniques used at ends of braided fringe elements on dog hair sashes.

Class C (1 fragmentary). Tie on a skin sack in a medicine pouch; 2-yarn, Z-twist strand, dark brown in color. Provenience: Broken Flute Cave (General).

Class D (1 whole; Fig. 52 *g*). This cord, which wrapped the bundle of sashes together, is a 12-thread, over-2, under-2 square braid. Each end is finished with two 6-thread braided fringes, 3–4 cm in length (Fig. 53 *a*). Five or six tassel threads are lashed to the ends of each fringe with very fine cord. Each lashing is wrapped around 20 or 30 times, and the color alternates between brown and yellow every four or five wraps (Fig. 53 *b*).

Cache of Material

One mass of short tufts of dog hair cached in a small wide-mouth jar. Some prepared cordage in jar. Provenience: Cave 8 (General).

HUMAN HAIR

Human hair was made into twisted and braided string. Some of this was used as cordage, for the same purposes to which yucca fiber cordage was put. The rest was braided or woven into anklets or bags. Masses of hair were saved as cut, presumably for future use. Some of these cut hanks show the method of hairdressing utilized by the Prayer Rock Basketmaker people. A similar range of uses is listed by Kidder and Guernsey (1919: 171).

Anklets or Leggings

Class A (4 fragmentary; Fig. 58 *e*). Cylinders manufactured by a coil-without-foundation technique. Edge

TABLE 7
Analysis of Dog Hair Sashes from Prayer Rock Caves

	Sashes Illustrated in Figure 52					
	a	**b**	**c**	**d**	**e**	**f**
Color of thread	white	brown	white	brown, white	brown, white	brown
Total length of sash	270 cm	270 cm	270 cm	270 cm	203 cm	147 cm
Total width of sash	7.3 cm	4.5 cm	6.5 cm	6.7 cm	2.2 cm	5.6 cm
Total number of threads	103	79	99	111–119	35	111
Length of a single thread	3.7 m	3.9 m	3.7 m	3.6 m	2.7 m	2.1 m
Total length of thread per sash	389 m	288 m	378 m	427 m	91 m	215 m
Number of threads per inch of weave	13	20	17	17	12	24
Length of plaited part of sash	170 cm	161 cm	170 cm	155 cm	103 cm	78 cm
Number of braided fringes per end of sash	13	10	12	14–15	8	14
Length of fringe elements	57 cm	50 cm	57 cm	49 cm	31 cm	27 cm
Total length of fringe elements per sash	11.3 m	9.2 m	11.2 m	12 m	9.2 m	9.4 m
Number of threads per braided fringe element	8 in 24 7 in 2	8 in 12 10 in 2 9 in 2 6 in 4	8 in 19 9 in 4 10 in 1	8 in 24 12 in 1 9 in 1 7 in 1	4 in 13 5 in 2 6 in 1	8 in all
Lashing method used on fringes, as shown in Fig. 57	25 of *a* 1 of *i*	14 of *f* 3 of *g* 3 of *h*	20 of *a* 1 of *b* 1 of *c* 1 of *d* 1 of *e*	26 of *i* 1 of *j*	knotted instead of lashed	all of *h*
Average length of fringe	7.3 cm	20.3 cm	7.3 cm	14.7 cm	21.5 cm	4.0 cm

formed from an unaltered edge of the fabric. Cordage used was a 2-ply, S-twist cord of human hair. One specimen was mended in prehistoric times by sewing the edges of a hole together with yucca fiber cord. Two specimens found in the fill of Pit House 9, Broken Flute Cave, seem to be a pair.

Length, 13–17 cm; diameter, 10–11 cm. Provenience: Broken Flute Cave (General, 1; Pit House 9, 2); Cave 1 (General, 1).

Bag

Class A (1 fragmentary). Rim of a piece of coil-with-out-foundation weaving. Made like anklets described above, but larger. Edge formed from an unaltered edge of the fabric.

Length unknown; diameter, 17 cm. Provenience: Cave 10 (General).

Gourd Carrying Net

Class A (1 fragmentary). Long cylindrical bag without a bottom. Made from loose coil-without-foundation weave. Three-ply, Z-twist yucca fiber cordage circle used as rim at bottom end, the coiled elements being looped around it. The ends of the yucca ring are tightly intertwined so that the joint is almost indiscernible. A similar circle is used for the top rim, with the strands tied in a square knot, and the ends looped for a handle and tied to the opposite side of the ring. The handle loops have been twined together with a 2-ply, S-twist hair string, with two yucca fiber strings serving as a core around which this cord is twined. Top of handle has remnant of a 2-ply Z-twist cord, knotted with a half knot, that probably served to suspend the net, with its gourd, from the handle.

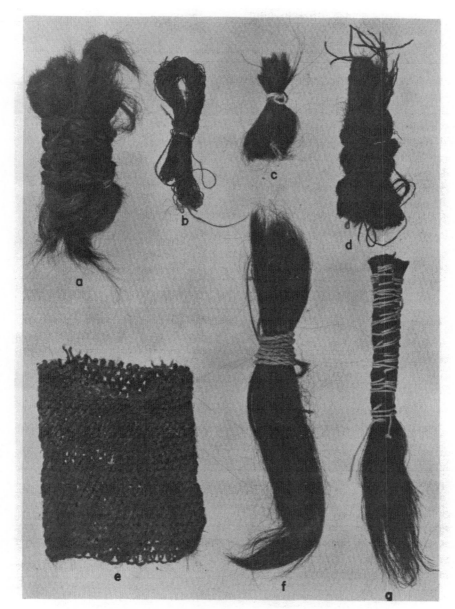

Fig. 58.   Artifacts of human hair. *a*, cut braid wrapped around two hanks of hair; *b*, bundle of cordage; *c*, mass of hair; *d*, braided strap bundle; *e*, anklet or legging; *f*, cut hank of hair wrapped with yucca cord; *g*, cut hank of hair, three bunches wrapped separately then tied together. Length of *g*, 22 cm.

Total length, 22 cm; handle length, 11 cm; diameter, about 10 cm. Provenience: Broken Flute Cave (General).

Flat Braided Strap and Cordage Bundle

Class A (1 whole; Fig. 58 *d*). A flat braid of 14 2-ply, S-twist cords, wrapped with four bundles of 2-ply, S-twist string to prevent fraying. Braid is 85 cm long and 1.1 cm wide. Tassel is 1.5 cm long on one end and 1.7 cm long on the other.

Provenience: Broken Flute Cave (General).

Bundles of Cordage

Class A (2 whole). Bundles of about 35 strands of 2-ply, S-twist cord, with a 2-ply, Z-twist yucca fiber cord tied through loop at one end. Bundle of hair cords, slightly twisted, frayed at intervals, and with ends missing.

Provenience: Cave 10 (General, 2).

Cordage

Class A (4 whole; Fig. 58 *b*). Fine 2-yarn, Z-twist and S-twist cordage in single lengths, bundles, or a loop loosely twisted around on itself.

Diameter, about 0.1 cm. Provenience: Broken Flute Cave (General, 3; Pit House 8, 1).

Hair Bundles Tied as When Worn

Class A (5 whole; Fig. 58 *a, f, g*; Guernsey and Kidder 1921: Plates 19, 32). Before being cut off, these bundles were tied while on the head of an individual. One had three bunches of hair that were wrapped separately with yucca cord, then tied together with the same kind of string; one end shows cutting strokes (Fig. 58 *g*). Another bundle was loosely wrapped in the center with an irregularly made yucca fiber cord, one end cut off (Fig. 58 *f*). One bundle had a 3-strand braid 65 cm long, with cutting strokes visible at the thick end and the small end tapered to a point. The braid was used to tie two shorter hanks of hair in the middle (Fig. 58 *a*).

Length, up to 25 cm. Provenience: Cave 10 (General, 1); unknown (4).

Bundles of Hair

Class A (3 whole; Fig. 58 *c*). Masses of hair, occasional tufts showing cutting strokes. One mass (illustrated) tied with yucca fiber cord.

Length, 7–18 cm; width, 1.4–1.5 cm. Provenience: Broken Flute Cave (General, 2; Cist 20, 1).

YUCCA

Yucca leaves and fiber were perhaps the most widely used of all the materials to which the Basketmakers had access. Available in quantity, and strong and flexible in any form, this plant was used for a tremendous variety of tasks. Slightly modified whole plants were used as carrying nets and containers; leaves were woven or tied together with various techniques to make containers, straps and fabrics; and the fiber was made into clothing and into cordage, which had a myriad of uses.

Yucca Leaves

Tump Bands

Class A (2 whole, 1 fragmentary; Figs. 59 *b*, 60). Two or three wide leaves, edges sewn together with yucca fiber cord in a zigzag running stitch. Ends of leaves split several times and used as warps for a weft of plain twined yucca fiber cords. After the twining had narrowed somewhat, the leaf tips were divided into two strands, each about 1 cm wide, which were brought around and overlapped with each other; the hole thus formed was covered with simple wrapping. In one specimen the ends were only wrapped and had no plain twining.

Length, 23–47 cm; width, 3–11 cm; thickness, 0.2–1.0 cm. Provenience: Broken Flute Cave (General, 1); Obelisk Cave (General, 1); Pocket Cave (General, 1).

Class B (4 fragmentary). Ten to 16 leaves of narrow-leaf yucca sewn together with a zigzag running stitch of

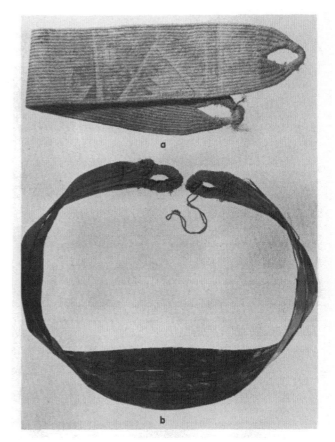

Fig. 59. Yucca tump bands. *a*, fiber band, tapestry weave with painted geometric design; *b*, two yucca leaves sewn together. Length of *b*, 47 cm.

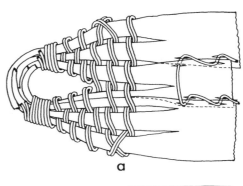

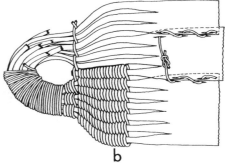

Fig. 60. Construction of yucca leaf tump bands. Drawing by Robert F. Burgh.

over-1, under-1 yucca fiber cordage. Ends narrowed by plain twining for a distance of about 2 cm, then elements wrapped in two parts to form hole and spliced together at end. One half of one end of a specimen wrapped with red cord.

Length, 13–24 cm; width, 6–7 cm; thickness, 0.5–1.0 cm. Provenience: Broken Flute Cave (General, 3; Pit House 10, 1).

Mats

Class A (1 whole, 1 fragmentary). Thirty-four narrow leaf yucca leaves diagonally plaited in an over-1, under-1 weave. Leaves cut near stalk, base ends at one end of mat, tips at the other. Joined at base end by plain twining with a yucca fiber cord, ends of cord tied in a square knot at one edge. Joined at tip ends by a plain twined yucca leaf tied in a square knot at one edge. Tips and bases of leaves left as fringe. Size of mats controlled by size of leaves.

Length, 36 cm; width, 22 cm; thickness, 1 cm. Provenience: Cave 3 (General, 1); Cave 10 (General, 1).

Bag

Class A (1 fragmentary). Bottom of twilled bag. Elements are whole narrow yucca leaves twilled in an over-2, under-1 weave. Rim missing; bottom made by joining parallel yucca leaves with plain twined yucca fiber string, twining spaced about 2.5 cm apart. Yucca leaf elements bent up to form sides of bag.

Height, 12 cm; diameter, 10 cm. Provenience: Obelisk Cave (General).

Containers

Class A (4 whole; Fig. 61 *a*). Narrow leaf yucca plant, head cut off at stalk so that some or all of the leaves remain naturally joined together. In one specimen, with only some leaves joined (not illustrated), the base is wrapped and tied with other narrow yucca leaves. These ends were left at the bottom with leaves coming straight from it or the leaves were folded back around the circumference forming the bottom of the container. At a distance of 8 to 14 cm from the base there is a row of plain twining with yucca leaves or string. The resulting form is a slender, roughly cylindrical net or container.

Two specimens: length, 19 cm, 29 cm; diameter, 4 cm, 5 cm; two specimens: length, 43 cm, 47 cm; diameter, 10 cm, 17 cm. Provenience: Broken Flute Cave (General, 3); General (1).

Class B (1 whole; Fig. 61 *b*). Two wide yucca leaves placed at right angles to each other and folded over once to form four sides and bottom of a container. Tips bound together with a narrow leaf tied in a square knot. Lump of pitch inside.

Length, 15 cm; width, 3 cm; thickness, 2.5 cm. Provenience: Broken Flute Cave (Cist 53).

Pot Rest

Class A (1 whole; Fig. 61 *f*). Narrow leaf yucca stalk cut off so bases of leaves remained naturally joined together. Tips wrapped around a coil of narrow yucca leaves that formed a hoop. Hoop tied in one place with a yucca fiber cord.

Diameter, 9 cm; thickness, 2 cm. Provenience: Broken Flute Cave (General).

Chains

Class A (1 whole). Twenty-nine interlocking loops, made of narrow yucca leaves, fastened together by half knots at the end of the leaves, and then tied with square knots.

Length, 107 cm; width, 4 cm; thickness, 0.6 cm; average loop diameter, 3.5 cm. Provenience: Broken Flute Cave (General).

Class B (3 whole). Rough coils of narrow yucca leaves tied end to end. Coils unfastened or secured with a piece of leaf.

Diameter, 8.5–11.5 cm; thickness, 2–3 cm. Provenience: Broken Flute Cave (General, 3).

Plaited Leaves

Class A (2 fragmentary). Three-ply flat braid of narrow yucca leaves. Ends unfinished.

Length, 52 cm, 57 cm; width, 0.7 cm, 1.2 cm; thickness, 0.5 cm, 0.7 cm. Provenience: Broken Flute Cave (General, 2).

Class B (1 whole). Six-ply flat braid of narrow yucca leaves. Made from three leaves folded over at finished end; working ends hanging loose.

Length, 15 cm; width, 2 cm; thickness, 0.4 cm. Provenience: Broken Flute Cave (General).

Class C (1 fragmentary). Eight-ply square braid of narrow yucca leaves. Made of four leaves folded over at finished end, two of them extended and tied to make a small loop. Working ends near base of leaves wrapped and tied with a narrow yucca leaf.

Length, 14 cm; width, 1.8 cm; thickness, 1.5 cm. Provenience: Cave 3 (General).

Loop

Class A (1 whole). Narrow yucca leaves bent to form hoop at end of straight handle. Hoop and handle loosely wrapped with split yucca leaves.

Length, 11.4 cm; width, 5.0 cm; thickness, 0.8 cm. Provenience: Cave 5 (General).

Miscellaneous Artifacts of Wide Yucca Leaves

Class A (1 whole). End of a wide yucca leaf tip folded over and tied with a yucca fiber string, each end of which was inserted through the loop and left dangling.

Length, 16.4 cm; width, 3.6 cm; thickness, 1 cm. Provenience: Broken Flute Cave (Pit House 7).

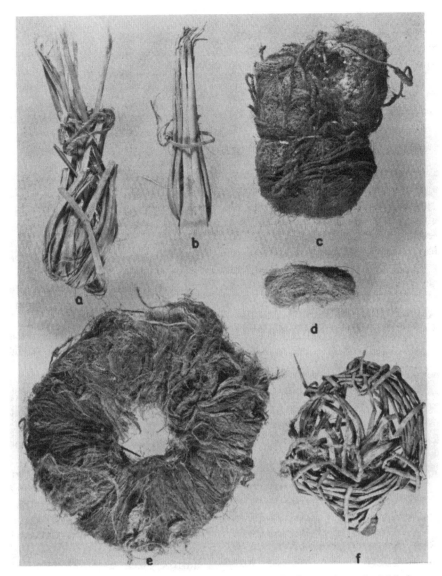

Fig. 61.   Miscellaneous artifacts of yucca. *a*, leaf container; *b*, folded leaf container; *c*, fiber bundle containing amorphous white mineral material; *d*, tobacco quid; *e*, fiber pot rest; *f*, leaf pot rest. Length of *a*, 19.5 cm.

Class B (1 whole). Wide yucca leaf folded double, tips wrapped and tied together with yucca fiber cord.

Length, 9 cm; width, 3 cm; thickness, 1.8 cm. Provenience: Pocket Cave (General).

Class C (1 whole). A fragment of wide yucca leaf with isolated cross-hatched diamonds painted in black at intervals along the length.

Length, 29 cm; width, 2 cm; thickness, 0.1 cm. Provenience: Pocket Cave (General).

Class D (1 whole). Wide yucca leaf split into seven pieces along three-fourths of its length. Split segments fastened together with nine rows of plain twining, two of narrow leaf yucca and seven of yucca fiber cordage.

Length, 26 cm; width, 6 cm; thickness, 1 cm. Provenience: Broken Flute Cave (General).

Bundles of Leaves

Class A (4 whole; Fig. 69 *a*). Bundles of parallel narrow leaves tied in middle with another leaf or with yucca fiber cord. One bundle has all base elements at one end and tips at other end; the leaves in another bundle have been folded over and over again and tied to make a neat package.

Length, 6.6–50 cm; diameter, 1–5 cm. Provenience: Broken Flute Cave (General, 4).

Yucca Fiber

Cordage

The analysis of yucca fiber cordage includes both the separate pieces of cordage that were found in the sites and pieces that were utilized as a part of other artifacts.

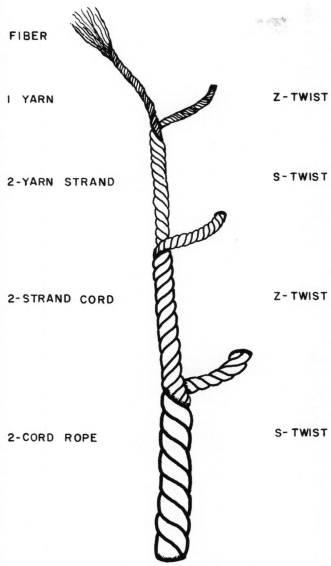

FIBER

1 YARN   Z-TWIST

2-YARN STRAND   S-TWIST

2-STRAND CORD   Z-TWIST

2-CORD ROPE   S-TWIST

Fig. 62. Diagrammatic definition of terminology used in cordage analysis. Adapted from Burgess and Irving (1934).

Each specimen of cordage was classified according to manufacture, diameter, color, and context in which it was found. The great majority of the specimens were manufactured by one or more consecutive twisting operations; a few were braided cords. A diagrammatic definition of the terminology employed in the analysis is given in Figure 62. This definition was adapted from that used by Burgess and Irving (1934). In the pieces whose size and strength were increased by compound manufacturing techniques, the twist usually alternated between S and Z. It was noted that the specimens in which the alternation did not occur tended to unravel and presented a looser, weaker finished product. By far the most commonly occurring finished cordage types were 2-yarn Z-twist strands, and 2-yarn S-twist strand, 2-strand Z-twist cords (Table 8).

The sample was examined in detail for patterned regularities in the classification units. No significance in the distribution of samples from different caves or from different areas of a single cave was noted. There was little correlation between the diameter of a given piece of string and the complexity of the manufacturing technique; some specimens of the most complex types are of the smallest diameter. Factors that seemed to correlate with string diameter were the size and function of the article on which the string was utilized.

About 75 percent of the specimens were loose pieces of string and 10 percent were used in articles manufactured from cords such as aprons and nets. The remainder were mostly ties and wraps on bundles, artifacts, suspension strings, and sewing materials.

Some of the larger pieces of cordage were wrapped with the split feathers of turkeys (85 specimens) or narrow strips of thin-skinned fur-bearing animals (16 specimens). These were not tabulated separately, since the type of cordage did not vary appreciably from unwrapped specimens.

Some pieces of cordage were dyed; the colors used were red, yellow, black, and several shades of brown. These specimens were notable in that they were of the smallest diameters found. While some were incorporated into ties and wrappings, they were mostly of the kinds used in sandals and textiles.

Knots

Knots were analyzed according to material and provenience, but no significant distribution was noted. Out of a total of 244 knots, 129 were square knots, 88 were overhand knots, 14 were granny knots, 11 were slip knots, and two were bow knots.

Quids

Class A (27 whole; Fig. 61 *d*). Bundle of finely prepared yucca fiber, carefully wrapped around cores of finely divided leaves and stems of tobacco (*Nicotiana attenuata*). Incrustation of lime on at least some specimens. The fiber bundles were secured with a twist on each side. They are oblong in shape and oval through the long and short axes. Some of them appear to have been matted from sucking and chewing. The practice of chewing tobacco mixed with lime as an agent to hasten the release of the alkaloid is known from ethnographic accounts from the southwestern United States (Driver and Massey 1957), but is unknown from previous archaeological work in the Southwest. This is the first reported occurrence of tobacco in any form in the Anasazi area.

Length, 4.0–6.5 cm; width, 2.5–3.5 cm; thickness, 1.3–2.8 cm. Provenience: Broken Flute Cave (General, 22; Pit House 8, 2; Pit House 10, 1; Cist 13, 1; Cist 55, 1).

TABLE 8

Frequency of Cordage Types from Prayer Rock Caves
(Diameter: 0.1–2.8 cm)

Number of Specimens			
2	1-yarn S-twist		
16	1-yarn Z-twist		
63	2-yarn S-twist strand		
409	2-yarn Z-twist strand		
10	3-yarn S-twist strand		
4	3-yarn Z-twist strand		
4	4-yarn Z-twist strand		
379	2-yarn S-twist strand	2-strand Z-twist cord	
10	2-yarn Z-twist strand	2-strand Z-twist cord	
2	3-yarn S-twist strand	2-strand Z-twist cord	
1	3-yarn Z-twist strand	2-strand Z-twist cord	
17	2-yarn S-twist strand	3-strand Z-twist cord	
9	2-yarn S-twist strand	4-strand Z-twist cord	
29	2-yarn Z-twist strand	2-strand S-twist cord	
1	2-yarn S-twist strand	2-strand S-twist cord	
1	3-yarn S-twist strand	2-strand S-twist cord	
1	2-yarn S-twist strand	3-strand S-twist cord	
3	2-yarn Z-twist strand	3-strand S-twist cord	
9	2-yarn Z-twist strand	2-strand S-twist cord	2-cord Z-twist rope
4	2-yarn Z-twist strand	3–14 strand S-twist cord	2-cord Z-twist rope
3	2-yarn S-twist strand	2-strand Z-twist cord	2-cord Z-twist rope
2	2-yarn S-twist strand	2-strand S-twist cord	2-cord Z-twist rope
2	2-yarn Z-twist strand	2-strand Z-twist cord	2-cord Z-twist rope
3	2-yarn S-twist strand	2-strand Z-twist cord	3-cord Z-twist rope
6	2-yarn S-twist strand	2-strand Z-twist cord	2-cord S-twist rope
2	2-yarn S-twist strand	3-strand Z-twist cord	2-cord S-twist rope
1	2-yarn S-twist strand	4-strand Z-twist cord	2-cord S-twist rope
1	2-yarn Z-twist strand	2-strand Z-twist cord	2-cord S-twist rope
2	2-yarn Z-twist strand	3-strand Z-twist cord	2-cord S-twist rope
1	2-yarn S-twist strand	4-strand Z-twist (wrapped with 2-yarn, S-twist strand)	
15	3-ply flat braid		
1	3-yarn Z-twist 3-ply flat braid		
2	2-yarn Z-twist 6-strand 3-ply flat braid		
1	2-yarn S-twist 7, 9, 9, 3-ply flat braid		
1	1-yarn S-Z-twist 6, 8, 9, 3-ply flat braid		
1	1-yarn S-twist strand, 3-ply braid, 2-braid S-twist rope		
2	4-ply round braid		
1	2-yarn S-twist 4-ply round braid		
1	2-yarn S-twist strand, 4-ply square braid		
1022	Total number of specimens		

Container Carrying Nets

Class A (9 whole and fragmentary; Fig. 63 *d*). Flexible, loosely woven, open-ended cylindrical nets with a loop handle of cordage tied to one end. Ends are circular loops of string, usually of greater diameter than the cord used in the wall mesh. Wall mesh is formed by two twined elements looped back and forth between the end loops to form a crisscross mesh. These nets would have been useful in carrying gourds and pottery vessels. Possibly, they were made on the container.

Length, 5–17 cm; diameter, 5–17 cm. Provenience: Broken Flute Cave (General, 4; Surface, 1; Pit House 8, 1; Cist 20, 1); Cave 3 (General, 1); General (1).

Aprons

Nearly all of the aprons were stained in the central portion of their length, indicating their use by women during the menstrual period. Most of them were subsequently folded and tied into a neat bundle so that the stain was hidden.

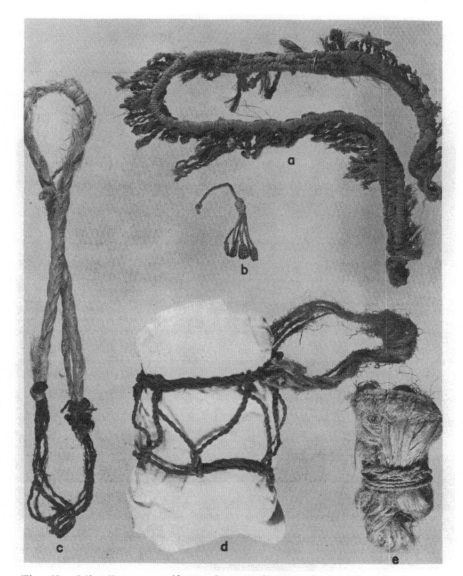

Fig. 63. Miscellaneous artifacts of yucca fiber. *a*, feathered strap; *b*, tassel base, sockets perhaps intended to hold quills of feathers; *c*, loops of yucca cordage and human hair cordage; *d*, gourd carrying net; *e*, apron. Length of *c*, 30 cm.

Class A (4 whole, 4 fragmentary; Figs. 64, 65, 66). Tapestry weave panel, warps folded over belt. Hanging warps below panel body of apron. Polychrome woven and painted designs in black, red, yellow, blue, pink, and brown. One specimen (Fig. 65 *b*) utilizes dog(?) hair as a light colored woven element.

Size range of panel: length, 10–14 cm; width, 5–7 cm. Provenience: Broken Flute Cave (General, 7); Pocket Cave (General, 1).

Class B (1 whole). Body of apron composed of narrow width of unwoven cordage; strands folded in middle, suspended from belt of human hair, and tied in place with a strand of human hair cordage.

Measurements unavailable. Provenience: Broken Flute Cave (General).

Class C (104 whole; Fig. 63 *e*). Body of apron composed of hanks of soft fiber. Ends of hanks folded over belt and tied in place with cordage. A few belts dyed red.

Unfolded size range: length, 40–65 cm; width, 13–22 cm. Bundle size range: length, 9–16 cm; diameter, 4–9 cm. Provenience: Broken Flute Cave (General, 59; Surface, 3; Pit House 4, 1; Pit House 8, 2; Pit House 9, 3; Pit House 10, 6; Pit House 12, 2; Cist 13, 3; Cist 20, 1); Obelisk Cave (General, 1); General (23).

Tump Bands

Class A (2 whole; Fig. 59 *a*). Tapestry weave tump bands, 25 and 30 warps, tightly woven cordage wefts. Polychrome painted designs in black, red, and yellow on one surface. Wrapping at each end where warp ends were joined to form loop.

Fig. 64.   Tapestry weave yucca fiber aprons. *a*, polychrome painted geometric designs (see reverse in Fig. 65*c*); *b*, polychrome woven geometric design (see Fig. 66*d*). Width of *a*, 13.5 cm.

Length, 46 cm, 52 cm; width, 6 cm, 8 cm. Provenience: Broken Flute Cave (Pit House 10, 1; Pit House 11, 1).

Class B (2 whole, 1 fragmentary; Fig. 67 *b, c*). Oblong straps, coarsely woven. Warp strands are cords and ropes of yucca fiber, weft is composed of yucca fiber, fur, or feathers. Holes made at ends by separating warps and wrapping weft elements around edges of hole. Central part of one strap has no weft present, apparently by intention.

Length, 40–51 cm; width, 5–10 cm. Provenience: Broken Flute Cave (General, 2); Cave 4 (General, 1).

Nets

Class A (3 whole, 3 fragmentary; Fig. 68). Mesh is composed of cordage fastened with square knots. Edges have a heavy cord run through loops. One specimen is sack-shaped. The specimens illustrated were recovered by the Bernheimer Expedition and are in the collection of the American Museum of Natural History.

Mesh size: 3.0–3.3 cm. Provenience: Obelisk Cave (General, 3); Prayer Rock area (General, 3).

Base of Tassel

Class A (1 fragmentary; Fig. 63 *b*; Kidder and Guernsey 1919: 164). Seven cords suspended from a knot, each cord braided in a round braid to form a tiny socket. It is thought that at one time these sockets held the quill tips of feathers.

Length, 8.5 cm; diameter, 7.0 cm. Provenience: Broken Flute Cave (General).

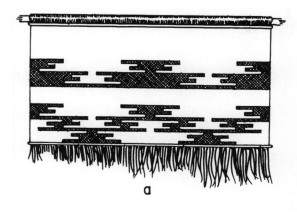

a

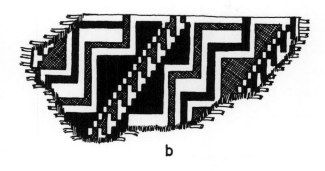

b

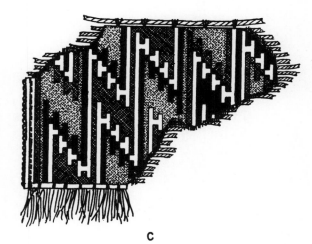

c

Fig. 65. Designs in tapestry weave yucca fiber aprons. *b*, white dog (?) hair used for white decorative element; *c*, with horizontal warp arrangement (see reverse in Fig. 64*a*). Solid black represents black or dark brown, solid cross hatching represents red, broken cross hatching represents yellow, white represents natural yucca fiber. Drawing by Robert F. Burgh.

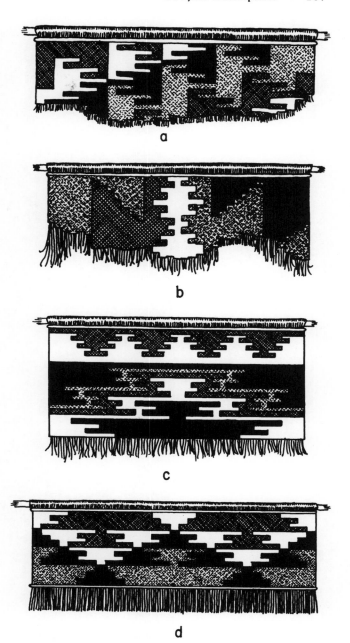

a

b

c

d

Fig. 66. Designs in tapestry weave yucca fiber aprons. Solid black indicates black, solid cross hatching indicates red, broken cross hatching indicates yellow, white indicates natural yucca fiber. In *b*, the natural yucca center panel has been divided vertically and painted blue on one side, pink on the other; *d* shows design of Figure 64*b*. Drawing by Robert F. Burgh.

Feces

This fragmentary specimen consists of a few seeds, crushed bone, and a large thick piece of yucca fiber cordage running through the center of the piece. It was examined by Volney Jones of the Ethnobotanical Laboratory, University of Michigan, who thought it was a piece of feces from a human or possibly from an animal scavenger or camp follower of man.

Length, 18.0 cm; diameter, 2.5 cm. Provenience: Broken Flute Cave (Cist 20).

Cordage Loops

Class A (6 whole, 3 fragmentary; Fig. 63 *c*). Knotted and spliced cordage loops of various diameters and sizes.

Fig. 67.   Woven yucca fiber artifacts. *a*, crude textile fragment;
b, c, coarsely woven yucca fiber tump bands. Length of *c*, 41 cm.

Some specimens have a double loop; three include a short length of human hair cordage at one end.

Diameter of loop, 5–17 cm; diameter of cord, 0.35–2.4 cm. Provenience: Broken Flute Cave (General, 1; Pit House 9, 1); General (1). No provenience available for 6 whole specimens.

Pot Rests

Class A (1 whole; Fig. 61 *e*). Doughnut-shaped coils of soft fiber and cordage, completely wrapped with soft fiber.

Diameter, 16 cm; thickness, 3 cm. Provenience: Broken Flute Cave (General).

Class B (1 whole). Cord looped three times into a hoop and coated with pitch.

Diameter, 10.3 cm; thickness, 2.4 cm. Provenience unknown.

Miscellaneous Cordage Artifacts

Class A (1 whole). A cord with one strand intentionally left out of twist to form free loops, fastened to cord at intervals with knots.

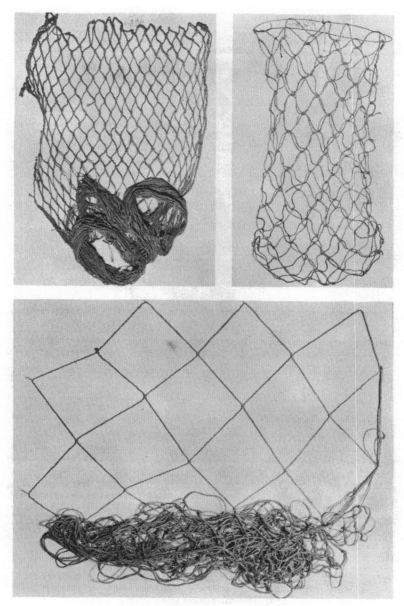

Fig. 68.   Yucca fiber nets (collection of the
American Museum of Natural History).

Length, 14 cm. Provenience: Broken Flute Cave
(General).

Class B (1 whole). Three-ply flat braid with slip knots
tied in each end.

Diameter, 1.0 cm; length, 25.0 cm. Provenience: Cave
3 (General).

Class C (1 whole). Series of yucca fiber cords folded
over string and tied down. Each folded element had
been wrapped with sinew, hide, or fine cordage. This
specimen may have been a headband or garter.

Length, 27 cm; width, 10 cm; thickness, 1 cm. Pro-

venience: Pocket Cave (General).

Class D (1 whole). Three-yarn S-twist strand loosely
wrapped around end of twig. Both ends of twig broken
off short.

Length, 25 cm; diameter, 1.6 cm. Provenience
unknown.

Class E (1 whole). Two-yarn Z-twist cord looped
around end of twig. Both ends of twig broken off short.

Length, 24 cm; diameter, 3.5 cm. Provenience: General.

Class F (2 whole). Short lengths of cordage. One

Fig. 69. Bundles of yucca materials. *a*, leaves; *b*, cordage; *c*, finely prepared fiber; *d*, coarsely prepared fiber. Length of *b*: twist as illustrated, 35 cm; continuous strand, about 42 cm.

length has a series of consecutive knots and a slip knot at one end. The other, a small bundle of parallel cords, has a knot at each end.

Length, 9 cm, 15 cm; diameter, 2 cm, 4 cm. Provenience: Broken Flute Cave (General, 1); General (1).

Bundles of Cordage

Class A (2 whole; Fig. 69 *b*). One three-ply braid of cordage and one twist of cordage. Braid has both ends broken off; twist has a continuous strand of about 42 cm of cordage.

Length, 23 cm, 42 cm; diameter, 1.5 cm, 2.0 cm. Provenience: Broken Flute Cave (Pit House 7, 1); General (1).

Feather Blankets

Class A (1 whole, 6 fragmentary; Fig. 70; Kidder and Guernsey 1919: 174). Twined nets wrapped with strips of feathers to form soft fluffy cloth. Typically a single long piece of cordage serves as a continuous warp, arranged in overlapping loops. Feather-wrapped elements are twined across them at intervals. At the end of a weft crossing, the two twining elements are twisted around each other as they are brought down the side to the next crossing. Usually one end of the blanket is neat and orderly where the warp threads must have been suspended from a string and the weave started. Toward the other end the warps got crossed and the edge is not so regular.

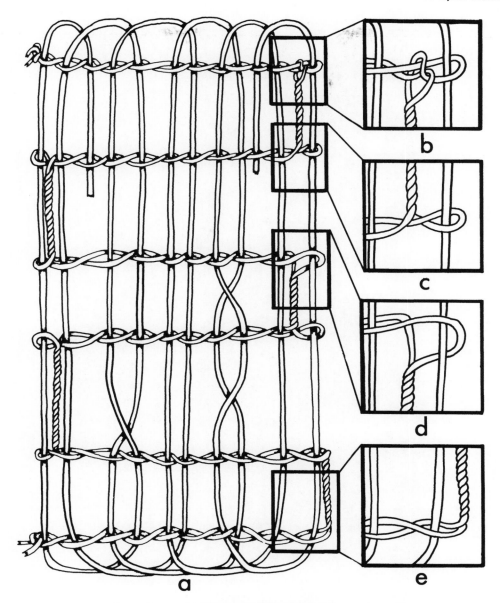

Fig. 70. Yucca fiber cordage framework for feather cloth blanket.

Length present, 0.26–1.05 m; width present, 0.18–0.40 m. Provenience: Broken Flute Cave (General, 1; Burial 3, 1; Burial 4, 1); Cave 3 (General, 1); unknown (3).

Fur Blankets

Class A (2 fragmentary). The fur blankets were made in the same fashion as the feather blankets so far as could be determined.

Length, 36 cm; width, 27 cm. Provenience: Broken Flute Cave (General, 2).

Bundles

Class A (31 whole; Fig. 69 *c*). Large bundles of well-prepared fiber, the hank twisted around itself and usually secured at one end by wrapping. One twist contains a bundle of feathers.

Length, 10–25 cm; width, 2–11 cm; thickness, 1.5–6.5 cm. Provenience: Broken Flute Cave (General, 4); Obelisk Cave (General, 1); Cave 3 (General, 1); Cave 4 (General, 3); General (22).

Class B (27 whole; Fig. 69 *d*). Irregular to oblong bundles of fiber presenting a partly cleaned, matted appearance, as if they had been soaked in water. These may have been waste materials from soap-using activities.

Length, 6.0–9.5 cm; width, 2.0–4.3 cm; thickness, 1.0–3.0 cm. Provenience: Broken Flute Cave (General, 10; Pit House 10, 1; Cist 13, 2; Cist 55, 9; Cist 57, 1); Obelisk Cave (General, 2); General (2).

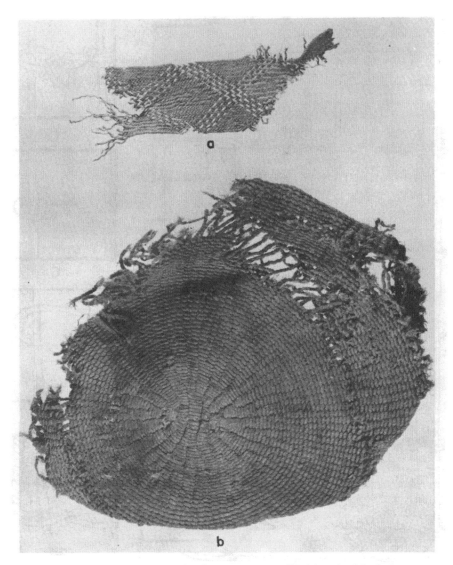

Fig. 71.   Yucca fiber textile fragments. *a*, twilled band with design in black, red, natural, and yellow; *b*, bottom fragment of twined bag. Length of *a*, 13 cm.

Class C (4 whole; Fig. 61 *c*). Soft fiber wrapped around bundles of juniper bark (2 specimens) or a white amorphous clay (2 specimens).

Diameter, 6.5–17.0 cm; length, 8.0–14.4 cm. Provenience: Broken Flute Cave (General, 2); Pocket Cave (Pit House 4, 1); Cave 10 (General, 1).

Feathered Strap

Class A (1 fragmentary; Fig. 63 *a*). Three 2-yarn Z-twist strands twined together with 2-yarn S-twist strands. Ends of bunches of small feathers were wrapped in fine string and sewn together. Judging from the size of the remaining portions of the quills, the feathers were probably short. This specimen may have been a head band or a garter.

Length, 19 cm; width, 1.5 cm; thickness, 0.6 cm. Provenience: Cave 10 (General).

Textile Fragments

Class A (1 fragmentary). Finely woven plain weave textile fragment. Manufactured of 2-yarn S-twist warps and 2-yarn S-twist wefts. No edges present. Intricate geometric design in one color, including diagonal rows of dots and solid stepped triangles. Five warp elements per centimeter.

Length, 15 cm; width, 6.5 cm. Provenience unknown.

Class B (1 fragmentary; Fig. 71 *a*). Wide flat twilled band of over-2, under-2 weave with design woven in red, black, yellow, and natural. Edges straight, work neatly done.

Fig. 72.   Twined bags of yucca fiber. The shell jewelry was
found in the bags. Length of *a*, 17.5 cm.

Length, 13 cm; width, 4.2 cm. Provenience unknown.

Class C (1 fragmentary; Fig. 67 *a*). Wide flat twilled strap fragment. Warps knotted at one end. Weave changes in texture and form at intervals along the length of the specimen, one portion including red twined elements, another with thickened ridges across the warps. Edges pulled in irregularly. Many errors present in weave. This specimen looks like a "sampler" woven by a child.

Length, 22 cm; width, 6 cm. Provenience: Broken Flute Cave (Pit House 7).

Class D (1 fragmentary). Coarse-twined strap; two warps per centimeter.

Length, 9 cm; width, 9 cm. Provenience: Broken Flute Cave (General).

Twined Bags

Class A (5 whole and fragmentary; Figs. 71 *b*, 72). Bags were roughly egg-shaped, tapering toward both ends. Warp elements were added at intervals from the bottom to the area of greatest circumference, and subtracted from this point to the mouth. No portion of the rim remains on any bag. On one specimen three warp elements are braided in a flat braid to form a strap handle. Horizontal bands of design were woven in red and black, separated by bands of naturally colored fiber. Two of the bags held strings of shell beads.

Length present, 13–17 cm; diameter, 7–11 cm. Provenience: Broken Flute Cave (General, 4); Obelisk Cave (General, 1).

Fig. 73.   Coil-without-foundation bag of yucca fiber.
Length, 35 cm.

Coil-Without-Foundation Bags

Class A (3 fragmentary; Fig. 73). Bags were roughly egg-shaped, tapering toward both ends. Only the specimen illustrated retains a portion of the original rim, which was a self rim. It also has the remnants of yucca leaf loops inserted in the fabric near the edge, presumably for carrying straps. Two specimens have indications of solid horizontal black and red bands of design at intervals along the length of the bag.

Length present, 33–35 cm; diameter present, 19–30 cm. Provenience: Broken Flute Cave (General, 1; Cist 20, 1); Cave 10 (General, 1).

Cordage and Stick Fragment

Class A (1 specimen). Warps of thin wooden twigs, weft of fine 2-yarn Z-twist strands tightly twined on warps. Edges and ends missing.

Length, 29 cm; width, 7.5 cm. Provenience: Broken Flute Cave (Pit House 8).

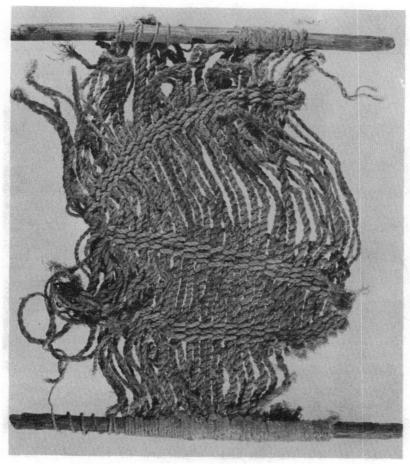

Fig. 74. Unfinished textile of yucca fiber on a loom (?). Length, 24.5 cm.

Textile on Loom (?)

Class A (1 whole; Fig. 74). Warps are fastened at each end by being passed through the lashing around a stick. A weft composed of three parallel pieces of cordage is twined across the warps three times in a roughly zigzag fashion.

Length, 24.5 cm; width, 23.5 cm. Provenience: Broken Flute Cave (Cist 44).

Sandals

Sandals woven of yucca fiber are one of the most abundant kinds of remains. About 220 whole and fragmentary specimens were recovered. The majority of these were found in trash deposits, and the presence of large holes in the heels suggests that they were worn out and discarded by the ancient people.

Most of the sandals are made with a multiwarp tapestry weave technique, with intricate geometric designs formed in colors and in the patterns of the weave. A summary description of the multiwarp type is presented below.

Several other kinds of sandals were present in small quantities. Plaited and twilled sandals made of wide yucca leaves, the second most abundant type, appear to have been used for winter wear or as overshoes, as indicated by their size and the nature of their wear.

Some of the remaining types may have been discarded or lost in one of the caves by a later wearer, or they may represent intrusive sandals in use in other areas during Basketmaker III times, or they may be an actual part of the Prayer Rock Basketmaker III sandal complex.

Class A. Multiwarp tapestry weave sandals. These sandals are similar in most aspects of composition, manufacture, decoration, and method of fastening to the foot. They are woven of 15 to 36 warps of yucca fiber cordage and finely twisted wefts of the same material. The wefts in the central portion of most specimens are woven with a plain weave technique. The toe and heel

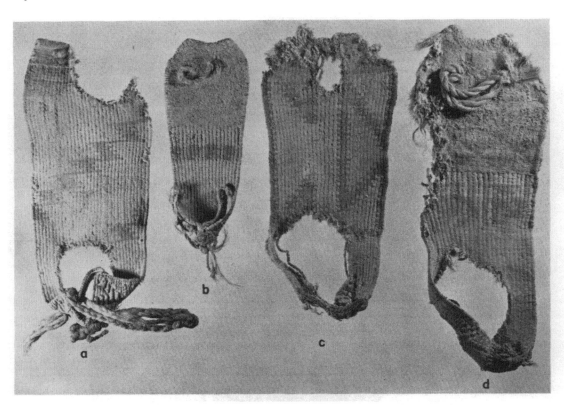

Fig. 75. Multiwarp tapestry weave sandals of yucca fiber cordage. Woven geometric designs in red, yellow, and black on the upper surface. Length of *d*, 27.5 cm.

areas are reinforced or thickened by a complex and varied series of wraps made by the weft strands on warp and weft elements in these portions of the sandals. The details of the manipulation of the warp and weft elements are the major bases for the classification used below.

The upper surfaces of most sandals exhibit geometric designs woven into the textile with dyed weft elements in red, yellow, and black; these occur in a toe panel, in a central band, or as an allover pattern (Fig. 75). Some sandals have thin solid-color stripes on their upper surfaces, and some are plain. The lower surfaces of most sandals have textured designs in the toe area, the heel region, or both areas (Fig. 76). These were made by one or several of a complicated series of weft-wrapping techniques, and the decorative techniques seem to cross-cut the classification below. This texturing is an effective method of forming a tread for walking on slippery sandstone, and it certainly would lend uniqueness to each individual's tracks. Also, it would serve to thicken the portion of the sandal that received the greatest wear.

The sandals were fastened to the foot by one of two basic methods (Fig. 77). The most common device involved a toe loop, located in the center of the sandal, large enough to hold two toes. Single or multiple pieces of cordage connected the toe loop to an ankle loop, which was tied through the fabric of the sandal on each side near the heel and passed in front of the ankle. On some specimens a piece of cordage connected the ends of the ankle loop in back of the heel as well. The other method of tying the sandal to the foot involved the use of a continuous row of loops sewn through the fabric on each side of the sandal. These loops were then connected by various systems of lacing across the top of the foot. Both varieties of fastening occur in each of the types below.

Type 1 (42 whole and fragmentary; Fig. 77 *b*). Multiwarp tapestry weave straight-toed sandals. The warps have been folded over a string suspended from two points, and the ends included in the weave for a short distance. The heel is flat and the warps are manipulated in a band of false braid, with the ends worked back into the weave or tied in a single large knot and allowed to trail behind the foot.

Length, 17–25 cm (average, 23.5 cm); width of heel, 5–9 cm (average, 7.3 cm); width of toe, 8–12 cm (average, 9.0 cm). Provenience: Broken Flute Cave (General, 18; Surface, 4; Pit House 16, 5); Obelisk Cave (General, 5); Pocket Cave (General, 5); Cave 3 (General, 5).

Type 2 (131 whole and fragmentary; Figs. 75 *c*, 77 *c*). Multiwarp tapestry weave scallop-toed sandals. The warps were folded over a string loop suspended from a

Fig. 76. Multiwarp tapestry weave sandals of yucca fiber cordage. Textured geometric designs on the lower surfaces. Length of *a*, 27 cm.

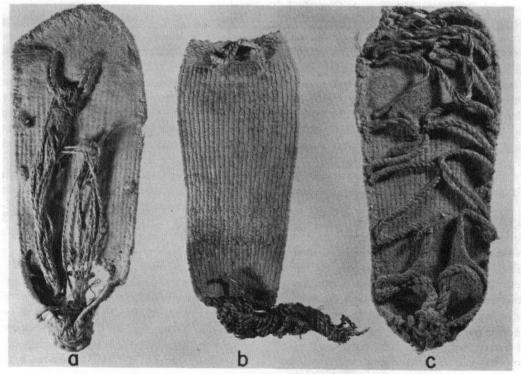

Fig. 77. Multiwarp tapestry weave sandals of yucca fiber cordage. *a*, toe loop–ankle loop method of fastening to the foot; *b*, toe loop only remains; *c*, side loop–lace method of fastening to the foot. Length of *a*, 26.5 cm.

single point, and the ends included in the weave for a longer distance than in the previous category. The scalloped nature of the toe is due to the curve of the suspension string. The heel is a ring heel, the outside warps serving as a core for the remainder of the warps to be looped over before being wrapped around themselves and ending. The corners of the heel end were touching when this process was completed.

Length, 20–28 cm (average, 25 cm); width of heel, 6–9 cm (average, 7.7 cm); width of toe, 8–12 cm (average, 11 cm). Provenience: Broken Flute Cave (General, 70; Pit House 4, 4; Pit House 8, 1; Pit House 9, 7; Pit House 10, 6; Pit House 11, 1; Cist 6, 11; Cist 16, 11; Cist 20, 5; Cist 52, 4; Cist 55, 1; Cist 57, 2); Pocket Cave (General, 1; Pit House 3, 1; Pit House 4, 1); Ram's Horn Cave (General, 1); Cave 8 (General, 1); Cave 10 (General, 3).

Type 3 (44 whole and fragmentary; Fig. 77 *a*). Multiwarp tapestry weave round-toed sandals. The warps were folded double and turned around the toe lying flat and parallel, with the ends brought down the opposite side to the heel. The ends form a ring heel as described for Type 2, except that in some specimens the warp ends are tied in a great knot and allowed to trail.

Length, 21–30 cm (average, 25 cm); width of heel, 6–10 cm (average, 8 cm); width of toe, 8.5–13.0 cm (average, 10.8 cm). Provenience: Broken Flute Cave (General, 27; Pit House 8, 1; Pit House 9, 1; Pit House 10, 3; Pit House 11, 2; Cist 6, 3; Cist 9, 1; Cist 16, 1; Cist 20, 2; Cist 52, 1; Cist 57, 1); Cave 10 (General, 1).

Class B. Plaited and twilled sandals. These sandals were woven from whole or split yucca leaves using a flat plaiting technique in an over-1, under-1 weave and a twilling technique in an over-2, under-2 weave. They are undecorated except for the texture of the plait. Both of the tie techniques described for the multiwarp sandals — the toe loop–ankle loop combination and the side loop–lacing arrangement — are found in most of the types. The details of manufacture and the size of the yucca leaves utilized differ significantly from one type to another and are the basis of the following classification.

Type 1 (10 whole and fragmentary; Fig. 78). Plaited sandals, wide leaves. From 4 to 12 yucca leaves are folded over at the toe end, forming a straight or nearly straight toe. The short ends are tied down on the lower or upper side of the sandal, inserted into the plait or, rarely, left projecting on the lower surface of the sandal and frayed out to form an additional pad under the foot. At the heel the ends are left trailing or are folded directly back into the weave, with an outside warp used as a base for folding the other over. Several specimens have irregular stitching with yucca leaves up the center portion, evidently to thicken the body. Two sandals, presumably a pair, have bundles of corn husks tucked inside the laced tie and arranged so that the foot would fit

inside the bundle (Fig. 78 *c*). Two other partly worn sandals are lashed together; they are uniformly larger than those in the other categories, and the lower surfaces are coated with mud. Also, despite their rectangular shape when manufactured, these sandals are stretched into foot-shapes as if they had been worn while wet. These features, combined with the corn husk pads noted, make these sandals appear to be overshoes to be worn in wet weather over other sandals or pads of material.

Length, 24–33 cm; width, 9–12 cm. Provenience: Broken Flute Cave (Cist 10, 8; Cist 50, 1); Pocket Cave (General, 1).

Type 2 (15 whole and fragmentary; Fig. 79 *a, c*). Twilled sandals, split or narrow leaves. From 8 to 16 leaves folded over at the toe end forming a straight toe. Short ends are incorporated into the over-2, under-2 twilled weave. Heels are finished by tying the warp elements into a large trailing knot. One specimen has rows of coarse stitching through the body of the sandal across the heel and toe areas, presumably for reinforcement. Two of these specimens probably constitute a pair. One miniature sandal was apparently a child's toy. Both of the previously described tie techniques are present on this group of sandals.

Length, 9–31 cm; width, 4–12 cm. Provenience: Broken Flute Cave (General, 6; Cist 44, 1; Cist 51, 1; Cist 52, 1; Cist 54, 2); Pocket Cave (General, 1; Pit House 4, 1); Cave 2 (Pit House 2, 1); Cave 11 (General, 1).

Type 3 (3 whole; Fig. 79 *b*). Twilled sandals of split or narrow leaves, with pointed toes. From 13 to 20 leaves are folded over at one end, forming a straight end on the sandal, and the ends of the leaves are incorporated into the weave. The other end is finished in a point that is off center. The ends are included in the weave or tied in a knot. The weave is an over-2, under-2 twilled technique. Two specimens are fastened to the foot by the loop–lace tie. Edges of one sandal trimmed in false braid by turning leaves alternately to the top and bottom of the sandal. Continuous rows of loops through which a tie might be passed for fastening the sandal to the foot are present along the edges.

Length, 24–29 cm; width, 11–13 cm. Provenience: Broken Flute Cave (General, 1); Pocket Cave (General, 1); Cave 2 (General, 1).

Type 4 (1 whole, 1 fragmentary). Twilled sandals of split or narrow leaves; round toes. About 25 strips of yucca tightly twilled in an over-2, under-2 weave. Toe rounded by shortening length of rows of twilling. Heels cupped and rounded; ends, not visible, included in twill. Edges finished in false braid or wrapped. The sandals were fastened onto the foot with a toe loop–ankle loop tie.

Length, 16 cm, 24 cm; width, 10 cm, 11 cm. Provenience: Cave 6 (General, 1); General (1).

Class C. Wickerwork sandals. These sandals have four

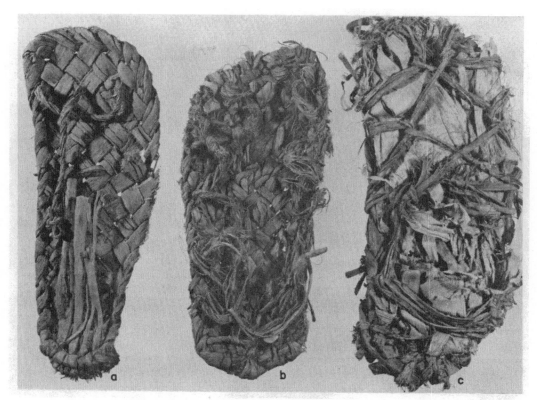

Fig. 78. Plaited sandals of yucca leaves. *c*, padded with corn husks. These may
have been sandals for wet or winter wear. Length of *c*, 30 cm.

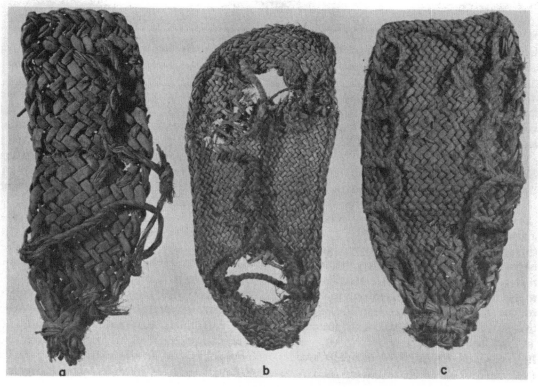

Fig. 79. Twilled sandals of yucca leaves. *a, c*, straight toe; *b*, pointed toe,
false braided edge. Length of *c*, 25 cm.

Fig. 80.   Wickerwork sandals. *a*, six warps of yucca leaves, crushed leaf weft; *b*, four warps of yucca fiber cordage, twisted fiber weft; *c*, six warps and weft of yucca leaves. Length of *c*, 29 cm.

or six parallel warps, and wefts that are twined over the outer warps and woven through the other warps with a plain weave. Weft ends are brought to the under side of the sole and frayed out, providing an additional pad for the foot. The toe loop–ankle loop tie and a variation of the side loop–lace tie are both used. The sandals differ in material, number of warps, and methods of lashing the ends.

Type 1 (1 whole; Fig. 80 *c*). Six-warp wickerwork sandals. Warps and wefts are composed of yucca leaves. Adjoining pairs are tied at one end and knotted to form a continuous finished edge at the other, with the ends brought back on top of the sandal. At intervals along the sides, two weft elements are pulled out to hold a single twisted yucca leaf lying parallel to the edge of the sandal; this probably served as part of the means of fastening it to the foot.

Length, 29 cm; width, 12 cm. Provenience: Cave 1 (Pit House 1).

Type 2 (2 whole; Fig. 80 *a*). Six-warp wickerwork sandals. Warps composed of yucca leaf strands, left as frayed out fringe at the toe end without being tied, knotted at heel end to form continuous finished band, ends folded under heel and frayed out to form an addi-

tional pad. The weft is composed of twisted crushed yucca leaves. At irregular intervals up one side of the sandal, a piece of crushed yucca leaf is brought up and over two weft elements and returned to the under side. The lack of wear on the sandal makes it doubtful that these elements were ever joined; apparently they served to add to the pad under the sole. Both specimens utilized a toe loop–ankle loop tie.

Length, 23 cm, 26 cm; width, 13 cm, 14 cm. Provenience: Obelisk Cave (General, 1); Cave 11 (General, 1).

Type 3 (1 whole; Fig. 80 *b*). Four-warp wickerwork sandals. Warps composed of two continuous strands of yucca fiber cordage, starting and finishing at the heel and running parallel around the toe. Warp pairs are knotted at the heel and resulting ends are knotted again. Weft composed of slightly twisted yucca fiber. The toe loop–ankle loop tie was utilized.

Length, 26 cm; width, 9.5 cm. Provenience: Pocket Cave (General).

Class D. Continuous outer warp sandal.

Type 1 (1 whole). This sandal is an anomalous type and may represent a temporary improvisation. The warp is a wide yucca leaf running in a horseshoe shape around

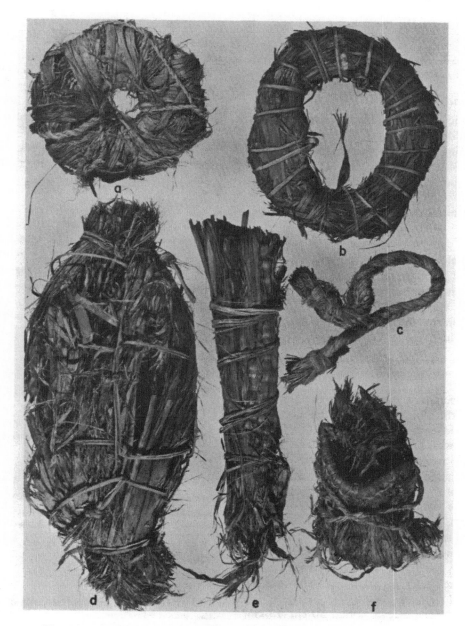

Fig. 81. Artifacts of juniper bark. *a*, head rest on cradle board; *b*, pot rest; *c*, braid; *d*, container; *e*, torch; *f*, apron. Length of *d*, 26 cm.

the bottom of the toe of the foot and left trailing at each end. Weft elements are wide yucca leaves folded over warp strands and plaited in an over-1, under-1 weave. The ends of the weft elements are left unaltered on the under side. Five wide yucca leaves are sewn through the plaited center section, forming a crude, open plain weave pattern over the plait, presumably to thicken the sandal. The only indications of fastenings are a set of holes that could have held a centrally located tie loop for two toes, and two holes at the sides near the heel where the ankle loop may have been secured.

Length, 16 cm; width, 8 cm. Provenience: Broken Flute Cave (General).

JUNIPER BARK AND SEEDS

Juniper bark was stripped from the trees and used as it was or shredded into a fine soft fiber. Large quantities of this material were a major constituent of the amorphous trash deposits in the caves.

Torches

Class A (6 whole and fragmentary; Fig. 81 *e*). Bundles of partly shredded bark, held together with individual ties spaced some distance apart or by a loose spiral wrap of juniper bark, yucca leaves, or fiber cordage. The individual fibers are tied parallel to one another, and the ends of all except the longest specimen are charred by burning.

Length, 22–40 cm; diameter, 3–8 cm. Provenience: Broken Flute Cave (General, 4); Cave 11 (General, 2).

Head Rests on Cradle Boards

Class A (3 whole; Fig. 81 *a*). Flat rings made of rolls of variously shredded bark. Base of ring formed with individual fibers, ring completely wrapped with bark tied in place by strands of yucca fiber and yucca fiber cord. These differ from pot rests by being markedly flattened.

Diameter, 9–20 cm; thickness, 2.5–3.5 cm. Provenience: Broken Flute Cave (General, 3).

Pot Rests

Class A (4 whole; Fig. 81 *b*). Ring-shaped rolls of variously shredded bark. Ring of individual fibers tied in place at intervals or spirally wrapped with pieces of yucca fiber.

Diameter, 13–20 cm; thickness, 2.2–4.5 cm. Provenience: Broken Flute Cave (General, 1; Cist 11, 1; Cist 54, 2).

Mats

Class A (2 fragmentary). Parallel strips of unshredded bark of equal width, joined at intervals by a single or double row of plain twined yucca leaves. One or two yucca leaves were woven across the bark elements with plain twining technique, presumably to the opposite side. The twining elements on one specimen are knotted at one edge; on the other, they are crossed over the end of the existing row of twining and are twisted on themselves for 3 to 5 cm, forming a slight loop along the edge before reentering the bark element. When a yucca leaf ended, a new one was inserted by twisting it or tying it onto the old one. A remaining mat end shows that bark elements were turned back on themselves and inserted into the end twined element.

Length present, 20 cm, 50 cm; width, 50 cm, 13 cm; thickness, 1 cm, 3 cm. Provenience: Broken Flute Cave (General, 1); Cave 10 (General, 1).

Container

Class A (1 whole; Fig. 81 *d*). A bundle of shredded bark, oblong in shape and round in section, is secured by a netting of yucca leaves. The interior cavity was filled with squash seeds. The yucca netting that wraps the bundle has a few elements running along the long axis, looped by others running along the short axis. Leaves were added on with square knots.

Length, 26 cm; diameter, 9.5 cm. Provenience: Cave 11 (General).

Aprons

Class A (5 whole and fragmentary; Fig. 81 *f*). Long flat bundles of finely shredded bark, one end looped over a string of 2-ply, S-twisted yucca fiber yarn. On some specimens the ends of the bark are folded over the string and the ends inserted in the bundle; on others they are fastened in place with a row of plain twining with cordage. The staining of the central portion of the bark strips indicates that they were worn by women during the menstrual period. Most were found rolled into neat bundles tied with the belt string.

Length of bundles, 10–12 cm; width, 4.8–7.5 cm. Provenience: Broken Flute Cave (General, 4); General (1).

Braided Cordage

Class A (9 fragmentary; Fig. 81 *c*). Bundles and pieces of 3-ply braided shredded bark. These strings were tightly made and had considerable strength. Because of the fragility of one charred bundle, its length could not be measured, but it was estimated at 250 cm.

Length, 20–250 cm; diameter, 1.0–1.5 cm. Provenience: Broken Flute Cave (General, 5; Cist 16, 1); Cave 10 (General, 1); unknown (2).

Strips Folded Over Stick

Class A (1 whole). Nine parallel pieces of bark folded over a stick and fastened in place with plain twined yucca cordage.

Length, 13.2 cm; width, 4.5 cm; thickness, 1.4 cm. Provenience: Broken Flute Cave (General).

Sandal Pad

Class A (1 whole). Bundle of juniper bark of a size and shape to act as a pad and cover for the foot in a sandal. The portion that would have been under the sole is matted and hard, as if used for some time.

Length, 23.5 cm; width, 10 cm; thickness, 2 cm. Provenience: General.

Knots

The four types recovered correspond to the types in the yucca fiber cordage.

Bundles of Bark

Class A (12 whole and fragmentary). These are lengths, rolls, twists, and masses of variously shredded bark, collected against time of need. Some are tied with cordage.

Length, 4.8–50.0 cm; diameter, 1.0–20.0 cm. Provenience: Broken Flute Cave (General, 2; Pit House 7, 1; Pit House 9, 2; Pit House 11, 1); Obelisk Cave (General, 1); unknown (5).

Juniper Seed Beads

Class A (2 lots). Juniper seed beads perforated for suspension. Drilling done from one side. One lot found in a small vessel with lateral spout.

Diameter, about 0.5 cm. Provenience: Broken Flute Cave (Pit House 9).

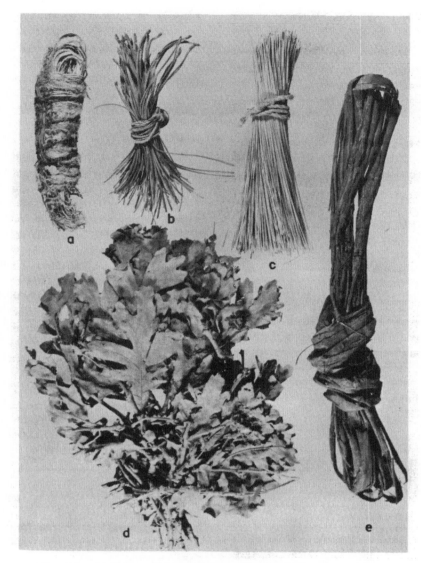

Fig. 82. Artifacts of sinew, pine needles, grass, oak leaves, and bark. *a*, sinew bundle; *b*, ponderosa pine needle broom; *c*, grass broom; *d*, bundle of oak leaves; *e*, bundle of bark. Length of *e*, 32 cm.

GRASS

Bunch grass growing on the valley floor was brought into the caves for occasional use. When dry it would have been too brittle to use as yucca fiber and juniper bark were used.

Mat

Class A (1 fragmentary; Nusbaum, Kidder, and Guernsey 1922: 98). Bundles of long grass stems fastened together by a plain twining technique. One end cut off or possibly broken off, other end folded over and caught in nearest three or four rows of twining; this edge has many seed heads of grass remaining. One side is frayed; to finish the other side, the ends of the twined elements were tied in a square knot and then crossed over each other and apparently lashed into the next twining element. The unfinished end has large loops of yucca leaf tied to the last row of twining and stretched as if a second layer of large loops had been fastened to them and used to suspend the mat off the ground.

Length, 65 cm; width, 60 cm; thickness, 2.5 cm. Provenience: Broken Flute Cave (General).

Brooms

Class A (4 whole and fragmentary; Fig. 82 *c*). Bundles of grass tied together with string or fiber. Tips on one end worn smooth through use.

Length, 15–25 cm; diameter, 1.0–2.5 cm. Provenience: Broken Flute Cave (General, 2); unknown (2).

PONDEROSA PINE NEEDLES

Broom

Class A (1 whole; Fig. 82 *b*). Bundle of ponderosa pine needles tied together with yucca fiber cordage. Pointed ends worn smooth through use.

Length, 13 cm; diameter, 1.4 cm. Provenience unknown.

OAK LEAVES

Bundle

Class A (1 whole; Fig. 82 *d*). Bundle of branch ends of Gambel oak with leaves remaining. Stems tied together with a piece of yucca leaf.

Length, 24.5 cm; width, 18 cm; thickness, 3 cm. Provenience: Broken Flute Cave (Cist 20).

BARK

Bundle

Class A (1 whole; Fig. 82 *e*). Bundle of lengths of dark brown bark stripped off thin twigs with very few branches, possibly elder. Bundle tied together with a strip of the same material. This could have been a source of dye, medicine, food, or construction material; whatever its purpose, it was recognized as useful and collected.

Length, 32 cm; diameter, 4.2 cm. Provenience: Broken Flute Cave (General).

ROOT

Class A (1 fragmentary). Piece of fibrous root.

Length, 24 cm; width, 4 cm; thickness, 1.5 cm. Provenience: Broken Flute Cave (General).

WOOD

Wood was one of the most commonly used materials in the artifactual inventory. The U.S. Bureau of Agriculture Forest Products Laboratory, Madison, Wisconsin, identified a selected sample of wood specimens as to genus, and in some cases, species. Most artifact classes included a range of kinds of wood, but there were some artifact groups in which material was a selective factor. A considerable variety of bushes, shrubs, and trees were identified:

Barberry, *Berberis*
Carrizo cane, *Phragmites vulgaris*
Cypress, *Cupressus*
Hop sage, *Grayia*
Mountain Mahogany, *Cercocarpus*
Oak, *Quercus*
Silk tassel, *Garrya*
Willow, *Salix*
Yellow pine, *Pinus ponderosa*

The selection of certain plants for particular items implies a recognition of the limitations and potentialities, in terms of size and physical characteristics, of each

kind. Some wooden artifacts retained none of the original shape of the pieces from which they were fashioned, but they were in the minority. Most of the specimens were sticks of varying lengths and diameters with one or both ends altered. In most cases, the protuberances on the shafts were cut or broken off, and the shafts of some were polished by repeated handling.

Bows

Class A (1 whole, 6 fragmentary; Fig. 83 *a*). Long slender pieces of wood, rectanguloid to plano-convex in section, tapering toward ends. Single whole specimen is unfinished. Slightly curved, convex side flattened, longitudinal cutting scars remaining on face. Concave surface is unaltered peeled branch. Fragmentary specimens are five tips and a midsection. Tips taper toward end, are rectanguloid in section, have squared off ends, and are smoothed on all surfaces. One end has notches in sides to hold string. Absence of notches in other specimens may be a pattern or may indicate misidentification. One specimen has pitch on untapered end, as if used to stir or apply pitch after being broken. The midportion is rectangular in section and broken at both ends; all surfaces are smoothed by grinding.

Length of whole specimen, 173 cm; width of tips, 1.0–1.8 cm; width of middles, 1.8–3.5 cm; thickness of ends, 0.4–1.1 cm; thickness of middles, 1.0–2.5 cm. Provenience: Broken Flute Cave (General, 2; Cist 54, 1); Obelisk Cave (General, 4).

Arrow Parts

The remains of the arrows, although numerous, are largely fragmentary. All are portions of compound arrows composed of wooden foreshafts and cane mainshafts. Rarely, a feathered wooden aftershaft is fitted into a proximal end of a cane mainshaft. The proximal ends of the solid wood foreshafts are tenoned and tapered, or gradually tapered to fit into the hollow cane mainshafts. The distal ends are ground to a point, notched to take a projectile point, or left with a large flat head (for stunning small game). The mainshafts are made of cane bound with sinew at the ends and at frequent intervals to prevent splitting. Some have shallow V-shaped nocks cut in the proximal end to hold the bow string. In some specimens, a wooden nock plug is set into the proximal end with its end flush with the cane and both members grooved. Other mainshafts are squared off and wrapped, presumably to receive aftershafts. Aftershafts are solid pieces of wood with a shallow nock in the proximal end and feathers tied along the shaft. The narrow, deep, U-shaped notches for projectile points are easily distinguished from nocks for strings, which are shallow, wide, and V-shaped in section. The size of the sample and the lack of gradation between the types make this distinction clear. One fore-

Fig. 83. **Bow and arrow specimens.** *a*, tip of bow stave; *b*, atlatl(?) mainshaft; *c*, atlatl(?) foreshaft, notched; *d*, foreshaft, tapered proximal end, notched tip; *e*, *f*, foreshafts, tenoned proximal end, rounded tip; *g*, foreshaft bunt; *h*, mainshaft, distal end; *i*, mainshaft, nocked proximal end; *j*, mainshaft, nocked proximal end, nock plug remaining; *k*, aftershaft. Length of *b*, 32.2 cm.

shaft, one mainshaft, and one solid wooden dart are classified as parts of atlatl shafts on the basis of size, but no other indication of the presence of atlatls was found.

FORESHAFTS

Class A (18 whole and fragmentary; Fig. 83 *e*, *f*). Pointed tip; tenoned (4), tapered (9), or unfinished (5) proximal end; sharp tapered tip at distal end. Surfaces smoothed by grinding, some polished by use. Two

specimens bound with sinew at intervals along shaft for decoration or to prevent splitting. Mountain Mahogany and other materials were used.

Length, 16–35 cm; length from shoulder to proximal end, 4.7–10.4 cm; diameter, 0.5–1.1 cm. Provenience: Broken Flute Cave (General, 6; Pit House 10, 1; Pit House 16, 1; Cist 54, 1); Pocket Cave (General, 6); Obelisk Cave (General, 2); Cave 3 (General, 1).

Class B (14 whole and fragmentary; Fig. 83 *d*).

Notched tip; tenoned (2), tapered (9), or unfinished (3) proximal end. Shoulder to proximal end tapered and roughly smoothed by grinding. Remainder of shaft polished. Two specimens split at tip, half of notch missing. One specimen shows traces of pitch in notch and of ties on exterior for fastening point in place.

Length, 19.1–50.0 cm; diameter, 0.4–0.9 cm. Provenience: Broken Flute Cave (General, 1); Obelisk Cave (General, 4); Pocket Cave (General, 7); Cave 3 (General, 1); General (1).

Class C (4 fragmentary). Tapered proximal ends, distal ends unfinished.

Length, 21.5–27.9 cm; diameter, 0.6–0.7 cm. Provenience: Broken Flute Cave (General, 2); Pocket Cave (General, 1); General (1).

FORESHAFT BUNTS

Class A (5 whole, 1 fragmentary; Fig. 83 *g*). Large cylindrical tips, tapered proximal ends. Bunt ends made from original branch, slightly smoothed. Ends flat with rounded edges somewhat battered.

Length, 6.8–15.5 cm; diameter, 1.1–1.9 cm. Provenience: Broken Flute Cave (General, 1; Pit House 6, 5).

FORESHAFTS AND MAINSHAFTS

Class A (5 fragmentary). Distal ends of cane mainshafts, with tapered wooden foreshafts firmly inserted. Ends of cane wrapped with sinew. Tips of all except one specimen broken off, foreshafts inserted at least 3.5 cm into mainshafts.

Maximum length, 9.0–36.4 cm; maximum diameter, 0.7–1.2 cm; length of mainshaft, 9.0–15.4 cm; diameter of foreshaft, 0.4–0.6 cm. Provenience: Broken Flute Cave (General, 3); Obelisk Cave (General, 2).

MAINSHAFTS

The mainshafts are made of carrizo cane (*Phragmites vulgaris*), bound at intervals to prevent splitting.

Class A (15 fragmentary; Fig. 83 *h, i*). Fragments of mainshaft with one nocked end remaining. Shaft unaltered, end ground thin on exterior of socket and bound with sinew.

Length, 10.2–43.0 cm; exterior diameter, 0.8–1.3 cm; interior diameter, 0.5–0.8 cm. Provenience: Broken Flute Cave (General, 5); Obelisk Cave (General, 6); Cave 4 (General, 3); General (1).

Class B (2 fragmentary; Fig. 83 *j*). Mainshaft fragments with nock plug remaining. Wooden plug jammed firmly into proximal end. Wide, shallow, V-shaped nock has been cut into mainshaft and nock plug after insertion.

Length, 16.2 cm, 23.2 cm; diameter, 1 cm; length of plug, 10.3 cm, 15.2 cm; diameter of plug, 0.6 cm, 0.7 cm. Provenience: Obelisk Cave (General, 1); Cave 3 (General, 1).

Class C (2 whole). Nock plugs for proximal ends of cane mainshafts. Roughly smoothed by grinding.

Length, 10.9 cm, 17.6 cm; diameter, 0.5 cm, 0.6 cm. Provenience: Broken Flute Cave (Cist 16, 1); Obelisk Cave (General, 1).

AFTERSHAFTS

Class A (1 fragmentary; Fig. 83 *k*). Distal end tenoned and tapered to point. Three Red-shafted flicker feathers tied onto shaft with sinew. Tip of proximal end missing. Shaft may have been painted red along entire length.

Length, 29 cm; length from shoulder to tip, 7.9 cm; diameter, 0.5 cm. Provenience: Broken Flute Cave (General).

Atlatl Darts

The specimens described below were judged to be atlatl dart parts on the basis of their large diameter.

FORESHAFT

Class A (1 whole; Fig. 83 *c*). Smooth wood cylinder notched at distal end, tapered to rounded point at proximal end. Two thin dark lines painted around short axis of shaft.

Length, 25.4 cm; diameter, 1 cm. Provenience: Broken Flute Cave (Cist 13).

MAINSHAFT

Class A (1 whole; Fig. 83 *b*). Large piece of cane, bound at ends and at intervals with sinew.

Length, 32.2 cm; diameter, 1.2 cm. Provenience: Cave 3 (General).

DART (?)

Class A (1 whole). Solid shaft made from single piece of wood, tip slightly tapered and battered. V-shaped nock in proximal end.

Length, 10.5 cm; diameter, 1.2 cm. Provenience: Broken Flute Cave (General).

Snares

Class A (1 fragmentary; Fig. 84 *h*). Tapered wooden stake with groove cut around top. Heavy yucca fiber cord looped around stake with slip knot; the loose end, although lengthened by a square knot attaching another string, is broken off short. Probably this led to another stake.

Length, 21.6 cm; diameter, 1.8 cm. Provenience: Cave 3 (General).

Class B (1 whole; Guernsey and Kidder 1921: Plate 32). Long thin unworked stick. Yucca fiber cord tied to one end, run through a short piece of hollow cane, and tied to outside of cane, forming an easily closed loop. A short twig is tied midway along cord to keep cane from sliding up too far.

Length of stick, 80 cm; diameter of stick, 1.0 cm; length of string, 30 cm; diameter of string, 0.2 cm. Provenience unknown.

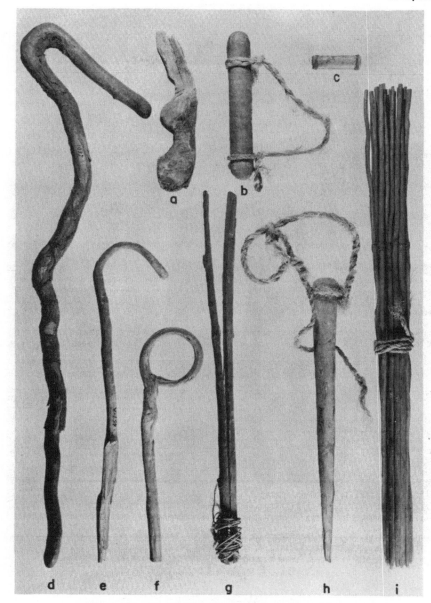

Fig. 84. **Miscellaneous artifacts of wood.** *a*, deeply grooved cylinder; *b*, grooved cylinder; *c*, game call; *d*, medium-length digging stick, cane-shaped head; *e*, *f*, prayer sticks (?); *g*, tongs; *h*, stake snare; *i*, bundle of snare sticks. Length of *d*, 41 cm.

Class C (2 bundles and 29 individual sticks; Fig. 84 *i*; Guernsey 1931: 82). Bundles of snare sticks. Two bundles of matched sticks, one with 16 and one with 18 pieces, each bundle tied together with yucca fiber cord. Bark removed from sticks, surface smoothed, one end tapered to point and other end squared off by grinding. Sticks wrapped with narrow band of sinew at some point between 9 and 12 cm from the squared end. Often the shaft near the tie is stained red. A number of individual sticks that were found fit this description specifically and must be from scattered sets. Most commonly used material is Hop-sage.

Length, 25.5–38.5 cm; diameter, 0.3–0.4 cm. Provenience: Broken Flute Cave (General, 3; Pit House 4, 2;

Pit House 10, 2); Obelisk Cave (General, 12 and 2 bundles); Pocket Cave (General, 2); Cave 3 (General, 3); General (5).

Awls

Class A (11 whole; Fig. 85 *c*, *f–h*). Split sticks, bark usually removed. Working end ground to tapering point, shaft smoothed by grinding and use, head rounded. One specimen has a knobbed head (Fig. 85 *g*); one head is wrapped with string (Fig. 85 *f*). Two specimens have identically crooked shafts.

Length, 12.0–23.5 cm; diameter, 1.0–2.8 cm. Provenience: Broken Flute Cave (General, 1; Pit House 8, 1; Pit House 10, 1; Cist 46, 1; Cist 50, 3); Pocket Cave (General, 1); Obelisk Cave (General, 3).

Fig. 85. Miscellaneous artifacts of wood. *a, b, l,* spatulas; *c,* awl, crooked shaft; *d, e,* grooved pointed sticks (butchering tools?); *f,* awl, head wrapped with string; *g,* awl, knob on head; *h,* awl; *i, j, k,* wedges. Length of *d,* 28 cm.

Long Pointed Sticks

Class A (2 whole). Slender sticks or split branches, one end ground to tapering tip, shaft slightly smoothed.

Length, 30 cm, 50 cm; diameter, 0.6 cm, 1.3 cm. Provenience: Broken Flute Cave (General, 1); Obelisk Cave (General, 1).

Long Grooved Pointed Sticks

Class A (12 whole and fragmentary; Fig. 85 *d, e*). Slender twigs or split branches, one end ground to tapered tip, other end roughly rounded. Shafts irregularly grooved at intervals from middle to tip; these grooves are V-shaped, some deep and some shallow. Shafts and tips do not show much polishing. The tools are covered with a crust of some organic material. It is

possible that they were used in skinning and butchering animals.

Length, 16–43 cm; diameter, 0.7–1.7 cm. Provenience: Broken Flute Cave (General, 4; Pit House 8, 2; Pit House 9, 1; Cist 16, 1; Cist 20, 1; Cist 47, 1; Cist 54, 1); General (1).

Spatulas

Class A (3 whole; Fig. 85 *a, b, l*). Split branches, one end ground to thin rectangular blade the same width as the shaft, the other smoothed by grinding. One specimen (Fig. 85 *l*) has a large head. Smoothed all over by grinding, not polished through use, working surface distinctly rough.

Length, 17.6–27.6 cm; width, 1.4–2.2 cm; thickness,

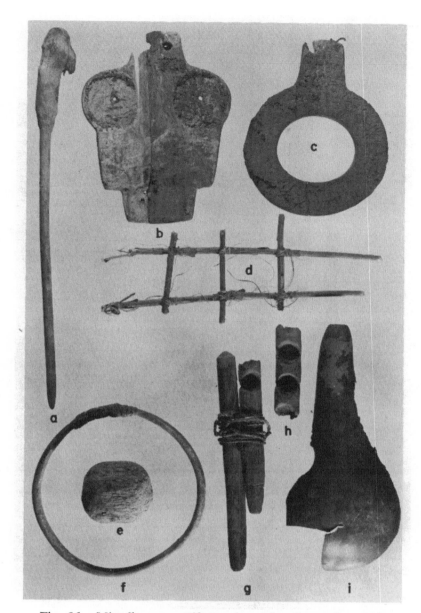

Fig. 86. Miscellaneous artifacts of wood and gourd. *a*, hair ornament; *b, c*, mosaic pendant backs; *d*, miniature ladder; *e*, ball; *f*, hoop; *g*, fire hearth and drill set; *h*, fire hearth; *i*, gourd bottle fragment. Length of *a*, 23 cm.

0.8–1.9 cm. Provenience: Obelisk Cave (General, 2); Cave 3 (General, 1).

Fire Drills and Hearths

Class A (19 whole and fragmentary, 3 sets; Fig 86 *g, h*). Cylindrical pieces of wood, surfaces smoothed, ends rounded off. Drills and hearths often made of the same piece of wood. Ends of drills rounded by grinding and blackened through use. One prepared but unused tip is slightly more conical in shape. Hearths have conical fire-blackened sockets placed irregularly along length.

Sides of holes are broken and holes almost perforate hearth. Unblackened sockets are shallow and one side is notched by cutting. Hearths are frequently broken at a used socket. One hearth end is grooved and has a string tied around it. Three examples of a drill and hearth tied together were noted. Wood used was willow root.

Length, 3.1–45.0 cm; diameter, 0.7–1.5 cm. Provenience: Broken Flute Cave (General, 12; Pit House 4, 1; Pit House 8, 1; Pit House 9, 2; Pit House 11, 2); Pocket Cave (General, 2); Cave 3 (General, 1); Cave 6 (General, 1).

Fig. 87.   Miscellaneous artifacts of wood. *a*, one-hole flute; *b*, miniature five-hole flute; *c*, *d*, *e*, prayer sticks; *f*, scarifier with chalcedony blade and piece of corncob lashed on as handle; *g*, scarifier with bone sliver blade; *h*, *i*, twig loops. Length of *g*, 19 cm.

Scarifiers or Lancets

Class A (2 whole; Fig. 87 *f*, *g*; Guernsey 1931: 109). Split twigs, with blade inserted perpendicular to long axis — a sliver of long bone in one twig and a chalcedony flake in the other. The blades are held in place by a string or yucca leaf binding the halves of the twig together. Sticks otherwise unworked; bone tapered at tip by grinding, flake slightly chipped on one side of point. Corn cob tied to one twig to make handle.

Length of stick, 19 cm, 38 cm; length of flake, 1.4 cm; length of bone, 5.8 cm; diameter of stick, 0.8 cm, 1.2 cm; width of blade, 0.8 cm, 1.3 cm. Provenience: Broken Flute Cave (Cist 54, 1); Obelisk Cave (General, 1).

Spoons

Class A (1 whole, 1 fragmentary). Branches, smoothed on all surfaces, symmetrical oblong depression gouged out of one side of one end. Edges and sur-

Fig. 88. Cylindrical wooden box for feathers, shown both closed and open, and its contents (collection of the American Museum of Natural History). Length, 50 cm.

faces smoothed by grinding. Whole specimen has a shoulder, with the handle smaller in diameter; other specimen has thinner walls on bowl of spoon.

Whole specimen: length, 31.5 cm; length of bowl, 8.5 cm; width, 4 cm; width of bowl, 3 cm. Provenience: Broken Flute Cave (Pit House 6, 1; Pit House 9, 1).

Cylindrical Boxes

Class A (1 whole, 1 fragmentary; Fig. 88; Nusbaum, Kidder, and Guernsey 1922: 116). Branch with bark removed, ends cut off square. Center hollowed out by cutting, leaving solid portion at each end. An oval slit on one side the same length as the cavity serves as opening; its edges are rounded and smoothed. The interior of the cylinder is rough and shows scars of the manufacturing process. The whole specimen was filled with bundles of feathers and a prayer stick. The opening was covered with a piece of hide, which was tied in place with string. The specimen was recovered by the Bernheimer Expedition and is in the collection of the American Museum of Natural History. Material is oak and box elder.

Length, 32 cm, 50 cm; length of cavity, 17 cm, 44 cm; diameter, 4 cm, 6 cm; diameter of cavity, 3.3 cm, 4.2 cm. Provenience: Obelisk Cave (General, 1); General (1).

Cradle

Class A (1 whole; Fig. 89). Made of slender parallel twigs tied across the back of an oval wooden hoop. Eight parallel twigs are closely laid together at right angles to the backing twigs near the center of the cradle. These are held in place with string looped around the two sets of twigs to form a design of contiguous diamonds (see Fig. 89). This specimen was recovered by the Bernheimer Expedition and is in the collection of the American Museum of Natural History.

Dimensions are unavailable and its provenience is unknown.

Dice Set

Class A (17 in set, and one disk; Fig. 44 *a, a', f*). Smooth oblong pieces of wood and a round disk in a hide sack. Dice and disk have a light side and a dark

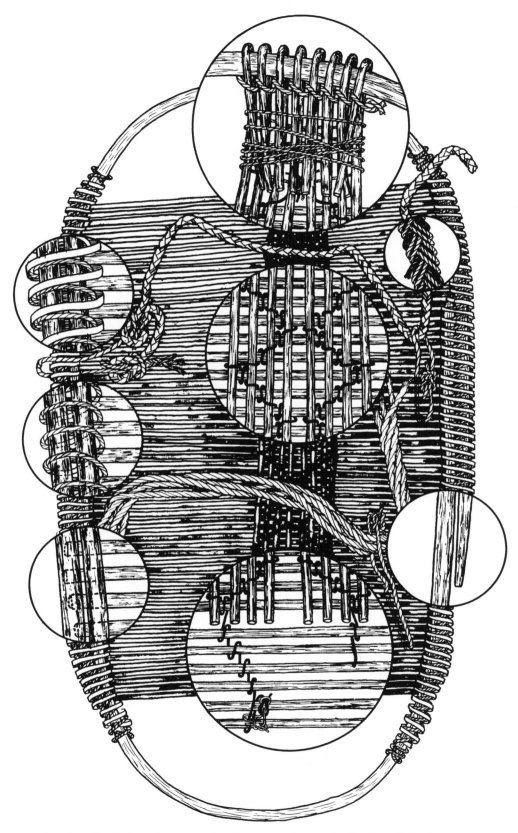

Fig. 89. Cradle board showing details of manufacture (collection of the American Museum of Natural History). Drawing by Robert F. Burgh.

side. Most of the dark sides formed by scoring at right angles to the long axis and rubbing with some substance. On two dice the dark side is unaltered bark. The light sides of two dice have burned decorations (see Fig. 44 *a'*).

Length of dice, 2.7–4.5 cm; width of dice, 0.7–0.9 cm; thickness of dice, 0.2–0.3 cm; diameter of disk, 1.5 cm; thickness of disk, 0.8 cm. Provenience: General.

Hair Ornaments

Class A (4 whole and fragmentary; Fig. 86 *a*). Long thin skewers, one end gradually tapered to blunt point, formed from natural twigs. Heads slightly smoothed, bent naturally to one side, with or without bark. Two specimens have hooklike protuberances on concave sides; these resemble foreshaft bunts but lack the battering on the cylindrical end and would have flown an irregular course because of the marked lack of symmetry.

Length, 13.4–23.0 cm; diameter, 1.6–2.1 cm. Provenience: Broken Flute Cave (General, 3); Obelisk Cave (General, 1).

Mosaic Pendant Backs

Class A (2 whole, 2 fragmentary; Fig. 86 *b, c*). Circular rings of wood with a rectanguloid projection on one side; one whole specimen has a geometric shape. Smoothed on all surfaces and edges by grinding. Both whole specimens perforated in two places for suspension, with one of the holes on each broken out. One side of each smeared with pitch, which held the decorative material in place. Two similar rings, set with turquoise, lignite, and shell, were found in Basketmaker burials in Canyon de Chelly by Earl Morris (1925: 273). The decorative materials must have been removed from the Prayer Rock pieces when the suspension holes broke. Several of the carefully worked disks and rectangles of shell and bone would have served nicely, but no suitable pieces of turquoise were found.

Length, 10.2–11.7 cm; width, 4.6–8.7 cm; thickness, 0.7 cm. Provenience: Broken Flute Cave (Pit House 8a, 3); Obelisk Cave (General, 1).

Human Figurines

Class A (3 whole, 1 fragmentary; Fig. 92 *a–c*). Three tabular rectangular pieces split from larger branch, and one cylindrical piece of wood smoothed by grinding. Each has a loin cloth of corn husk that is wrapped around the waist, passed down as if through the crotch and back up through the belt, and then tucked under the vertical element in back in the shape of a large coil. No features or limbs are discernible.

Length, 4.7–7.7 cm; width, 1.4–2.1 cm; thickness, 0.7–1.0 cm. Provenience: Broken Flute Cave (in front of the Great Kiva Circle, 3); Cave 8 (General, 1).

Prayer Sticks

Class A (3 whole; Figs. 87 *c–e*, 88; Guernsey 1931: Plate 49; Guernsey and Kidder 1921: Plate 18). Bundle of two to four smoothed and pointed sticks bound together. On one specimen (Fig. 87 *c*), many feathers and pieces of bird skin held by tiny strings fastened into the bindings in many places. Other specimens fastened with string or carrizo cane leaf.

Length, 7.7–22.7 cm; diameter, 1.2–2.2 cm. Provenience: Pocket Cave (Pit House 4, 1); Obelisk Cave (General, 1); Cave 4 (General, 1).

Class B (1 whole). Thin twig, feather lashed to one end with a yucca leaf. Tip of stick and tip of feather missing.

Length, 17 cm; diameter, 0.5 cm. Provenience: Broken Flute Cave (Pit House 7).

Class C (2 fragmentary; Fig. 84 *e, f*). Thin prayer sticks (?), one with cane-shaped head like miniature digging stick, the other with a looped head. Sticks unsmoothed.

Length, 18 cm, 24 cm; diameter, 1 cm. Provenience: Broken Flute Cave (Pit House 7, 1; Pit House 11, 1).

Twig Loops

Class A (6 whole and fragmentary; Fig. 87 *h, i*). Thin twigs with bark remaining, bent double, and the ends tied together for some distance, leaving a loop at the end.

Length, 9.4–26.0 cm; width, 0.8–5.2 cm; diameter of loop, 2–6 cm. Provenience: Broken Flute Cave (General, 3; Pit House 11, 1; Cist 13, 1; Cist 57, 1).

Class B (1 whole). Bundle of looped twigs. Seven tiny single twigs looped by tying ends together with split yucca leaves. Loops tied together with a knotted yucca leaf.

Length, 11 cm; width, 0.6 cm. Provenience: Broken Flute Cave (Cist 54).

Hoops

Class A (2 whole; Fig. 86 *f*). Twigs bent into a circle and tied together. The illustrated hoop is a complete twig and has been neatly tied with sinew. The other is a split twig and has been crudely tied with a yucca leaf.

Diameter, 6.8 cm, 10.4 cm; thickness, 0.5 cm, 0.7 cm. Provenience: Broken Flute Cave (General, 1); Cave 9 (General, 1).

Ball

Class A (1 whole; Fig. 86 *e*; Kidder and Guernsey 1919: 186; Guernsey and Kidder 1921: Plate 36). Nearly spherical piece of soft wood, from the heart of a branch, shaped by grinding.

Diameter, 3.8 cm. Provenience: Broken Flute Cave (General).

Rabbit Stick

Class A (1 whole; Guernsey 1931: 89). Gently curved, flattened stick, oval in section, surfaces and edges rounded by grinding. Handle has groove near end. The piece was split in prehistoric times and was tied together with sinew near the handle. Each surface has four parallel carved grooves following the shape of the curved wood; these are discontinuous, leaving a smooth surface on both faces slightly toward handle from middle of specimen. Handle end smeared with pitch. The possibility that these are fending sticks for atlatl darts is supported by the unscarred surface of this specimen.

Length, 51.5 cm; width, 3 cm; thickness, 1.3 cm. Provenience: Cave 10 (General).

Flutes and Whistles

Class A (4 whole, 4 fragmentary). Long cylindrical tubes of box elder wood, polished through use. Six holes placed as two groups of three holes each nearer one end than the other. Bird feathers tied with yucca fiber cord to ends of two flutes found tied together in cache. Ends tied with sinew and insides smeared with pitch to prevent splitting. See Morris (1959a) for complete discussion and illustration.

Length, 68–74 cm; diameter, 2.6–2.8 cm. Provenience: Broken Flute Cave (General, 1; Pit House 4, 2; Cist 7, 2; Cist 20, 1); Obelisk Cave (General, 1); unknown (1).

Class B (1 whole; Fig. 87 *b*). Piece of carrizo cane with five holes of varying sizes burned in irregular row up the side, ends rough. May be child's copy of a flute.

Length, 12.3 cm; diameter, 0.8 cm. Provenience: Cave 3 (General).

Class C (2 fragmentary; Fig. 87 *a*). Piece of carrizo cane and piece of hollowed-out box elder wood, each with one hole. Ends ground off square and thinned through grinding on the exterior. Hole in cane near one end; hole in box elder near center. Shrill notes can be produced by blowing diagonally against far wall of one end.

Length, 17.8 cm, 19.3 cm; diameter, 0.9 cm, 1.4 cm. Provenience: Broken Flute Cave (General, 1); Obelisk Cave (General, 1).

Reworked Flute Fragments

Class A (2 fragmentary). Pieces of box elder, of the size and shape of flute barrels, split along long axis. Ends ground off square.

Length, 3.5 cm, 7.8 cm; width, 2.3 cm, 2.5 cm; thickness, 0.8 cm, 1.2 cm. Provenience: Broken Flute Cave (General, 2).

Game Call

Class A (1 whole; Fig. 84 *c*). Short cylindrical piece of wood, split down the center, faces smoothed and tied together with sinew so that membrane is held between them by the ends. Rounded sides of ends grooved for sinew. Blowing on crack produces reedy, high-pitched call, like the sounds produced by various modern game calls.

Length, 3.5 cm; diameter, 1 cm. Provenience: Pocket Cave (General).

Tongs

Class A (4 whole; Fig. 84 *g*). Split unworked branches bent double. Ends on each pair about the same length, charred through use. The specimen illustrated has string tied around it near head.

Length, 22–30 cm; diameter, 1.1–2.0 cm. Provenience: Obelisk Cave (General, 3); Cave 3 (General, 1).

Drill Shaft

Class A (1 whole). Piece of cane with chert drill set into one end and lashed in place with yucca fiber cord. Cane unworked.

Length, 47 cm; diameter, 0.7 cm. Provenience unknown.

Beamer

Class A (1 whole). Split branch, flattened by cutting with a stone blade. Ends unaltered, center of one edge thinned by grinding on both sides, polished on edge and immediate faces by use.

Length, 28.8 cm; width, 1.9 cm; thickness, 1.1 cm. Provenience: Cave 9 (General).

Knife Hafts

Class A (2 whole). Somewhat tapered oval and cylindrical sticks, smoothed all over by grinding. Groove in large end to take blade. One specimen has stone blade set in place with pitch and tied with sinew. One has four rows of short cuts on one side.

Length, 9.5 cm, 10.0 cm; width, 1.7 cm; thickness, 1.2 cm, 1.5 cm. Provenience: Broken Flute Cave (Pit House 9, 2).

Wrench

Class A (1 whole). Heavy unshaped piece of branch, flattened on one side by cutting. Perforated through center with large hole, which shows signs of some smoothing through use on interior edge.

Length, 31.5 cm; width, 5.8 cm; thickness, 3.7 cm. Provenience: Broken Flute Cave (Pit House 7, 1).

Digging Sticks

Digging sticks like these have been found in most Basketmaker caves (Guernsey and Kidder 1921: Plate 37).

Class A (7 whole, 6 fragmentary; Fig. 90 *a*). Straight, slender shaft, pointed tip. Smoothed all over from grind-

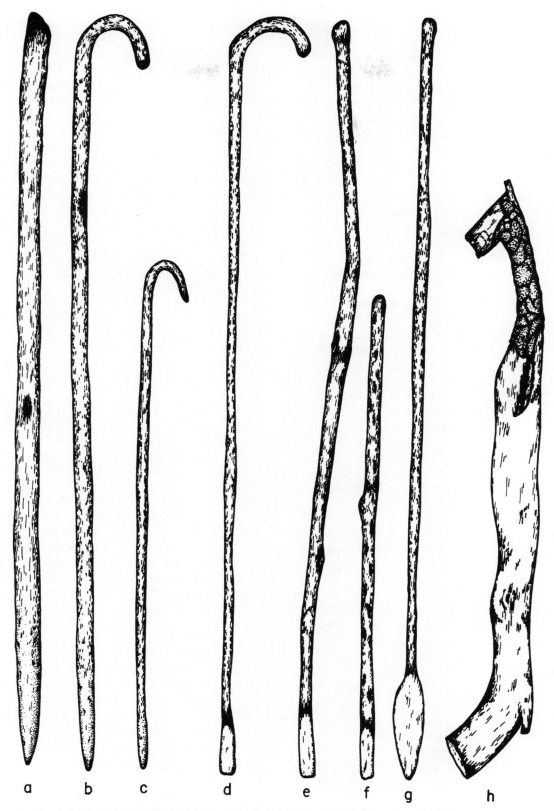

Fig. 90.   Digging sticks. *a*, long straight shaft, pointed tip; *b*, long shaft, cane-shaped head, pointed tip; *c*, medium length shaft, cane-shaped head, pointed tip; *d*, long shaft, cane-shaped head, blade tip; *e*, long crooked shaft, blade tip; *f*, medium length shaft, blade tip; *g*, long shaft, wide blade tip; *h*, seed beater(?). Length of *c*, 36.4 cm.

ing and use. Tip tapered and rounded. Material mostly Hop-sage and Mountain mahogany.

Length, 60.0–128.5 cm; diameter, 1.0–1.8 cm. Provenience: Broken Flute Cave (Pit House 4, 1; Pit House 9, 1; Pit House 16, 2; Cist 7, 2); Obelisk Cave (General, 6); Pocket Cave (General, 1).

Class B (6 whole, 5 fragmentary; Figs. 84 *d*, 90 *b*, *c*). Cane-shaped, pointed tip. Shafts and ends smoothed by grinding and polished through use. Tips ground to rounded point. Two specimens naturally bent at head.

Length, 36.4–89.5 cm; diameter, 0.6–3.2 cm. Provenience: Broken Flute Cave (General, 1; Pit House 7, 1; Pit House 11, 3; Cist 9, 1; Cist 20, 1); Pocket Cave (General, 1; Pit House 4, 1); Cave 10 (General, 1); General (1).

Class C (1 whole; Fig. 90 *d*). Cane-shaped, blade-tipped. Tip of point flattened to rounded edge by grinding.

Length, 146 cm; diameter, 2 cm. Provenience: Broken Flute Cave (Cist 7).

Class D (6 whole, 8 fragmentary; Fig. 90 *e*). Straight or somewhat crooked shaft, often knobby; smoothed by grinding and polished through use. Blade pointed with rounded edges, flattened by grinding on both sides.

Length, 90–108 cm; diameter 1.5–3.0 cm. Provenience: Broken Flute Cave (General, 4; Cist 20, 3; Cist 57, 1); Obelisk Cave (General, 2); Pocket Cave (Pit House 3, 3); Cave 8 (General, 1).

Class E (10 whole and fragmentary; Fig. 90 *f*). Straight shaft, flat blade, intermediate length. Shaft and proximal end smoothed by grinding, blade flattened by grinding on both sides, edges and tip rounded.

Length, 41.5–61.0 cm; diameter, 1.8–2.5 cm. Provenience: Broken Flute Cave (General, 2; Pit House 8, 1; Pit House 9, 1; Cist 44, 1); Obelisk Cave (General, 3); Cave 10 (General, 1); unknown (1).

Wedges

Class A (4 whole; Fig. 85 *i*, *k*). Straight short shaft, flat blade, end tied with cord or yucca leaves to form handle and to keep from splitting. Shafts smoothed by grinding or through use, blades flattened by grinding on both surfaces. Heads battered and flattened by pounding.

Length, 18.8 cm, 30.0 cm; diameter, 2.0 cm, 2.7 cm. Provenience: Broken Flute Cave (General, 1); Pocket Cave (General, 3).

Class B (3 whole). Straight short shaft, flat blade, natural knob left on end for handle. Shafts smoothed by grinding and through use. Blade flattened by grinding on both sides, tip and edges rounded, head battered and flattened.

Length, 16.8–29.8 cm; diameter, 1.6–2.5 cm. Provenience: Broken Flute Cave (General, 2); Obelisk Cave (General, 2); Cave 3 (General, 2).

Class C (10 whole; Fig. 85 *j*). Straight short shaft, flat blade. Shafts and ends slightly smoothed, blades

flattened by grinding on both sides. Head battered and flattened.

Length, 18.4–34.8 cm; diameter 2.0–3.2 cm. Provenience: Broken Flute Cave (General, 3; Cist 9, 1; Cist 20, 1; Cist 50, 1); Obelisk Cave (General, 3); Cave 3 (General, 3).

Seed Beaters

Class A (1 whole, 4 fragmentary). Long shaft with wide blade at distal end. Tip at one edge of blade, curved convex sharpened edges along other edge. Blade shouldered onto shaft, flattened by grinding on two surfaces.

Length, 11.1–96.5 cm; width, 5–7 cm; thickness, 0.8–1.5 cm. Provenience: Broken Flute Cave (General, 1; Pit House 6, 1); Obelisk Cave (General, 1); Cave 2 (Pit House 2, 1); Cave 5 (General, 1).

Class B (1 whole; Fig. 90 *h*). Specimen with long shaft, concave working surface, is probably a seed beater. Tip of blade shaped like hockey stick. Blade flattened on both sides by grinding. Edges, except for concave edge, squared off. Bark left on short round handle, hook on end formed by cut branch.

Length, 74.4 cm; width, 11.5 cm; thickness, 3.5 cm. Provenience: Obelisk Cave (General).

Boards

Artifacts of this type have been found in many Basketmaker sites — for instance, DuPont Cave (Nusbaum, Kidder, and Guernsey 1922: Plate 59).

Class A (2 whole). Curved thin boards. Made of split branches, ground very thin. Surfaces, edges, and ends somewhat rounded and smoothed by grinding.

Length, 22.4 cm, 38.6 cm; width, 3.3 cm, 5.3 cm; thickness, 0.8 cm, 1.0 cm. Provenience: Broken Flute Cave (General, 1); Cave 11 (General, 1).

Class B (2 whole). Paddle-shaped boards with short handle. Blade rectanguloid with rounded corners, shaped by grinding and cutting. Blade as thick as handle and a little wider.

Length, 17.3 cm, 16.9 cm; width, 3.9 cm, 5.3 cm; thickness, 1.0 cm, 1.7 cm. Provenience: Broken Flute Cave (General, 2).

Class C (16 whole and fragmentary). Oblong to rectangular in shape and section. Surfaces worked by cutting and grinding. Possibly some shaping by burning.

Measurements unavailable. Provenience: Broken Flute Cave (General, 8; Cist 13, 1; Cist 16, 1; Cist 20, 1; Cist 52, 1); Pocket Cave (Pit House 3, 1); Cave 3 (General, 1); Cave 11 (General, 2).

Class D (4 whole). Split boards, ends cut off. No smoothing or signs of use on three; one long specimen ground smooth on both surfaces at one end.

Length, 16.4–21.5 cm and 99 cm; width, 5.0–9.9 cm; thickness, 1.4–3.6 cm. Provenience: Broken Flute Cave (Pit House 11, 1; Cist 54, 1); Pocket Cave (General, 1); Obelisk Cave (General, 1).

Ladder Pole

Class A (1 fragmentary). Long straight pole with a light stick bound to it at regular intervals with split twigs. At one end of each gap in the binding, the light stick has been pulled out of shape by the now-missing rung. The light stick is thinned by cutting on the inside where it is warped out of shape. Rungs would have been about 27 cm apart and 1.1 cm in diameter.

Length, 86 cm; diameter, 4.1 cm. Provenience: Broken Flute Cave (Cist 9).

Miniature Ladder

Class A (1 fragmentary; Fig. 86 *d*). Uprights formed from twigs, rungs of same material tied between uprights with split yucca leaves. Ends unsmoothed, tying neatly done.

Length, 17.5 cm; width, 6.4 cm; thickness, 1.1 cm. Provenience: Broken Flute Cave (General).

Hook

Class A (1 whole). Stick with branch projecting near one end. Bark removed, surface of stick unaltered, ends cut off. Acute angle where branch juts out deeply worn by abrasion as if by a cord or a narrow strip of hide.

Length, 31 cm; diameter, 2 cm. Provenience: General.

V-Shaped Object

Class A (1 whole). Split branch fork, flattened and smoothed by grinding, ends rounded, edges somewhat smoothed. Base of fork slightly protuberant and rounded.

Length, 18 cm; width, 14 cm; thickness, 2.2 cm. Provenience: Broken Flute Cave (General).

Grooved Cylinders

Class A (6 whole and fragmentary; Fig. 84 *b*). Short thick cylindrical sticks, surfaces well smoothed by intention and use, ends irregularly rounded off. Midsections deeply to barely grooved by abrasion from a cord. The grooves are narrow, spiraled noncontinuously, and only roughly parallel. The illustrated specimen has a short braided yucca cord tied from one end to the other. One specimen has deep conical holes along the long axis in each end. Most specimens are Mountain mahogany.

Length, 10.7–15.0 cm; diameter, 1.4–4.3 cm. Provenience: Broken Flute Cave (General, 1; Pit House 16, 1); Obelisk Cave (General, 2); Cave 3 (General, 2).

Class B (5 whole; Fig. 84 *a*). Short thick sticks, ends smoothed by abrasion, surfaces smoothed by use. All specimens have a deep, wide, V-shaped groove worn parallel to short axis on one side; the illustrated specimen has a second groove, broken through at one end. Working surfaces and parts of sticks seem to be stained yellow from natural dye in the wood. Material is Barberry.

Length, 7.1–12.8 cm; diameter, 1.7–4.2 cm; width of grooves, 2.2–4.5 cm; depth of grooves, 0.4–1.0 cm. Provenience: Obelisk Cave (General, 4); Cave 3 (General, 1).

Worked Cylinders

Class A (12 whole and fragmentary). Short, thick worked cylinders. Some shafts and ends are smoothed by grinding or show marks of cutting.

Length, 7.8–15.6 cm; diameter, 0.8–2.5 cm. Provenience: Broken Flute Cave (General, 3; Pit House 4, 1; Pit House 9, 2; Cist 44, 1; Cist 52, 2); Obelisk Cave (General, 2); Cave 3 (General, 1).

Incised Sticks

Class A (11 whole and fragmentary). Cylindrical sticks with bark removed and ends cut off. Ends and surfaces somewhat smoothed. Many short nonparallel incisions on one side or all sides, as if stick had been held behind something being cut.

Length, 5.7–46.0 cm; diameter, 0.7–3.6 cm. Provenience: Broken Flute Cave (General, 3; Pit House 4, 3; Pit House 11, 1; Cist 16, 1); Cave 3 (General, 3).

Class B (1 whole). Cylindrical branch incised all over surface with continuous lines forming cross-hatched design. One end rounded.

Length, 5.4 cm; diameter, 1 cm. Provenience: Pocket Cave (General).

Class C (1 fragmentary). Cylindrical stick, surface and remaining finished end smoothed by grinding. Other end shouldered, tapering to slender shaft, which is broken. Incised zigzag line around complete end, two parallel rows of dots a short distance below it.

Length, 13.8 cm; diameter, 3.9 cm. Provenience: Obelisk Cave (General).

Stick with Burned Decoration

Class A (1 fragmentary). Split twig with bark left on, ends ground off square. Flat surface has burned line along short axis near each end. Space between lines filled with closely spaced burned dots.

Length, 12.5 cm; width, 1.3 cm; thickness, 0.6 cm. Provenience: General.

Worked Sticks

Class A (38 whole and fragmentary). Sticks and twigs of varying lengths and diameters. Ends usually rounded, flattened, squared off, or pointed by grinding. Some shafts rough, some split, and some polished. Some have string, yucca leaves, or juniper bark tied around shaft.

Length, 7.6–66.6 cm; diameter, 0.5–3.5 cm. Provenience: Broken Flute Cave (General, 17; Pit House 4, 2; Pit House 9, 1; Pit House 11, 3; Cist 16, 1; Cist 54, 2); Pocket Cave (General, 3; Pit House 4, 1); Obelisk Cave (General, 7); General (1).

Worked Poles

Class A (1 whole, 1 fragmentary). Long poles slightly smoothed by use. Branches and ends show somewhat worn scars of cutting.

Length, 112 cm, 116 cm; diameter, 3.5 cm, 3.8 cm. Provenience: Broken Flute Cave (General, 1); Obelisk Cave (General, 1).

Roof Support

Class A (1 fragmentary). Base of post, unburned because it was beneath the floor level. End, tapered to point, shows scars from cutting with stone tool.

Length, 13.2 cm; diameter, 11 cm. Provenience: Broken Flute Cave (Surface).

Worked Cane

Class A (1 whole). One end of string run through hole in side of short piece of carrizo cane and knotted on inside, other end run through length of another piece of cane and looped on the far end. String dyed red, cane ends burned or cut.

Length of each piece, 2 cm; diameter, 0.7 cm. Provenience: Broken Flute Cave (General).

Class B (4 fragmentary). Worked carrizo canes, some ground smooth or wrapped with sinew at one or both ends.

No dimensions taken. Provenience: Broken Flute Cave (General, 1); Obelisk Cave (General, 1); General (2).

Cane Stem on String

Class A (1 whole ?). String run through hole in carrizo cane stem, as if for suspension.

Length, 3.5 cm; diameter, 0.8 cm. Provenience: Broken Flute Cave (General).

Braid of Cane Leaves

Class A (2 fragmentary). Bundle of leaves of carrizo cane joined in 3-ply braid.

Length, 12.0 cm, 27.5 cm; diameter, 1 cm, 2 cm. Provenience: Broken Flute Cave (General, 2).

Knot of Cane Leaves

Class A (1 whole). Bundle of a few leaf sheaths of carrizo cane joined in a square knot.

Length, 10 cm; diameter, 3 cm. Provenience: Broken Flute Cave (General).

BASKETRY

An analysis of the basketry from the Prayer Rock district formed the basis for the detailed descriptive compilation presented in "Anasazi Basketry" (Morris and Burgh 1941). A summary review is included here to indicate the range of materials recovered and the provenience of the specimens.

Coiled basketry with foundations of various combinations of materials sewn together with splints of split twigs in an over-and-over stitch were found in the following forms: trays, bowls, conical carrying baskets, and globular containers of various sizes with incurving rims. Design forms include elements that are direct radii or spiral radii in a quartered or halved field, and elements that form an encircling band. These elements are in black or black and red.

Two-rod-and-bundle, Close Coiling

Class A (49 whole and fragmentary). Two-rod-and-bundle foundation, rods laid side by side, bundle on top. Close coiled with a simple, uninterlocked stitch.

Provenience: Broken Flute Cave (General, 20; Pit House 7, 2; Pit House 9, 1; Pit House 11, 1; Cist 20, 2; Cist 50, 1); Obelisk Cave (General, 9); Cave 2 (Pit House 4, 2); Cave 4 (General, 2); Cave 6 (General, 1); Cave 10 (General, 1); Cave 11 (General, 1).

Two-rod-and-bundle, Spaced Coiling

Class A (3 whole and fragmentary). Two-rod-and-bundle foundation, rods laid side by side, bundle on top. Uninterlocked spaced coiling with intricate stitch and wrap.

Provenience: Broken Flute Cave (Pit House 7, 1; Pit House 16, 1); Obelisk Cave (General, 1).

Bundle foundation, Close Coiling

Class A (1 whole). Bundle foundation. Close coiled with simple uninterlocked stitch.

Provenience: Broken Flute Cave (General).

One-rod foundation, Close Coiling

Class A (1 fragmentary). One-rod foundation. Close coiled with interlocked stitch and wrap.

Provenience: Cave 2 (Pit House 4).

One-rod foundation, Spaced Coiling

Class A (1 fragmentary). One-rod foundation. Spaced coiling, intricate interlocked stitch and wrapped.

Provenience: Cave 8 (General).

Twilled Ring Baskets

Class A (6 whole and fragmentary). Some baskets were manufactured by first weaving split or whole yucca leaves into mats with an over-3, under-3 or an over-2, under-2 technique. These flat woven mats were then passed up through an osier ring and the ends bent over and tied down on the outside. Most specimens were large shallow trays. Designs were woven into the fabric by introducing dyed yucca leaves into the weave.

Provenience: Broken Flute Cave (General, 4); Cave 8 (General, 2).

Toy Basket

Class A (1 fragmentary). Two split basket splints placed at right angles to each other, ends folded up. The resulting four warps were crudely joined by plain weaving, using the same materials, with numerous errors. Piece unfinished, warp and weft elements left dangling.

Height, 9 cm; diameter, 3.6 cm. Provenience: Broken Flute Cave (General).

Basket Rods

Class A (1 bundle). Large bundle of slender branchless twigs, one end cut off near tip, the other near ground or main stem. Twigs are all about the same length. Bundle is tied in two places with split twigs of the same material.

Length, 95 cm; diameter, 10 cm. Provenience: Broken Flute Cave (Cist 13).

Basket Splints

Class A (10 bundles). Large bundles of split twigs of the same material used for the rods. The split portions are less than half of the original diameter of the twigs. Several bundles are tied near each end or at intervals down their lengths with yucca leaves, yucca fiber cord, or some of the pieces of the splints. Two of the bundles are composed of smaller bundles tied together, apparently showing increment through a period of time. One shorter bundle is heavily wrapped with the same material, and the splints protruding from one end are folded back over the wrapping on all sides.

Length, 53–117 cm and 19.5 cm; diameter, 3–16 cm. Provenience: Broken Flute Cave (Cist 13, 9; short bundle, Cist 54, 1).

CORN

Corn was the staple agricultural food of the Prayer Rock Basketmaker people, and the stalks, leaves, and cobs occupied a place in their technology. A hollowed out piece of stalk served as a container. The leaves were used as a binder for clay and mud, and were made into mats. The cobs were used in myriad ways; they were most commonly found with feathers or sticks stuck into the ends, probably relics of some ritual use.

A botanical analysis of the corn specimens was prepared by Paul C. Mangelsdorf of the Botanical Museum, Harvard University (see Appendix). Some of the specimens are artifacts and as such are included in the descriptions below. An examination of the provenience of the four species of corn shows mixing of all species in all caves where corn was recovered.

Cobs with Sticks or Feathers in the Ends

The corn cobs with sticks or feathers inserted in one or both ends may have been game darts, prayer sticks, or other ceremonial material.

Class A (9 whole and fragmentary; Fig. 91 *g*). Cobs with sticks inserted in one end (4) or inserted clear through the center and left protruding from both ends (5). Apparently the kernels were removed in prehistoric times. Most sticks are unworked and very firmly placed in the cobs. One stick was tapered to a point by grinding, and one was painted red at the tip. Cobs are mostly broken sections.

Length, 10–24 cm; length of cob, 3.5–14.0 cm; diameter, 2.0–2.8 cm. Provenience: Broken Flute Cave (General, 6; Pit House 4, 1; Pit House 9, 1; Cist 57, 1).

Class B (2 whole; Fig. 91 *h*). Cobs with a stick in one end and a large turkey or hawk feather in the other. Sticks unworked.

Length, 5.0 cm, 26.5 cm; length of cob, 5.0 cm, 8.0 cm; diameter, 1.9 cm, 2.4 cm. Provenience: Broken Flute Cave (General, 1; Pit House 7, 1).

Class C (1 whole; Fig. 91 *f*). Cob with a piece of cordage wrapped around it twice and tied in a square knot.

Length, 10.8 cm; diameter, 2.4 cm. Provenience: Broken Flute Cave (Cist 54).

Perforated Cob Fragment

Class A (1 whole). Short section of cob with large hole bored through center. Yucca fiber cord passed through hole and tied with a granny knot.

Length, 1.7 cm; diameter, 2 cm. Provenience: Broken Flute Cave (General).

Split Cobs with Leaf Wrapped Around One End

Class A (2 whole; Fig. 91 *e*). Sections of split cobs, each with a leaf wrapped around one end. One leaf is tied with a piece of yucca. The field notes state that the Navajo workmen had an explanation for objects of this kind, saying that they were dipped into mush or some liquid and given to children to suck.

Length, 9 cm, 12 cm; width, 1.4 cm, 2.2 cm; thickness, 0.8 cm, 1.1 cm. Provenience: Broken Flute Cave (Cist 16, 2).

Cob Handle on Scarifier

Class A (1 piece; Fig. 87 *f*). Length of broken cob lashed onto split stick holding chalcedony chip scarifier.

Length, 8 cm; width, 3 cm. Provenience: Broken Flute Cave (Cist 54).

Container Made from Stalk

Class A (1 whole; Fig. 91 *c*). An internodal piece of corn stalk, with the pith removed from a part of the center. The opening was covered with a leaf wrapped in place with a string.

Length, 10.2 cm; diameter, 1.8 cm; length of cavity, 4 cm; diameter of cavity, 1 cm. Provenience: Broken Flute Cave (Surface).

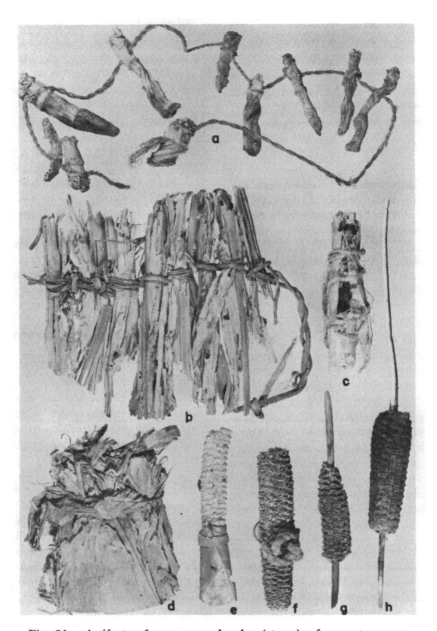

Fig. 91.   Artifacts of corn. *a*, peduncles (stems) of ears strung on string; *b*, twined leaf mat fragment; *c*, stalk container; *d*, package of husks; *e*, cottonwood leaf wrapped around split cob; *f*, string tied around cob; *g*, stick inserted through pith of cob; *h*, feather inserted in one end of cob, stick in the other.

Stems Strung on Cord

Class A (1 whole; Fig. 91 *a*). Eleven peduncles (stems) of corn ears, each perforated near one end and strung on a cord 68 cm long. They are shriveled as though they were picked green, and some of the ends have been charred. E. H. Morris (1919: 180) pictures a similar specimen and states: "The Pueblos still string ears of green corn in this fashion and hang them up to dry. When an ear is wanted for use it is broken off, and when all have been consumed the string with the stubs attached is thrown away."

Package of Husks

Class A (1 whole; Fig. 91 *d*). Corn husks are flattened and folded over, the loose ends tied with a piece of 2-ply, Z-twist cord.

Length, 11.5 cm; width, 8 cm; thickness, 2.4 cm. Provenience: Broken Flute Cave (Pit House 9).

Leaf Mat

Class A (1 fragmentary; Fig. 91 *b*). Corn leaves laid in parallel bundles twined together with plain strips of yucca leaf. Another yucca leaf has been tied to the twined element in large loops. This may have been used to hang the mat, or since the length of the loops correspond to the edge of the mat, they may have been joined to corresponding loops on another mat to fasten them together.

Length, 14.2 cm; width, 15 cm; thickness, 0.9 cm. Provenience: Cave 11 (General).

SQUASH AND GOURDS

Only a few fragments of squash and gourd shells were found in the excavations. The gourds, at least, must have been present in greater numbers than the fragments indicate, to judge from the large number of carrying nets that were found. The fragile nature of their shells, especially when charred, is probably the reason for their scarcity in the collection.

Bottles

Class A (2 fragmentary; Fig. 86 *i*). Neck fragments of long thin gourd (*Lagenaria siceraria*) bottles. The tip of the neck has been removed to make an aperture. The edge is smoothed by grinding and polished through use.

Length present, 5.0 cm, 15.5 cm; diameter present, 3.0 cm, 7.1 cm. Provenience: Broken Flute Cave (General, 1; Pit House 9, 1).

Plate

Class A (1 fragmentary). Fragment of a large gourd (*L. siceraria*), oval in shape, edges smoothed by grinding. Concave surface shows irregular striations at all angles, possibly resulting from the manufacturing technique or from use.

Length present, 11.5 cm; thickness, 0.8 cm. Provenience: Broken Flute Cave (Pit House 9).

Perforated Gourd

Class A (1 fragment). Piece of circular bowl-shaped gourd (*L. siceraria*) artifact with a round hole in the center and a round edge, both smoothed by grinding. Perforation near outer edge, diameter 0.2 cm. Interior shows no working; exterior smoothed and polished.

Diameter, 9.5 cm; thickness, 1.0 cm. Provenience: Broken Flute Cave (General).

Cut Gourd

Class A (1 fragmentary). Piece of neck of gourd (*L. siceraria*), one edge irregular but somewhat smoothed by use, the other edge freshly cut. Scars from cutting instruments are shallow and numerous beside edge.

Estimated diameter, 8.5 cm; thickness, 3.8 cm. Provenience: Broken Flute Cave (General).

CLAY

These artifact classes are composed of untempered clay. In some cases this is red, formed from the decomposed red sandstone; in others it is the finer clay used in the pottery vessels. Most of the specimens have been fired to some extent, but it is believed that the baking was unintentional, occurring as the houses burned or as fire spread through trash deposits. The clay vessels have been included in Chapter 6.

Human Figurines

This collection is described in detail by E. H. Morris (1951) and is presented in summary form here. The female features present on most of the figurines suggest that they had some ritual significance. Their lack of uniformity of details is probably not significant, but merely a result of random variation in their manufacture.

Class A (2 whole; Fig. 92 *j*, *l*). Oval in shape and section. A nose ridge at one end of one side was produced by pinching up a portion of clay. One specimen (Fig. 92 *l*) has cactus thorns stuck into the clay at regular intervals over the whole surface, suggesting the intriguing possibility of witchcraft.

Length, 4.6 cm, 5.0 cm; width, 2.8 cm, 3.3 cm; thickness, 1.6 cm, 2.6 cm. Provenience: Broken Flute Cave (Pit House 9, 1); Pocket Cave (General, 1).

Class B (3 whole and fragmentary; Fig. 92 *k*, *q*). Oval in shape and section, suggestion of crotch cleft present. Two specimens have prominent breasts, all specimens have nose ridge at one end. One specimen has two holes and a groove incised under the nose as if for nostrils and a mouth. One specimen (Fig. 92 *q*) has a double row of irregularly spaced holes around the edge of the face. One has eye slits extending outward from the nose ridge.

Length, 4.0–6.7 cm; width, 1.5–2.3 cm; thickness, 1.0–1.5 cm. Provenience: Broken Flute Cave (Pit House 8, 1); Cave 2 (Pit House 2, 1); Cave 3 (General, 1).

Class C (8 whole and fragmentary; Fig. 92 *m–p*). Rectangular with rounded corners or oval in shape, oval in section. Nose ridge, breasts, and crotch cleft usually prominent. Two are wearing fiber aprons. Four show demarcation between head and body, all except one have eye slits or holes extending outward from the nose ridge. Six have punctate bands, possibly representing necklaces, circling the face area or, in one case, located beneath the lower half of the face. Two have holes punched at the base of the nose. One has a geometric punctate design on the body (Fig. 92 *m*).

Length, 5.9–14.2 cm; width, 2.2–5.0 cm; thickness, 1.2–2.0 cm. Provenience: Broken Flute Cave (Pit House 9, 2); Cave 2 (Pit House 2, 1); Cave 8 (General, 3); Obelisk Cave (General, 1); Pocket Cave (Pit House 3, 1).

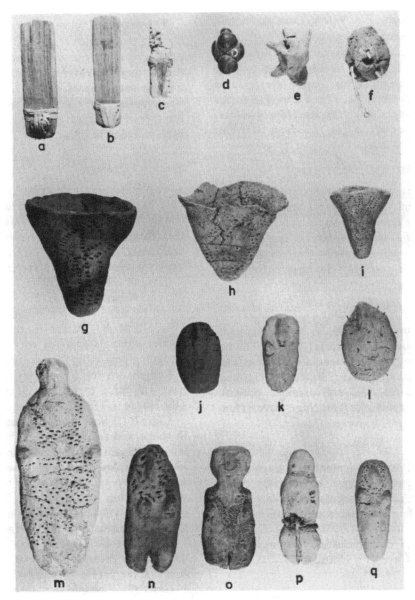

Fig. 92. Effigies of wood, stone, and clay. *a, b,* tabular human effigies of wood; *c,* cylindrical human effigy of wood; *d,* generalized animal or bird effigy of stone (note bead on back); *e,* clay turtle effigy; *f,* feather standard base of clay; *g, h, i,* miniature clay carrying basket effigies; *j, k, m–q,* clay human effigies; *l,* clay effigy of human head, stuck in many places with cactus spines. Length of *m,* 14 cm.

Class D (6 fragmentary). These specimens could belong to any of the above classes. Most show one or more features found on the other figurines.

Provenience: Broken Flute Cave (General, 4; Pit House 7, 1); Pocket Cave (Pit House 4, 1).

Carrying Basket Effigies

Class A (10 whole and fragmentary; Fig. 92 *g–i*).

These specimens are roughly funnel-shaped, the constricted portion of the funnel being solid in all except two instances. Most specimens have a crude punched geometric design on one or occasionally both sides. Most specimens are perforated in two places on one side, presumably for suspension. The shape and the decorative elements resemble those of actual carrying baskets.

Length, 3.2–9.7 cm; width, 2.4–8.0 cm; thickness,

2.3–6.3 cm. Provenience: Broken Flute Cave (Pit House 9, 3; Pit House 10, 1; Pit House 16, 1); Cave 2 (Pit House 1, 2; Pit House 2, 1); Cave 8 (General, 2).

Pipes

Class A (18 whole and fragmentary; Figs. 41 *g, i–n*; 42 *g, i*; Kidder and Guernsey 1919: 188). Roughly conical in shape with irregular sides. Bits rounded to oval with small central perforation. Bowls wide and shallow, sometimes as deep as half of the length, typically considerably less. Most specimens flare slightly at the bowl end, some flare considerably. Walls of bowl are variously thick or thin. Surfaces rough or well smoothed.

Length, 3.7–11.5 cm; diameter, 2.2–4.0 cm. Provenience: Broken Flute Cave (General, 1; Pit House 9, 4); Obelisk Cave (General, 3); Pocket Cave (General, 3; Pit House 3, 1); Cave 2 (Pit House 1, 2; Pit House 2, 1; Pit House 4, 1); Cave 8 (General, 2).

Pot Stoppers

Class A (2 whole; Fig. 25 *f*). Cylindrical in shape, molded from clay. The inner sides are covered with corn husks and yucca fiber stuck into the clay. Found in position in the tops of jars.

Diameter, 5.5 cm, 8.0 cm; thickness, 2.8 cm, 3.5 cm. Provenience: Pocket Cave (General, 1); Cave 10 (General, 1).

Feather Standard Base

Class A (1 whole; Fig. 92 *f*). Lump of clay pressed on flat surface. One large feather shaft hole in center, three smaller ones with portions of the feathers remaining around it.

Length, 3.5 cm; width, 2.7 cm; thickness, 2.0 cm. Provenience: Broken Flute Cave (General).

Turtle Effigy

Class A (1 whole; Fig. 92 *e*). Flat roundish effigy form with four legs, a flat tail, and raised head, crudely pinched out. Surface unfinished.

Length, 3.5 cm; width, 3.0 cm; thickness, 1.9 cm. Provenience: Cave 2 (Pit House 2).

8. PRAYER ROCK BASKETMAKERS IN NORTH AMERICAN PREHISTORY

The well-preserved Prayer Rock Basketmaker remains constitute a focal point for the study of prehistoric development on the North American continent, illuminating the nature of seventh century occupancy in the northern Southwest.

ARCHAIC CULTURE

The Archaic culture served as the continent-wide base for later prehistoric developments in North America. Archaeologists define it as a hunting, gathering, collecting level of subsistence that developed after the extinction of the large Pleistocene fauna. Hunters who had depended on these animals were forced to adapt their subsistence activities to other foods available in their home regions. This stage of development was largely preagricultural. The people lived in small wandering groups hunting the available animals, birds, and reptiles, and collecting any plant food that was edible (Byers 1959, Fowler 1959, Kelley 1959, Willey and Phillips 1958: 107). The climate is considered to have been similar to modern conditions. This period was one of regional adaptation. In some coastal, riverine, and lacustrine areas, fish, shell fish, or water fowl became important; people in forested areas lived on small animals, roots, and berries. In the Great Plains, bison were hunted. In the more arid west, hunting of smaller game was supplemented with the collection of grass seeds and other plant foods.

DESERT CULTURE

The Desert culture has been defined by Jennings as that part of the Archaic which reflects a human adaptation to the arid environment of the western United States (Jennings 1957, Jennings and Norbeck 1955). Radiocarbon dates from Danger Cave, one of the major Desert culture sites, indicate that a Desert culture subsistence pattern was utilized there 11,000 years ago. The small number of prehistoric remains are diverse, but they reflect technological adaptations to subsistence problems in a semiarid area that link the Great Basin into a single unit. The Desert culture way of life is particularly well known·because ethnographic accounts are available for tribes whose subsistence depended on this pattern (Steward 1938, 1940).

The Desert culture people were foragers, utilizing a tremendous variety of plant and animal resources for food and technological purposes. Small groups of people traveled from place to place, living temporarily where a particular type of plant or animal food was available. Probably they returned to favorable locations year after year. Their belongings were limited to what they could carry or easily make. Most characteristic among these were baskets, artifacts of plant fibers, and flat milling stones indicating the orientation of the culture toward seed collecting. Snaring and hunting game were well-developed. Camps were made near water, preferably next to overhanging cliffs, and surpluses of food were stored for later use. These people exploited the whole environment, finding no one food or group of foods which would sustain them. The collection and preparation of wild seeds involved techniques that could easily be adapted to the cultivation of maize.

The Desert culture traits present in the Basketmaker complex are numerous. These include the products of an intensive adaptation to the semiarid environment — that is, the collection of diverse plant and animal foods, and the utilization of a wide range of the available materials in their technology. The traits that distinguish Basketmaker II culture are the cultivation of corn, squash, and probably beans, and the related village architecture. The acquisition of a dependable staple food supply implemented the establishment of permanent dwellings and allowed the accumulation and elaboration of material culture.

Information indicating whether or not the Desert culture inhabitants of the Anasazi area had a particularly rich assemblage of material culture awaits the excavation of sites that can be dated in the first millenium B.C. If the presence of such items as intricately patterned tapestry weaving, flutes, ceremonial paraphernalia and other Basketmaker traits in a preagricultural context can be established on the Colorado Plateau, then the long-awaited definition of the Basketmaker I phase can be made. If, on the contrary, the artifactual inventory from preagricultural sites cannot be differentiated from Desert culture remains over the rest of the Great Basin, then the Basketmaker II development must be derived directly from the Desert culture base.

SOUTHWESTERN AREA

The Southwestern area becomes differentiated from the Desert culture area by the advent of a complex of traits including cultivation of corn, beans, and squash, the bow and arrow, pottery, grooved axes and mauls, and pit houses. Most of these were directly or indirectly derived from Mexico. The Southwestern area is subdivided into the Anasazi, Mogollon, and Hohokam regions on the basis of differences in pit house shape, pottery color and decoration, the axe form, and the general cultural complex present at any given time. The Anasazi region is characterized on an early time horizon by gray pottery and its relatively late time of development. The Basketmaker III period of Anasazi development is in turn subdivided on the basis of pottery decoration and details of pit house architecture. The Prayer Rock Basketmaker remains were at one time considered a part of the Mesa Verde regional sequence. Now, however, they appear to share more traits with remains of sites to the south — along the Arizona–New Mexico state line.

BASKETMAKER III PERIOD

The Basketmaker III cultural configuration consists of intensive adaptation to a semiarid environment derived from the Desert culture and a number of important additions from elsewhere. Many of these additions were ultimately derived from the high culture centers of Mesoamerica, some were probably acquired from other known sources, and the origins of still others are not known. Notable among the former group are maize agriculture and ceramic technology; among the second group are pit houses and the bow and arrow; and in the third group are full-grooved axes. This complex forms a dynamic base for Pueblo development in the Anasazi culture. The combination of the component parts was a fortunate accident of cultural diffusion and invention. In order to develop an understanding of the origins of this complex the individual traits will be considered in detail. The Desert culture base has been discussed above — the additions to it are described below.

The routes of the Mesoamerican innovations are not precisely known. Evidence is available suggesting that one or more avenues of diffusion existed, but the data are not conclusive for any of them (Jennings 1956). Briefly, these are: (1) up the west coast of Mexico to the Hohokam area and thence northward; (2) up the Central Plateau to the Mogollon and Hohokam areas; (3) up the east coast of Mexico, overland to the Mississippi Valley, with direct influence on the peoples in southern New Mexico; and (4) indirectly, with influence coming west from the Mississippi Valley up the tributary rivers which may have served as highways of human contact.

Corn. Maize agriculture is the most important and apparently one of the earliest additions to the Desert culture base. Probably more than any other factor, the acquisition of a nutritious staple food source affected the subsequent development of cultures in the Southwest. It contributed directly to the establishment of permanent villages and to the increase in population, factors that are basic to the expansion seen in Pueblo III times. The date of the advent of corn is not known. Probably the seed-gathering economy of the Desert culture involved a complex of skills that could be directly applied to the beginnings of maize agriculture. Corn was found in the earliest well-dated Basketmaker II sites in the Durango area (E. H. Morris and Burgh 1954), and in all other sites of known Basketmaker affiliation where perishable materials were found. This grain was found considerably earlier in the southern portion of the Southwestern area and in northern Mexico (Dick 1954, Lister and others 1958, MacNeish 1958, Mangelsdorf and Lister 1956, Martin and others 1952, Wellhausen and others 1952). Several kinds of maize have been recorded for the different sites, and botanical affiliations have been made to types of archaeological corn present in the Mississippi Valley and in Mexico. These probably have a direct correlation to the time and method of diffusion, but the archaeological picture is so fragmentary that the situation remains unclear (Jennings 1956). A recent suggestion has been made that at about A.D. 700 a new race of maize spread through the Southwest, giving a large yield and strengthening the agricultural dependence of the people (Galinat and Gunnerson 1963).

Squash. Squash is found with maize in Basketmaker II sites. The details of origin and distribution of species await further work.

Beans. Beans are first found in Basketmaker III sites in the northern Southwest (Kaplan 1956). A source of vegetable protein probably had a positive effect on the increasing population (Linton 1940). As with corn, a number of species and varieties have been recognized in the archaeological remains, but the affiliations of the separate groups with wild types and with each other are not known.

Turkeys. Evidence that turkeys were kept in captivity is first observed in a Basketmaker III context. The turkey litter in Pocket Cave indicates that the Prayer Rock people had these birds. Turkeys were not kept until later times in the Mogollon, Hohokam, Sinagua, and Fremont areas (Jennings 1956). It is not known whether the turkeys were actually domesticated and bred in captivity or were caught and kept alive in pens. Similarly, the problem of whether the birds were eaten or used merely as a source of feathers has not been settled. Isolated turkey bones have been found in trash and some have been made into artifacts. Also, turkey burials and occasional instances of the setting of broken turkey leg bones have been recorded. Certainly turkey feathers were widely used by the Basketmaker people whether or not the flesh was eaten.

Full-grooved Axes and Mauls. The origin and distribution of full-grooved axes and mauls is a problem (Woodbury 1954: 35–37). Grooved or notched axes are not reported from Basketmaker II sites. They occur sporadically at various relatively isolated Basketmaker III and early Pueblo I sites. The rather unformalized complex of notched and full-grooved axes and mauls present in the Prayer Rock caves indicates that both techniques were in use in this area in the early part of the seventh century.

Pottery. Basketmaker ceramic technology can be derived from the Mogollon area to the south. Early vessels from both areas exhibit marked similarities in shape, lug form, surface treatment, and general manufacture. The differences in paste color are geographically determined; the Mogollon vessels are brown because they are made from volcanically derived clays, while the gray Anasazi pots are manufactured from sedimentary clays. The appearance of pottery before A.D. 1 in the Mogollon area and about A.D. 500, or possibly earlier, in the Anasazi culture is interpreted as a slow diffusion of the trait northward.

The crude fiber-tempered vessels were probably not independently invented prototypes of true fired pots, as was once postulated by Morris (1927). They are interpreted as short-lived products of the diffusion of an idea rather than a method or a response to a specific need. The continued use of the clay vessels after the advent of true pottery may have occurred because they were bowls, while most of the fired vessels were jars. These vessels may have had a function that was not replaced by fired pots, a function that was still important after the better domestic containers were introduced. The eccentric vessel shapes that occur in Basketmaker III pottery perhaps were derived from somewhere in the drainage of the Mississippi River, where pottery had been made for centuries and where forms similar to the unusual Southwestern shapes occurred (Jennings 1956). This is an intriguing idea, both for its value in understanding the source of technological manifestations and in terms of what other traits may have accompanied the contact indicated by the ceramic evidence.

With the exception of the eccentric vessel forms, the only trait in the Prayer Rock Basketmaker pottery complex that does not have a direct affiliation to the Mogollon culture is the decoration of the La Plata Black-on-white pieces. Morris (1927) has derived designs of this nature from those utilized on baskets. This would seem a logical source and to have been an independent invention in the Basketmaker III culture.

Bow and Arrow. In the Anasazi area the bow and arrow replaced the atlatl sometime between A.D. 500 and 600. Its source is rather a greater problem than that of the other incoming traits of Basketmaker times. The manufacture and use of the bow and compound arrows was a complicated set of innovations, although the obvious utility of the weapon would have hastened its rapid spread. The trait appears in Tularosa Cave at a slightly later date (Martin and others 1952) and in Mesoamerica even later, where it had not completely replaced the atlatl, even at the time of Spanish contact. The absence of cave sites where perishable materials were preserved — dating in the first few centuries A.D. in the Great Basin, in the Plains, and in the Southwest itself — precludes the documentation of these areas as sources, but one or more are considered logical possibilities.

Pit Houses. The construction of complex pit houses of the type found in the Prayer Rock district may be linked to the same source as the bow and arrow or it may be of considerably earlier origin. The Basketmaker II houses noted at the Durango sites and in the Los Pinos phase were constructed by methods to which the complex features of the Prayer Rock houses could be added with a minimum of change. However, the intricate association of component parts in Basketmaker III houses can scarcely be called derivative. Wendorf (1953) traced the distribution of pit house features across the greater Southwest. One of his conclusions is that similar structures differing in details of size and composition are widely distributed in time and space. The earliest pit houses are rare and are rather generalized in form. The source of the whole idea is probably linked to the New World distribution of pit houses at an early time level with an ultimate source in Asia (Daifuku 1952). The earth lodges found at later times in the Plains are similar in form if not in size to the Prayer Rock pit houses. Their prototype, if such exists, may have been the source of this architectural pattern in the Southwest.

SUMMARY

The raising of corn, beans, and squash, the use of pit houses, the manufacture of thin pottery with increasing amounts of decoration, the use of a grooved axe, and the bow and arrow were shared throughout the Southwest. This complex differentiates this area from the surrounding areas of North America at that time. The regional subdivisions that are recognized within it are insignificant compared to the differences that existed between the Southwestern area and neighboring areas.

The Prayer Rock Basketmaker remains are the culmination of a long line of development. As a part of a continent-wide Archaic substratum, the Desert culture peoples learned to exist in the arid western United States. Through the centuries, their pattern of existence was refined to a complicated and intensive use of the resources available in their environment. To the part of the Desert culture that was in the Anasazi area were added maize agriculture, squash, beans, pottery technology, the bow and arrow, and grooved axes and mauls. The resulting complex distinguishes the Basketmaker III period.

The sites in the Prayer Rock caves are particularly revealing in their portrayal of this developmental level. The well-preserved houses found with a rich assemblage of material culture enable the reconstruction of the lives of the people and of their cultural heritage in satisfying detail. The intensive adaptation to a semiarid environment is portrayed in the great diversity of natural products that are used in Basketmaker technology. Specialized tools available in large numbers are an index to their manufacturing achievement. The bundles of raw materials cached for future use are an indication of the forethought necessary for more than mere existence in a dry country. Complex houses in groups, numerous pottery vessels, and quantities of other material remains indicate the importance of agricultural food in this economy. The bow and versatile arrows were an efficient hunting mechanism. Although the people did not wear many clothes, their sandals, aprons, jewelry, and feather robes were complex in manufacture and often decorated elaborately. The presence of an intricate social and religious life is indicated by the flutes, dog hair sashes, medicine kits, dice, tobacco quids, pipes, animal effigies, female figurines, miniature effigies of carrying baskets, and prayer sticks. The occurrence of this complex in a number of inhabited caves marks the beginning of the population increase and elaboration of the social structure made possible by an agricultural economy.

The new innovations imposed upon a Desert culture base blended into a prosperous society whose remains were portrayed in detail in the Prayer Rock caves. The development of this fortunate combination of traits culminated in the great Pueblo III villages in Chaco Canyon and Mesa Verde. The archaeologist is assisted in the reconstruction of the base from which this efflorescence developed by the fortunate conditions of preservation in the Prayer Rock caves.

9. SUMMARY AND CONCLUSIONS

The Prayer Rock caves are of particular interest because of the repeated association of pit houses and abundant artifactual remains. The more than 3000 specimens include a large proportion of perishable items, as well as enough stone, bone, and pottery to establish typological affiliations in detail. Most of these items came from ten caves that contained a total of at least 42 pit houses — Broken Flute, Ram's Horn, Pocket, and Obelisk caves, and Caves 1, 2, 3, 6, 7, and 8. Broken Flute, Pocket, and Obelisk caves, and Caves 1, 2, and 8, contained about 75 percent of the architecture and artifacts. Cave 4 was apparently only used for burials, most of them disturbed in antiquity, so that little information about the human remains and the association of grave goods was obtained. No data, except rare artifact proveniences, are available for Caves 5, 9, 10, 11, and 12, and it is assumed that these sites were only noted or tested by the expedition.

The architecture and artifactual remains have been classified as part of the Four Corners phase of the Mesa Verde branch as defined by O'Bryan (1950: 104). However, some similar pit houses and associated specimens have been found in Basketmaker III sites of the Chaco branch, Shabik'eschee Village (Roberts 1929), the Twin Lakes site, LA 2507 (Wendorf, Fox, and Lewis 1956: 57; Johnson 1962), in the Kayenta branch (Taylor 1954: 110), in the Cibola branch, White Mound Village (originally defined as part of the Chaco branch; Gladwin 1945), NA 3941A near Ganado, Arizona (excavated by Robert Euler), and Site 264 on Antelope Mesa, which probably would be placed in the Cibola branch.

This distribution, depending heavily on architectural details, thus overlaps the area of four Anasazi branches. It is probably significant that many of the sites listed are in the modern Juniper-Piñon Pine ecological belt. Interestingly, the major distribution extends from the forested area north of the Mogollon Rim, northward along the similarly forested Chuska-Lukachukai mountain range to the Mesa Verde plateau. This distribution supports the argument for a Mogollon source of ideas for some part of the Basketmaker III archaeological complex. The derivation of much of the subsistence pattern from the Desert culture has been emphasized in the text. The evidence for this is the large number of natural products used for a wide variety of mostly perishable goods and for the careful collection and storage of raw materials. The Basketmakers were veritable human packrats.

The tree-ring dates for the wall timbers and roof supports of the house structures are so internally consistent that the time of construction between about A.D. 620 and 670 seems to be reliably established. The green and yellow color of the carrizo canes used in some of the roofs and walls indicate that at least some houses were built in the fall and winter, although it is consistent with the Basketmaker character that the cane might have been gathered when it was ready and saved to be used when it was needed. The time of abandonment is more difficult to assess and the reasons for the departure of the people cannot be definitely determined.

Since many of the pit houses in several of the sites had burned while containing large quantities of food and personal belongings, but apparently no people, it is a very real possibility that the caves were visited by raiders who captured or drove off the local inhabitants. The destruction of usable foodstuffs and such portable items as jewelry, knives, and articles of clothing might be explained as an effort to wipe out a people who were so disliked that the acquisition of their possessions was considered undesirable. Or perhaps some of these things were taken according to the fancy or need of the raiders. It is more difficult to determine what portions of a cultural complex are absent from a site than it is to note the remains present. An alternative explanation is that all or most of the local people were away when the raiders struck.

It is an intriguing possibility that the presence of agricultural implements and containers full of foodstuffs and the relative absence of hunting gear, together with the absence of the byproducts of hunting such as unused portions of animals and waste products from chipping stone, indicate that much of the hunting was done away from the home caves. It is possible, of course, that the houses caught fire by accident, even in several unconnected caves, over a period of some years. In such a case, the conflagration could spread rapidly through the tinder-dry house structures and trash deposits. The people may have had no choice but to stand by helplessly as their dwellings, food stores, and personal belongings were destroyed. But there was a minimum of post-fire disturbance and it seems likely that the people would have searched through some of the remains for any unconsumed treasures, which, incidentally, were numerous and not deeply buried. Such an event might be such a tragedy that they would move away forever from such an unlucky place. It seems unlikely that the houses burned one at a time, accidentally, in the normal course of daily life. They were consistently full of harvested agricultural crops, indicating that they burned at about the same time, and they were mostly full of personal belongings indicating that the people had not intended to leave permanently. The scene reflects some measure of human tragedy serious enough so that a prosperous community ceased to exist in these valleys.

Whatever the cause of the burning of many of the structures, it was a fortunate occurrence for the archaeologist. The clay roofs collapsed onto the house floors as their supports burned and the flames were smothered before they could erase the many diverse objects that reflected the existence of the Prayer Rock Basketmakers. The clay formed a protective surface over these remains and shielded them from many of the destructive natural and cultural events of the subsequent centuries. The red vaulting cave roofs and the well-watered valleys were too useful to be ignored by the later Pueblo and Navajo peoples but the population was never as intense as it had been in Basketmaker times.

* * *

In the original version of this manuscript (E. A. Morris 1959b) the Prayer Rock remains were compared extensively to other Basketmaker assemblages in an effort to determine areal affiliations and regional differences. Since that time much new material has been added to our knowledge of the period. Of great importance are the current efforts of the Laboratory of Tree-Ring Research at the University of Arizona to publish all of the archaeological materials in its files, making available the raw data for a detailed synthesis of Basketmaker culture. Although not attempting such a synthesis herein, I shall present a summary of the materials from sites similar to the Prayer Rock caves, and certain suggestions about cultural affiliations.

As noted, the Prayer Rock remains were included in the definition of the Four Corners phase of the Mesa Verde branch (O'Bryan 1950). Remains from other excavations made north of the San Juan River in the Yellowjacket, Durango, and La Plata Valley regions might well be placed in this phase. However, I suggest that the Prayer Rock materials should be removed from the Four Corners phase. As opposed to these other sites, the Prayer Rock district is south of the San Juan River, and it exhibits more architectural similarities to excavated sites even further south than it does to the Mesa Verde sites.

Ceramic remains and tree-ring dates are the bases by which sites are judged to be contemporaneous. Unfired fiber-tempered bowls, Lino Gray, Lino Smudged, Lino Fugitive Red, La Plata Black-on-white, Lino Black-on-gray, and polished red vessels constitute the Basketmaker III ceramic assemblage. Neck-banded types, Abajo Red-on-orange and White Mound Black-on-white, appear at the end of the period and they become the hallmarks of the Pueblo I period. This complex is widely distributed in the Anasazi area in the seventh century. Its roots are found in sixth century sites but the details and earliest limits are yet to be determined.

Architectural remains are the basis for recognizing regionally affiliated sites. Pit houses, occurring in caves and open sites and reflecting an interrelated complex of preferences on the part of the people, are a useful distributional index. The Prayer Rock pit houses with floor features that include four main roof supports, a centrally-located clay-rimmed hearth, radial timbers, interior cists, often benches and pot-holding depressions, and walls and roofs of closely-spaced timbers covered with reeds, bark, or brush, with a layer of mud, form an internally consistent architectural style. In addition, there is a notable absence of antechambers, slab walls, deflectors, ashpits, and wingwalls.

Remains found at Jeddito 264 in the Awatovi area (Daifuku 1961) closely resemble the Prayer Rock assemblage. NA 3941 A, south of Ganado, Arizona, is another similar site, excavated by Robert Euler. The sequence of houses found at LA 2507, the Twin Lakes site, 15 miles north of Gallup, New Mexico, represents occupation immediately before, during, and just after the building of the Prayer Rock houses (Wendorf, Fox, and Lewis 1956: 57; Johnson 1962). Recently obtained tree-ring dates from all of these sites indicate close contemporaneity (Bannister, Hannah, and Robinson 1966; Bannister, Warren, and Robinson, 1970).

Earlier sites, apparently antecedent to this period, are found in the area. Salvage excavations at Arizona K:12:6 on the Puerco River just west of the Arizona–New Mexico line indicate a village that is ceramically and temporally earlier than the occupation in the Prayer Rock area (Wasley 1960; Bannister, Hannah, and Robinson 1966), and the early house at the Twin Lakes site is similar (Johnson 1962). Later remains differing only slightly in architectural features and even less in ceramics are more numerous. Remains at White Mound Village (Gladwin 1945) and Arizona K:12:8 (Wasley 1960), both in the Puerco River valley and both within ten miles of the Arizona–New Mexico state line, at Shabik'eschee Village (Roberts 1929), and probably at Half House (Adams 1951) in Chaco Canyon, represent the development of traits that started in Prayer Rock times.

Wasley (1960) discusses in some detail the interaction between Mogollon and Anasazi peoples during the Basketmaker III period. The Prayer Rock materials and the comparative data given above seem to support the Mogollon origin of much of the Anasazi architectural and ceramic cultural assemblage. Plotted on a map the distribution of the Prayer Rock type of pit house resembles a gigantic spearhead extending up the center of the Anasazi area to its northern limits. Some of the admittedly tenuous, earliest pottery dates for this region are from the Durango area at the northern edge. Also at the northern extreme are the red-on-orange pottery types of the San Juan Red Ware series that are almost certainly derived from Mogollon types. Earlier dates for ceramics in clear architectural associations have been reported by Eddy (Dittert, Eddy, and Dickey 1963) for the Navajo Reservoir area. It is suggested that the continental divide constituted a second highway of diffusion from the south to the north. It seems to be more than coincidental that this distribution follows modern belts of forested highlands extending from the Mogollon to the Anasazi area.

In summary, the following statements may be made about the cultural affiliations of the Prayer Rock Basketmakers.

1. The Prayer Rock Basketmaker remains should be removed from the Four Corners phase, defined for the Mesa Verde branch by O'Bryan (1950). While the pottery is similar to that found in other areas, the architectural remains more closely resemble those found in nearby areas to the south, southeast, and southwest.

2. The origins of many ceramic, architectural, and perhaps other traits in the Basketmaker III phase of Anasazi development may be derived from the Mogollon area to the south. I would postulate the existence of north-south pathways of ideas and possibly peoples along the forested uplands of the Carrizo Mountains and the continental divide.

Appendix

PLANT REMAINS FROM
THE PRAYER ROCK CAVES

PINON NUTS

Piñon nuts were found scattered through the fill of the caves and were found in quantity in Burial 2, Cave 4.

BEANS

The bean specimens were identified by Lawrence Kaplan, Department of Biology, Roosevelt University, Chicago. He provided the following statement.

The identifiable bean remains are of one of the most widespread types of the prehistoric Southwest. They are *Phaseolus vulgaris* Type Cl (Kaplan 1956: 189–251), and have been found most abundantly in P III sites in Mesa Verde and Tsegie Canyon. The Prayer Rock valley beans are the earliest of this type from northern Arizona but are antedated by Cl remains from Tularosa Cave in the Mogollon area.

The remaining, charred materials, while not identifiable as to variety or type, are all *P. vulgaris*. Limas and teparies are not represented.

Recent excavations (Brooks and others 1962) at the Rio Zape in the State of Durango, Mexico, radiocarbon dated 1300 ± 100 years ago, have yielded abundant bean remains, including seeds of the variety predominating in the Prayer Rock caves. The same variety appears in the Georgetown level of Tularosa Cave (Martin and others 1952) in western New Mexico. Because all of these occurrences date earlier than finds of this bean in the Sonoran-influenced Verde Valley, if this bean came to the Prayer Rock district diffusing by way of agricultural peoples, it came by way of Chihuahua.

149   *P. vulgaris*, about 34 valves, some slightly charred, probably bush types and may represent two varieties. Broken Flute Cave, Cist 11.

149a   *P. vulgaris*, 500 cc, pod fragments, some slightly charred; two varieties, probably bush types. Broken Flute Cave, Cist 11.

745   *P. vulgaris*, type Cl, about 80 seeds and fragments. Uncharred. Broken Flute Cave, General.

1148   *P. vulgaris*, seeds and pods, charred, 500 cc, most are probably type Cl. Cave 8.

1148b   *P. vulgaris*, seeds, charred, 150 cc. Cave 8.

SQUASH AND GOURDS

Squash and gourd remains were identified as to genus and species by Thomas W. Whitaker, U.S. Department of Agriculture, Crops Research Division, La Jolla, California. He contributed the following information.

The material consists almost entirely of "shell" fragments of *Lagenaria siceraria* (Mol.) Stand. (White-flowered Gourd) together with seeds and peduncles of *Cucurbita pepo* L. There is a single seed of C. Mixta Pang. in U-12, but this is probably a late introduction and may be relatively recent.

The evidence of the cucurbit material from this collection confirms the idea that *Cucurbita pepo* and *Lagenaria siceraria* were used by the people of this area at a comparatively early date. *Cucurbita moschata* Poir. came in about A.D. 1000, followed by *C. mixta* in the late 1100s and early 1200s (Cutler and Whitaker 1961).

25a, b   Stems. *C. pepo*, peduncle. Broken Flute Cave, General.

88   Shell fragment. *C. pepo*, peduncle and shell. Broken Flute Cave, Pit House 4.

116   Shell fragments. Most likely *C. pepo*. Broken Flute Cave, General.

202b   Seeds from mouse nest. *C. pepo*. Broken Flute Cave, Pit House 6.

1307   Seeds. *C. pepo*. Cave 11.

U-4   Charred and roasted seeds, very numerous. *C. pepo*, peduncle. *C. pepo*.

U-12   Seeds. *C. pepo*; one seed of *C. mixta*.

REPORT ON THE MAIZE SPECIMENS
IN THE MORRIS COLLECTION

Paul C. Mangelsdorf

The specimens of maize in this collection can be divided into five categories as follows: (1) cobs with kernels; (2) loose kernels; (3) cobs without kernels; (4) cob fragments with sticks or a feather; (5) miscellaneous specimens. The specimens in each category are described in detail in the corresponding Tables 9 to 13. Information to be gained from the specimens regarding the characteristics of the maize is greatest in Table 9, intermediate in Tables 10 and 11, and least in Tables 12 and 13.

The data from Table 9 which involve descriptions of all of the cobs still bearing kernels show that the collection contains four more or less distinct types or races of maize. These are: (1) Chapalote; (2) Modified Chapalote; (3) Modified Harinoso de Ocho; and (4) Mestizo.

TABLE 9
Description of Corn Cobs with Kernels
(Dimensions in millimeters)

Number	Description of specimen	Length	Diameter of Ear	Diameter of Cob	Diameter of Ped.	No. rows	Color	Kernels Length	Kernels Width	Kernels Thickness	Texture	Race
29	Branch of main ear	55	20	—	—	4	Red	6.4	6.6	6.0	Flint	Modern Chapalote
201a	Broken cob	130	34	18	12	14	Brown	9.8	6.8	4.5	Dent	Mestizo
201b	Intact cob	111+	29	19	9	14	Brown	8.1	6.6	4.7	Flint	Chapalote
201c	Intact cob	99	27	15	6	10	Brown	8.0	8.2	4.6	Flint	Modern Chapalote
201d	Intact cob	92	28	18	8	10	Brown	8.2	7.2	4.4	Flint	Modern Chapalote
201e	Broken cob	59+	31	22	14	10	Brown	7.8	8.2	4.6	Flint	Modern Chapalote
201f	Broken cob	48+	27	19	9	14	Brown	7.4	6.2	4.6	Flint	Chapalote
201g	Broken cob	43+	23	17	—	14	Brown	8.0	5.8	4.4	Flint	Chapalote
205	Intact cob	165	38	25	16	10	Variegated Red	8.4	9.0	5.0	Flour	Modified Ocho
395a	Intact cob	143	31	18	19	8	Brown	8.7	9.6	4.8	Flint	Modified Ocho
395b	Intact cob	106	32	19	11	12	Brown	8.4	7.4	4.5	Flour	Modified Chapalote
395c	Intact cob	98	31	21	7	12	Brown	7.2	7.4	4.8	Flour	Chapalote
U 11a	Intact cob	182	36	18	12	10	Red	8.9	9.4	4.9	Flint	Modified Ocho
U 11b	Intact cob	180	42	27	17	14	Brown	9.8	8.2	4.9	Dent	Mestizo

Chapalote is one of the ancient indigenous races of maize in Mexico described by Wellhausen (Wellhausen and others 1952). It is still found in parts of western Mexico and was distributed prehistorically throughout the American Southwest including Arizona, New Mexico, Colorado, Texas, Oklahoma, and perhaps even Nebraska. Chapalote is characterized by relatively low kernel-row numbers, usually 12 or 14 slender peduncles, small kernels which are about as wide as long, and a brown pericarp.

Modified Chapalote is the equivalent of early Basketmaker corn. It is the product of the introgression of an eight-rowed flour corn into Chapalote. Most ears of Modified Chapalote have brown pericarp although some are red. The kernels are larger than those of pure Chapalote and the peduncles usually thicker.

The Modified Harinoso de Ocho probably traces back to the Harinoso de Ocho of Mexico described by Wellhausen (Wellhausen and others 1952), and is probably originally from South America. It has both red and colorless pericarp.

The fourth type in this collection, designated as Mestizo, is the product of genetic recombination following hybridization of Chapalote and Harinoso de Ocho, perhaps with some introgression from teosinte. In the corn of northwestern Mexico (Mangelsdorf and Lister 1956), this combination gave rise to a race which still exists and which has been described by Wellhausen (Wellhausen and others 1952) under the name "Cristalino de Chihuahua." Some ears in the Prayer Rock collection could

be assigned to this race, but since the number of ears available for study is small it seems advisable to simply call them Mestizos rather than to assign them definitely to known races.

Table 10 lists all of the separate collections of loose kernels. Some collections containing a relatively small number of kernels can be definitely assigned to one of these four categories; others are clearly mixtures of two or more types. All but two of the individual collections contain both brown and red kernels, and it is to be noted that in the majority of these the red kernels are slightly larger than the brown. This supports the assumption that the original corn was a strain of Chapalote breeding true for brown pericarp, and that the red pericarp has resulted from hybridization with a more recent introduction, probably Harinoso de Ocho.

Table 11 is concerned with a description of cobs without kernels. Here the only data available are the diameters of the cobs and the peduncles. On the basis of these data the specimens have been assigned to one of the four types listed in Table 9, but the identifications are by no means as certain as in the case of specimens which have both cob and kernels. If the identifications in Table 11 prove to be meaningful in terms of sequence within the site, they should be retained, otherwise the last column in Table 11 should, perhaps, be deleted. These specimens are useful, however, in showing that everything in this collection can be assigned to one of the four categories recognized in Table 9.

The specimens listed in Table 12 involve pieces of cob

TABLE 10
Description of Loose Corn Kernels
(Dimensions in millimeters)

Number	Color	Texture	Count	Length	Width	Thickness	Probable Race
202	Brown	Flint and flour	1746	8.2	8.0	4.4	Modern Chapalote and Modern Ocho
202	Red	Flint and flour	82	8.7	7.4	4.4	Modern Chapalote
702	Light Brown	Flint	192	7.4	7.1	5.8	Chapalote
702	Dark Brown	Flint	127	7.2	7.2	5.4	Chapalote
702	Red	Flint	10	7.5	7.5	5.8	Chapalote
747	Brown	Flint	372	6.8	7.1	5.6	Chapalote
747	Red	Flint	84	7.6	7.4	5.9	Chapalote
1007	Brown	Flint	77	8.9	9.0	5.8	Modern Ocho
1007	Red	Flint	1	8.6	6.2	6.3	Modern Ocho
1364	Brown	Dent	16	11.7	8.2	4.8	Mestizo
U 2	Brown	Flint	2589	8.3	7.8	4.6	Modern Chapalote and Modern Ocho
U 2	Red	Flint	793	8.6	7.8	5.0	Modern Chapalote and Modern Ocho
U 3	Brown	Flint	375	7.4	7.2	4.6	Chapalote and Modern Ocho
U 3	Red	Flint	5	7.8	7.2	4.6	Chapalote and Modern Ocho
U 3	Mixed	Flour	75	9.6	8.6	4.7	Mestizo
U 5	Brown	Flint	4	6.5	6.5	5.0	Chapalote
U 5	Mixed	Flour	12	9.2	8.0	5.3	Modern Ocho
U 6	Brown	Flint	21	7.3	6.8	4.8	Chapalote
U 6	Red	Flint	1	7.4	8.3	4.6	Modern Chapalote
U 6	Yellow	Flour	31	9.5	8.2	4.6	Mestizo
U 7	Brown	Flint	8	7.1	6.4	4.9	Chapalote
U 7	Red	Flint	48	7.5	6.5	4.9	Modern Chapalote

with a stick thrust into one end or completely through the pith of the cob. The last specimen, No. 770, has a stick at one end and a feather at the other. It is difficult to imagine the purpose of these cobs unless they were used as darts in a game. The one with a feather might certainly have been used for this purpose (see description of corn artifacts). It is impossible to assign these cob fragments to the four races recognized in Table 9, however; all but one of them have a rather large cob diameter and probably are not Chapalote.

The items listed in Table 13 are described individually and the descriptions are self-explanatory. Items 162a and b are especially interesting, since I have never encountered either one of them before in any collection of vegetal remains. I cannot imagine what these were used for unless they represent a kind of crude brush used to apply paint to the skin or to basketry. These specimens show no evidence of having been immersed in paint, but

they may have been prepared for this purpose and not used (see description of corn artifacts).

The collection as a whole confirms the conclusions which Lister and I reached with respect to the corn from several caves in northwestern Mexico. Here the original race was Chapalote; this was strongly modified by the introgression of the eight-rowed flour corn, Harinoso de Ocho. At about the same time there was also evidence of the introgression of teosinte; the blending of these three elements resulted in a new hybrid race, Cristalino de Chihuahua. In the Prayer Rock collection we have the pure Chapalote and evidence of the influence of Harinoso de Ocho, although there are no specimens of the pure race. Finally, there is a new hybrid race which may or may not be a close counterpart of the Cristalino de Chihuahua of northwestern Mexico. The influence of teosinte introgression is by no means as conspicuous in the Prayer Rock collection as it was in the Chihuahua specimens.

TABLE 11
Description of Corn Cobs without Kernels
(Dimensions in millimeters)

Number	Length	Diameter Cob	Peduncle	No. Rows	Probable Race
28a	180	21	18	12	Mestizo
28b	120	22	15	12	Modified Chapalote
28c	153	21	15	12	Modified Chapalote
28d	215	20	15	10	Modern Ocho
28e	135+	19	14	12	Modern Ocho
28f	204	21	23	12	Mestizo
28g	135	18	12	12	Modern Chapalote
28h	120	17	8	10	Chapalote
269a	70	22	10	12	Chapalote
269b	108	19	6	8	Modern Chapalote
672a	80	25	17	16	Modern Chapalote
672b	67+	17	—	8	Modern Ocho
703	164	18	13	10	Modern Ocho
740	140	21	10	14	Chapalote
754	149	21	15	16	Modern Chapalote
767	164	20	16	14	Modern Chapalote
837	166	27	15	18	Modern Chapalote
U 1a	158	20	9	16	Mestizo
U 1b	150	23	8	16	Chapalote
U 1c	142	22	13	14	Chapalote
U 1d	145	20	10	14	Chapalote
U 1e	140	21	10	12	Chapalote
U 1f	130	19	12	10	Modern Ocho
U 1g	120	20	10	16	Chapalote
U 1h	125	21	10	16	Chapalote
U 1i	105+	21	—	14	Modern Chapalote
U 1j	100	22	13	12	Modern Chapalote
U 1k	86	21	12	14	Chapalote
U 1l	86	16	6	10	Chapalote
U 1m	70	16	3	10	Chapalote
U 11e	169	18	10	12	Modern Chapalote
U 11d	161	22	11	12	Modern Chapalote

TABLE 12
Description of Corn Cob Fragments with Stick or Feather

Number	Diameter (millimeters)	No. Rows
78	22	14
173	23	12
260a	24	14
260b	24	12
260c	23	16
366	19	10
464	23	14
487	24	14
513a	20	12
513b	24	12
770	23	14

TABLE 13
Description of Miscellaneous Specimens of Corn

Number	Description
171	Eleven pieces of peduncles of ears strung on a cord 68 cm in length. The peduncles are shriveled as though they were from ears picked green. The ends of some are charred as though the ears had been exposed to fire. The lengths of the peduncles are (mm) 38, 70, 55, 55, 50, 40, 70, 70, 55, 40, 35. The corresponding diameters are 13, 9, 7, 8, 10, 8, 9, 13, 9, 7, 12. With respect to both length and diameter all of these peduncles could be assigned to the race Chapalote.
162a, b	Pieces of split corn stalks with a leaf wrapped around one end of each.
259	A knot of several leaf sheaths. These, like No. 283, are probably *Phragmites communis* and not corn.
283	A braid of several leaf sheaths. These, like No. 259, are probably *Phragmites communis* and not corn.
382	A packet of corn husks folded and tied at the ends with coarse twine.
671	An internode of a corn stalk with the pith partly hollowed out, the opening covered with a piece of leaf sheath. Held in place with several turns of a coarse twine. This may be the counterpart of a modern pillbox or jewelbox.
1299	A mat of corn leaves rolled up and fastened together with a strip of bark.

REFERENCES

Abel, Leland J.
1955 Pottery Types of the Southwest: Wares 5A, 10A, 10B, 12A, San Juan Red Ware, Mesa Verde Gray, and White Ware, San Juan White Ware. *Museum of Northern Arizona, Ceramic Series* 3B. Flagstaff.

Adams, Richard N.
1951 Half House: A Pit House in Chaco Canyon, New Mexico. *Papers of the Michigan Academy of Science, Arts and Letters* 39: 273–95. Ann Arbor.

Amsden, Charles Avery
1949 *Prehistoric Southwesterners from Basketmaker to Pueblo.* Los Angeles: Southwest Museum.

Bakkegard, B. M., and Elizabeth Ann Morris
1961 Seventh Century Flutes from Arizona. *Ethnomusicology* 5 (3): 184–86.

Bannister, Bryant
1962 The Interpretation of Tree-Ring Dates. *American Antiquity* 27: 508–14.

Bannister, Bryant, Jeffrey S. Dean, and
Elizabeth Ann Morris Gell
1966 *Tree-Ring Dates from Arizona E: Chinle — De Chelly — Red Rock Area.* Laboratory of Tree-Ring Research. Tucson: University of Arizona.

Bannister, Bryant, John W. Hannah, and
William J. Robinson
1966 *Tree-Ring Dates from Arizona K: Puerco — Wide Ruin–Ganado Area.* Laboratory of Tree-Ring Research. Tucson: University of Arizona.

Bannister, Bryant, Richard Warren, and
William J. Robinson
1970 *Tree-Ring Dates from New Mexico A, G–H; Shiprock — Zuni — Mt. Taylor Area.* Laboratory of Tree-Ring Research. Tucson: University of Arizona.

Breternitz, D. A., A. H. Rohn, Jr., and E. A. Morris
1974 Prehistoric Ceramics of the Mesa Verde Region. *Museum of Northern Arizona, Ceramic Series* 5. Flagstaff.

Brew, John Otis
1946 Archaeology of Alkali Ridge, Southeastern Utah. *Papers of the Peabody Museum, Harvard University,* 21. Cambridge.

Brooks, Richard H., Lawrence Kaplan, Hugh C. Cutler, and Thomas W. Whitaker
1962 Plant Material from a Cave on the Río Zape, Durango, Mexico. *American Antiquity* 27: 356–69.

Burgess, J. Tom, and J. Irving
1934 *Knots, Ties and Splices.* New York: E. P. Dutton and Co.

Byers, Douglas S.
1959 An Introduction to Five Papers on the Archaic Stage. *American Antiquity* 24: 229–32.

Carlson, Roy L.
1963 Basket Maker III Sites Near Durango, Colorado. *University of Colorado Studies, Series in Anthropology 8. The Earl Morris Papers 1.* Boulder: University of Colorado Press.
1965 Eighteenth Century Navajo Fortresses of the Gobernador District: *University of Colorado Studies, Series in Anthropology 10. The Earl Morris Papers 2.* Boulder: University of Colorado Press.

Colton, Harold S.
1939 Prehistoric Culture Units and Their Relationships in Northern Arizona. *Museum of Northern Arizona, Bulletin* 17. Flagstaff.
1955 Pottery Types of the Southwest: Wares 8A, 8B, 9A, 9B, Tusayan Gray, and White Ware, Little Colorado Gray, and White Ware. *Museum of Northern Arizona, Ceramic Series* 3A. Flagstaff.

Colton, Harold S., and Lyndon L. Hargrave
1937 Handbook of Northern Arizona Pottery Wares. *Museum of Northern Arizona, Bulletin* 11. Flagstaff.

Cutler, Hugh C., and Thomas W. Whitaker
1961 History and Distribution of the Cultivated Cucurbits in the Americas. *American Antiquity* 26: 469–85.

Daifuku, Hiroshi
1952 The Pit House in the Old World and in Native North America. *American Antiquity* 18: 1–7.
1961 Jeddito 264. A Report on the Excavation of a Basketmaker III–Pueblo I Site in Northeastern Arizona with a Review of Some Current Theories in Southwestern Archaeology. *Peabody Museum Papers, Harvard University,* 33 (1). Cambridge.

Dick, Herbert W.
1954 The Bat Cave Pod Corn Complex: A Note on Its Distribution and Archaeological Significance. *El Palacio* 61 (5): 138–44.

Dittert, Alfred E., Jr., Frank W. Eddy, and Beth L. Dickey
1963 Evidences of Early Ceramic Phases in the Navajo Reservoir District. *El Palacio* 70 (1–2): 5–12.

Dixon, Roland B., and John B. Stetson, Jr.
1922 Analysis of Pre-Columbian Pipe Dottles. *American Anthropologist* 24: 245–46.

Douglass, A. E.
1936 The Central Pueblo Chronology. *Tree-Ring Bulletin* 2 (4): 29–34. Flagstaff.

Driver, Harold E., and William C. Massey
1957 Comparative Studies of North American Indians. *Transactions of the American Philosophical Society* 47 (2). Philadelphia.
Fowler, Melvin L.
1959 Modoc Rock Shelter: An Early Archaic Site in Southern Illinois. *American Antiquity* 24: 257–70.
Galinat, Walter C., and James H. Gunnerson
1963 Spread of Eight-Rowed Maize from the Prehistoric Southwest. *Harvard University Botanical Museum Leaflets* 20 (5): 117–60.
Gell, Elizabeth Ann Morris, and Volney H. Jones
1962 Seventh Century Evidence for the Use of Tobacco in Northern Arizona. *34th International Congress of Americanists*, Vienna 1960. Vienna: Ferlag, Ferdinand Berger, Horn.
Gladwin, Harold S.
1945 The Chaco Branch: Excavations at White Mound and in the Red Mesa Valley. *Medallion Papers* 33. Globe, Arizona.
Guernsey, Samuel J.
1931 Explorations in Northeastern Arizona. *Papers of the Peabody Museum, Harvard University*, 12 (1). Cambridge.
Guernsey, Samuel J., and Alfred V. Kidder
1894 Recent Finds in Utah. *The Archaeologist* 2 (5): 154–55. Waterloo, Indiana.
1921 Basket-Maker Caves of Northeastern Arizona. *Papers of the Peabody Museum, Harvard University*, 8 (2). Cambridge.
Harshbarger, J. W., C. A. Repenning, and J. H. Irwin
1957 Stratigraphy of the Uppermost Triassic and Jurassic Rocks of the Navajo Country. *Geological Survey Professional Paper* 291. Washington.
Haury, Emil W.
1938 Southwestern Dated Ruins: II. *Tree-Ring Bulletin* 4 (3): 3–4. Flagstaff.
1940 Excavations in the Forestdale Valley, East-Central Arizona. *University of Arizona Bulletin* 9 (4), *Social Science Bulletin* 12. Tucson.
Haury, Emil W., and E. B. Sayles
1947 An Early Pit House Village of the Mogollon Culture, Forestdale Valley, Arizona. *University of Arizona Bulletin* 18 (4), *Social Science Bulletin* 16. Tucson.
Hawley, Florence M.
1936 Field Manual of Prehistoric Southwestern Pottery Types. *University of New Mexico Bulletin* 291, *Anthropological Series* 1 (4). Albuquerque.
Hough, J. W.
1914 Culture of the Ancient Pueblos of the Upper Gila River Region, New Mexico and Arizona. Smithsonian Institution. *U.S. National Museum Bulletin* 87. Washington.
Jennings, Jesse D.
1956 The American Southwest: A Problem in Cultural Isolation. In Seminars in Archaeology: 1955, edited by Robert Wauchope. *Memoirs of the Society for American Archaeology*, 11: 59–127.
1957 Danger Cave. *Memoirs of the Society for American Archaeology* 14.
Jennings, Jesse D., and Edward Norbeck
1955 Great Basin Prehistory: A Review. *American Antiquity* 21: 1–11.

Johnson, Chester
1962 The Twin Lakes Site, L.A. 2507. *El Palacio* 69 (3): 158–73.
Johnson, V. C., F. L. Gager, Jr., and J. C. Holmes
1959 A Study of the History of the Use of Tobacco. 13th Tobacco Chemists Research Conference. Mimeographed. Lexington, Kentucky.
Jones, Volney H.
1944 Was Tobacco Smoked in the Pueblo Region in Pre-Spanish Times? *American Antiquity* 9: 451–56.
Jones, Volney H., and Elizabeth Ann Morris
1960 A Seventh-Century Record of Tobacco Utilization in Arizona. *El Palacio* 67 (4): 115–17.
Kaplan, Lawrence
1956 The Cultivated Beans of the Prehistoric Southwest. *Annals of the Missouri Botanical Garden* 43: 189–251.
Kelley, J. Charles
1959 The Desert Culture and the Balcones Phase: Archaic Manifestations in the Southwest and Texas. *American Antiquity* 24: 276–88.
Kidder, A. V.
1915 Pottery of the Pajarito Plateau and of Some of the Adjacent Regions of New Mexico. *Memoirs of the American Anthropological Association* 2 (6).
1924 *An Introduction to the Study of Southwestern Archaeology.* Papers of the Phillips Academy Southwestern Expedition 1, Andover. New Haven: Yale University Press.
1927 Southwestern Archaeological Conference. *Science* 66 (1716): 489–91.
1932 *The Artifacts of Pecos.* Papers of the Phillips Academy Southwestern Expedition 6, Andover. New Haven: Yale University Press.
Kidder, Alfred V., and Samuel J. Guernsey
1919 Archaeological Explorations in Northeastern Arizona. *Bureau of American Ethnology, Bulletin* 65. Washington.
Kluckhohn, Clyde, and Paul Reiter, editors
1939 Preliminary Report on the 1937 Excavations, Bc 50–51, Chaco Canyon, New Mexico. *University of New Mexico Bulletin* 345, *Anthropological Series* 3 (2). Albuquerque.
Kroeber, Alfred L.
1916 Zuni Potsherds. *Anthropological Papers of the American Museum of Natural History* 18 (1): 1–37.
Linton, Ralph
1940 Crops, Soil and Culture in America. In *The Maya and Their Neighbors.* New York: D. Appleton-Century.
Lister, Robert H., Paul C. Mangelsdorf, and Kate Peck Kent
1958 Archaeological Excavations in the Northern Sierra Madre Occidental, Chihuahua and Sonora, Mexico. *University of Colorado Studies, Series in Anthropology* 7. Boulder.
MacNeish, Richard S.
1958 Preliminary Archaeological Investigations in the Sierra de Tamaulipas, Mexico. *Transactions of the American Philosophical Society* 48 (6). Philadelphia.

Mangelsdorf, Paul C., and Robert H. Lister
1956 Archaeological Evidence on the Evolution of Maize in Northwestern Mexico. *Harvard University Botanical Museum Leaflets* 17 (6): 151–78.

Martin, Paul S., John B. Rinaldo, Elaine Bluhm, Hugh C. Cutler, and Roger Grange, Jr.
1952 Mogollon Cultural Continuity and Change: the Stratigraphic Analysis of Tularosa and Cordova Caves. *Fieldiana: Anthropology* 40. Chicago Natural History Museum.

Morris, Earl H.
1919 Preliminary Account of the Antiquities of the Region between the Mancos and La Plata Rivers in Southwestern Colorado. *Thirty-third Annual Report of the Bureau of American Ethnology*, pp. 157–206. Washington.
1921 Chronology of the San Juan Area. *Proceedings of the National Academy of Sciences* 7: 18–22. Washington.
1925 Exploring in the Canyon of Death. *National Geographic Magazine* 48 (3): 263–300.
1927 The Beginnings of Pottery Making in the San Juan Area; Unfired Prototypes and the Wares of the Earliest Ceramic Period. *Anthropological Papers of the American Museum of Natural History* 28 (2): 125–98.
1936 Early Date Archaeology. *Tree-Ring Bulletin* 2 (4): 34–36. Flagstaff.
1939 Archaeological Studies in the La Plata District. *Carnegie Institution of Washington Publication* 519. Washington.
1951 Basketmaker III Human Figurines from Northeastern Arizona. *American Antiquity* 17: 33–40.

Morris, Earl H., and Robert F. Burgh
1941 Anasazi Basketry. *Carnegie Institution of Washington Publication* 533. Washington.
1954 Basket Maker II Sites Near Durango, Colorado. *Carnegie Institution of Washington Publication* 604. Washington.

Morris, Elizabeth Ann
1958 A Possible Early Projectile Point from the Prayer Rock District, Arizona. *Southwestern Lore* 24 (1): 1–4.
1959a Basketmaker Flutes from the Prayer Rock District, Arizona. *American Antiquity* 24 (4): 406–11.
1959b Basketmaker Caves in the Prayer Rock District, Northeastern Arizona. Ph.D. dissertation, University of Arizona, Tucson.
1975 Seventh Century Basketmaker Textiles from Northern Arizona. *Proceedings of the 1974 Irene Emery Roundtable on Museum Textiles: Archaeological Textiles*, pp. 125–32. Washington: The Textile Museum.

Nelson, N. C.
1916 Chronology of the Tano Ruins, New Mexico. *American Anthropologist* 18 (2): 159–80.

Nordenskiöld, Gustav
1893 *The Cliff Dwellers of the Mesa Verde*. Stockholm: P. A. Norstedt and Sons.

Nusbaum, Jesse L., A. V. Kidder, and S. J. Guernsey
1922 A Basket-Maker Cave in Kane County, Utah. *Indian Notes and Monographs* 29. New York: Museum of the American Indian, Heye Foundation.

O'Bryan, Deric
1950 Excavations in Mesa Verde National Park, 1947–48. *Medallion Papers* 39. Globe, Arizona.

Pepper, George H.
1902 The Ancient Basket Makers of Southeastern Utah. *American Museum of Natural History Journal* 2, (4), Supplement. New York.

Prudden, T. M.
1897 An Elder Brother to the Cliff Dwellers. *Harper's New Monthly Magazine* 95: 55–62. New York.

Raffauf, Robert A., and Elizabeth Ann Morris
1960 Persistence of Alkaloids in Plant Tissue. *Science* 131 (3406): 1047.

Roberts, Frank H. H., Jr.
1929 Shabik'eschee Village. *Bureau of American Ethnology Bulletin* 92. Washington.
1930 Early Pueblo Ruins in the Piedra District, Southwestern Colorado. *Bureau of American Ethnology Bulletin* 96. Washington.
1931 The Ruins at Kiatuthlanna, Eastern Arizona. *Bureau of American Ethnology Bulletin* 100. Washington.
1935 A Survey of Southwestern Archaeology. *American Anthropologist* 37 (1): 1–35.
1937 Archaeology in the Southwest. *American Antiquity* 3: 3–33.

Smiley, Terah L.
1951 A Summary of Tree-Ring Dates from Some Southwestern Archaeological Sites. *University of Arizona Bulletin* 22 (4), *Laboratory of Tree-Ring Research Bulletin* 5. Tucson.

Spier, Leslie
1917 An Outline for a Chronology of Zuni Ruins. *Anthropological Papers of the American Museum of Natural History* 18 (3). New York.

Steward, Julian H.
1938 Basin-Plateau Aboriginal Sociopolitical Groups. *Bureau of American Ethnology Bulletin* 120. Washington.
1940 Native Cultures of the Intermontane (Great Basin) Area. *Smithsonian Miscellaneous Collections* 100: 445–502. Washington.

Steward, Julian H., and F. M. Setzler
1938 Function and Configuration in Archaeology. *American Antiquity* 4: 4–10.

Taylor, Walter W.
1948 A Study of Archaeology. *Memoirs of the American Anthropological Association* 69.
1954 An Early Slabhouse near Kayenta, Arizona. *Plateau* 26 (4): 109–16.

U.S. Department of Commerce
1931– *Climatic Summary of the United States, Supple-*
1961 *ments for 1931–61. Washington*: U.S. Weather Bureau.

Vivian, Gordon, and Paul Reiter
1960 The Great Kivas of Chaco Canyon and Their Relationships. *Monographs of the School of American Research and the Museum of New Mexico* 22. Santa Fe: The School of American Research.

Wasley, William W.
1960 Salvage Archaeology on Highway 66 in Eastern Arizona. *American Antiquity* 26: 30–42.

Wellhausen, E. J., L. M. Roberts, and E. Hernandez X;
in collaboration with Paul C. Mangelsdorf
1952   *Races of Maize in Mexico; Their Origin, Characteristics and Distribution.* Cambridge: Bussey Institution of Harvard University.

Wendorf, Fred
1953   Archaeological Studies in the Petrified Forest National Monument. *Museum of Northern Arizona Bulletin* 27. Flagstaff.

Wendorf, Fred, Nancy Fox, and Orian L. Lewis, editors
1956   *Pipeline Archaeology.* Santa Fe and Flagstaff: Laboratory of Anthropology and Museum of Northern Arizona.

Wetherill, Richard
1897   Letter to the Editor. *The Antiquarian* 1. Columbus.

Wheat, Joe Ben
1954   Crooked Ridge Village. *University of Arizona Bulletin* 25 (3), *Social Science Bulletin* 24. Tucson.

Willey, Gordon R., and Philip Phillips
1958   *Method and Theory in American Archaeology.* Chicago: University of Chicago Press.

Woodbury, Richard B.
1954   Prehistoric Stone Implements of Northeastern Arizona. Reports of the Awatovi Expedition 6. *Papers of the Peabody Museum, Harvard University*, 34. Cambridge.